I0465494

GROW BIG OR STAY SMALL

DEFY THE 'GROW OR DIE' PRESSURE
REDEFINE SUCCESS ON YOUR OWN TERMS

BY
LIM PEEK EEK

Copyright © 2024 by Peek Eek Lim
ISBN: 9798300224578

Publisher:
Lim Peek Eek
3417, Jalan Taman Bangi Jaya,
Taman Bangi Jaya,
43500 Semenyih, Selangor,
Malaysia.

All rights reserved.

No part of this book may be reproduced in any form or by any electronic or mechanical means, including information storage and retrieval systems, without written permission from the author, except for the use of brief quotations in a book review.

CONTENTS

INTRODUCTION

Purpose of This Book

In the ever-evolving landscape of business, entrepreneurs face numerous critical decisions that shape the future of their ventures. One of the most pivotal decisions is whether to scale up and grow their business into a large corporation or to maintain a smaller, more manageable size, even as a one-person operation. This choice transcends the mere act of expansion or staying as is; it is about aligning the business with personal goals, market demands, and the entrepreneur's vision.

This book is written to empower entrepreneurs who, like me, have grappled with the dilemma of growth versus stability. Having experienced this struggle firsthand, I decided to share insights and practical guidance to help other entrepreneurs navigate their unique paths. Within these pages, you will find a clear framework to evaluate the pros and cons of each direction, enabling you to make informed decisions that align with your personal aspirations and business goals.

This book is not just theoretical; it includes practical tools, checklists, and templates that you can use to assess your readiness for growth, plan strategically, and manage your resources effectively. These actionable insights are designed to empower you to take decisive steps toward your desired future. Additionally, the real-life case studies included in this book share the experiences of businesses that chose to grow big and those that opted to stay small. These examples and lessons learned can help you understand the potential outcomes of your decisions.

A significant strength of this book is its balanced perspective. While many business books focus solely on growth, this one acknowledges that staying small can be just as successful and fulfilling as scaling up. This balanced view ensures that you are aware of all possibilities and can choose the path that best suits your vision and circumstances.

The decision to grow or stay small impacts not only your business but also your lifestyle and personal fulfillment. That is why this book addresses the importance of aligning business decisions with personal values and goals, ensuring that you find satisfaction and balance in your professional and personal life. From strategic planning and resource management to marketing strategies and leadership development, this book covers all essential aspects of running a business. This comprehensive coverage ensures that you have a well-rounded understanding of what it takes to succeed, regardless of the path you choose.

Furthermore, this book offers strategies for building strong business networks, providing you with the support and resources needed to thrive.

In summary, this book is a guide for entrepreneurs at any stage of their journey. It equips you with the knowledge, tools, and confidence to make one of the most significant decisions in your business life, ensuring you choose the path that best aligns with your vision and goals. Whether you are aiming for rapid growth or finding fulfillment in a small niche market, this book provides the insights and support needed to succeed.

Is This Book for You?
Who Should Read This Book

This book is designed for entrepreneurs who find themselves at a crossroads, pondering the future direction of their business. Whether you are a self-employed individual running a one-person operation or the founder of a small but growing company, this book provides valuable insights and guidance tailored to your unique circumstances.

Entrepreneurs at a Decision Point

If you are an entrepreneur contemplating the next steps for your business, this book is for you. It addresses the crucial decision of whether to pursue rapid growth and expansion or to maintain a smaller, more manageable size. By exploring both paths, the book helps you weigh the benefits and challenges of each option, ensuring that your decision aligns with your personal and professional goals.

Self-Employed Individuals

For those who are self-employed, the decision to grow or remain a one-person business can be particularly challenging. This book offers strategies for optimizing solo operations while also presenting the opportunities and considerations involved in scaling up. Whether you are a freelancer, consultant, or artisan, you will find practical advice on how to thrive in your chosen path.

Small Business Owners

Small business owners who have already established their ventures but are unsure about the next steps will find this book especially useful. It provides real-life case studies of businesses that have successfully grown into large corporations and those that have chosen to stay small and profitable. By learning from these examples, you can gain insights into the potential outcomes of your own business decisions.

Aspiring Entrepreneurs

If you are at the beginning of your entrepreneurial journey and seeking guidance on how to shape your business's future, this book serves as an essential resource. It helps you understand the long-term implications of your choices and provides tools for making informed decisions right from the start. By considering the experiences of other entrepreneurs, you can better navigate the challenges and opportunities that lie ahead.

Business Consultants and Advisors

Professionals who advise entrepreneurs will also benefit from this book. It offers a comprehensive overview of the factors that influence the decision to grow or stay small, providing valuable insights that can be shared with clients. By understanding the nuances of both paths, consultants and advisors can better support their clients in makinng strategic decisions that align with their goals.

The Stage of Business Relevant to the Content

"Grow Big or Stay Small" is crafted to resonate with entrepreneurs at various stages of their business journey. Whether you are just starting out or have been in the market for a while, the insights and guidance offered in this book are designed to help you make informed decisions about the future direction of your business.

Startups and Early-Stage Businesses

For entrepreneurs who are in the initial stages of launching their business, this book provides foundational knowledge and strategic insights. Early-stage businesses often grapple with decisions about how to allocate limited resources, build a customer base, and create a sustainable business model. This book will help entrepreneurs at this stage understand the potential paths they can take, weighing the benefits of rapid growth against the advantages of staying small and focused. The book offers practical advice on how to build a solid foundation, whether your goal is to scale quickly or remain agile and responsive.

Growing Businesses

Businesses that have moved beyond the startup phase and are experiencing growth will find this book particularly valuable. At this stage, entrepreneurs face critical decisions about expanding their operations, entering new markets, and managing increased complexity. The content addresses the challenges and opportunities associated with scaling up, such as securing funding, developing infrastructure, and maintaining quality and customer satisfaction. Additionally, the book provides insights into the risks and rewards of expansion, helping business owners to plan strategically and sustainably.

Established Small Businesses

Entrepreneurs who have established small businesses and are content with their current scale, or are considering whether to expand further, will also benefit from this book. It discusses the strategies for optimizing operations, enhancing efficiency, and maximizing profitability without necessarily growing larger. For those who choose to remain small, the book highlights the importance of maintaining a strong brand identity, fostering customer loyalty, and creating a fulfilling work environment. It also explores how small businesses can leverage their unique advantages, such as personalized service and niche market focus, to thrive in competitive landscapes.

Mature Businesses Considering Transition

For mature businesses contemplating a transition—whether that means expanding, diversifying, or even downsizing—this book provides comprehensive guidance on evaluating the best course of action. At this stage, it often becomes necessary to reassess goals, adapt to market changes, and consider succession planning. This book offers tools and frameworks to help entrepreneurs navigate these transitions smoothly and effectively. By using these resources, business owners can ensure that their decisions are aligned with both their long-term vision and the current market conditions, enabling them to maintain stability and achieve continued success.u

CHAPTER 1

UNDERSTANDING YOUR VISION

The Importance of Having a Clear Business Vision

Imagine setting out on a journey without a map. You might eventually reach your destination, but the path would be uncertain, and you would likely encounter unnecessary obstacles. Similarly, a clear business vision is critical in determining whether you should scale up or stay small. When you have a well-defined vision, it becomes easier to set goals, develop strategies, and make decisions that align with your chosen path. This clarity helps navigate challenges and seize opportunities that fit your business size aspirations, ensuring your efforts remain consistent with your overall mission.

Moreover, a clear business vision helps in communicating your aspirations to stakeholders, including investors, customers, and partners. It builds trust and credibility, demonstrating that you have a clear plan for the future and the determination to achieve it. This can be particularly important when you are seeking funding or forging strategic partnerships.

A clear business vision goes beyond being a mere declaration; it serves as a strategic instrument that fosters growth, encourages innovation, and builds resilience. It enables you to navigate the complexities of the business world with confidence and clarity, ensuring every step you take moves you closer to your ultimate goals. By investing the time and effort to define and articulate your vision, you lay the groundwork for a successful and sustainable business. In the following sections, we will explore in detail how having a clear vision benefits various aspects of your business.

Benefit #1: Providing Clear Direction and Maintaining Focus

A clear business vision acts as your compass, whether you are aiming for significant growth or maintaining a small, efficient operation. This direction helps in resource allocation and prioritization, ensuring your strategic focus aligns with your business size goals. When you have a clear vision, you can avoid the pitfalls of drifting aimlessly and making reactive rather than proactive decisions.

Imagine embarking on a journey without knowing your destination. The lack of direction would make it easy to get lost or sidetracked. Similarly, your business vision provides the map that guides you and your team, ensuring that every effort contributes to your ultimate goals. By having a clear vision, you can make informed decisions that keep your business on track. It empowers you to decline opportunities that do not align with your goals, ensuring your time and resources are invested in what truly matters. This strategic focus not only enhances efficiency but also boosts morale, as your team understands and is motivated by the shared mission.

Benefit #2: Inspiring and Motivating Your Team

A compelling vision can inspire and motivate both you and your employees. It provides a sense of purpose and meaning, making daily tasks feel more significant and connected to a greater cause. When everyone understands and believes in the vision, it creates a powerful sense of unity and direction within the organization.

Think about those challenging times when the road ahead seems uncertain. A strong vision can be the beacon that keeps you and your team focused and driven. It reminds everyone why they started this journey and what they are working towards, helping to maintain morale and determination even when obstacles arise.

When you articulate a clear and compelling vision, you provide your team with a reason to believe in the work they do. This can lead to higher levels of engagement, productivity, and job satisfaction. Employees are more likely to go the extra mile when they feel their contributions matter and are part of something bigger.

Moreover, a strong vision can attract customers who share the same values and beliefs. People want to support businesses that stand for something meaningful. By clearly communicating your vision, you can build a loyal customer base that is not only interested in your products or services but also in the mission and values your business represents.

Benefit #3: Guiding Your Decisions with Clarity

Having a clear vision simplifies the decision-making process. When faced with choices, you can refer back to your vision to determine which option best aligns with your long-term goals, making sure your decisions are not just reactive but strategic. This helps in maintaining consistency and coherence in your business strategies and operations, ensuring that every decision supports your overall mission.

Additionally, a clear vision helps in communicating decisions to your team and stakeholders. When everyone understands the vision, they can see how each decision fits into the bigger picture, which fosters buy-in and support. This clarity helps in building a cohesive and motivated team that works together towards common objectives.

Benefit #4: Drawing in Investors, Partners, and Customers

A well-articulated vision can be a powerful tool for attracting investors, partners, and customers who resonate with your business's goals and values. When you clearly communicate your vision, you create a magnetic pull that draws in those who share your enthusiasm and belief in your mission. This can be crucial for building a strong brand identity and reputation, which are essential for gaining support and loyalty from various stakeholders.

Picture this: articulating your business's purpose and direction so clearly that investors are lining up to fund your projects, partners are excited to collaborate, and customers become loyal advocates of your brand. This is the impact of a compelling vision. It creates a compelling and motivating vision of your business's future, helping others recognize its potential and inspiring them to enthusiastically become part of the journey.

Take, for example, the case of Tesla. Elon Musk's vision to "accelerate the world's transition to sustainable energy" is more than just an ambitious objective; it is a powerful and persuasive narrative that has drawn substantial investment, forged strategic partnerships, and built a loyal customer following. Investors are drawn to the innovative and forward-thinking approach, partners are motivated by the potential for groundbreaking collaborations, and customers are inspired by the commitment to sustainability.

Having a well-defined vision allows you to attract the appropriate stakeholders to your business in a similar way. Investors are more likely to provide funding when they see a clear path to success and a purpose that aligns with their values. Partners are more inclined to collaborate when they understand and believe in your vision, knowing their efforts will contribute to something meaningful. Customers are more likely to remain loyal and become advocates for your brand when they resonate with your vision and feel a connection to your mission.

Also, a strong vision helps in building a cohesive brand identity. When your vision is consistently communicated across all aspects of your business, from marketing materials to customer interactions, it reinforces your brand's values and goals. This consistency builds trust and credibility, making it easier for stakeholders to commit to supporting your business.

Benefit #5: Uniting Your Team Around a Common Goal

A clear vision ensures everyone in your organization is working towards the same objectives, fostering alignment and cohesion. When employees understand how their roles contribute to the overall success of the business, it enhances collaboration, productivity, and morale. This unifying force helps your team coordinate activities, share resources, and support each other in achieving common goals, ultimately driving the business toward its shared mission.

Furthermore, a clear vision boosts morale by giving employees a sense of belonging and significance. They are not just doing a job; they are part of a meaningful journey. This sense of purpose can be incredibly motivating, leading to higher job satisfaction and retention rates.

Benefit #6: Staying Flexible and Growing with Purpose

While a clear vision provides direction, it also allows for flexibility and adaptability. As the business environment changes, having a strong vision can guide you in making necessary adjustments without losing sight of your ultimate goals. This balance helps your business remain relevant and competitive while staying true to its core purpose.

Your vision acts as a stable anchor that keeps you grounded even as you navigate through changes and uncertainties. This adaptability is crucial for long-term success and growth. When faced with new opportunities or challenges, you can refer back to your vision to determine the best course of action. This ensures any changes you make are aligned with your long-term objectives and core values. It helps you to innovate and expand thoughtfully, ensuring that growth is sustainable and purposeful.

Having a clear vision also empowers your team to embrace change. When everyone understands the overarching goals, they are more likely to support and adapt to new strategies and initiatives. This shared understanding fosters a culture of resilience and agility, where your team feels confident in navigating changes because they know it is all part of achieving the vision.

Aligning Personal and Business Aspirations

Achieving entrepreneurial success requires the alignment of personal and business aspirations. This harmony ensures that the journey of building and running a business is fulfilling, providing both financial gains and personal satisfaction. When personal and business goals are in sync, you become a more motivated, resilient, and effective leader for your ventures.

Think about the reasons that originally motivated you to start your business. Perhaps it was to pursue a passion, achieve financial independence, or create a positive impact in your community. Whatever the reason, it is important to ensure these personal aspirations are reflected in your business goals. When your business aligns with your personal values and dreams, every achievement becomes more meaningful and every challenge easier to overcome.

Take, for instance, an entrepreneur who is passionate about the environment and wants to make a difference through sustainable practices. If their business goals include becoming a leader in eco-friendly products, they will find greater satisfaction and motivation in their work because their personal values align with their professional objectives. This passion for sustainability will drive innovation and perseverance even in the face of obstacles. Additionally, this alignment can resonate with customers who share similar values, building a loyal customer base that supports the business's mission.

Conversely, a disconnect between personal and business aspirations can lead to burnout and dissatisfaction. Running a business solely for financial gain while sacrificing personal time, health, or values can eventually drain your motivation and affect your ability to lead effectively. That is why it is crucial to set business goals that also cater to your personal well-being and happiness.

Aligning personal and business aspirations also aids in making tough decisions. In challenging situations, your core values and long-term vision can serve as a dependable guide for your decisions. For instance, if one of your personal goals is to spend more time with family, you might prioritize business strategies that offer a better work-life balance, such as delegating responsibilities, implementing flexible work hours, or investing in automation.

Moreover, this alignment fosters authenticity and integrity in your business. Staying true to your personal values influences your leadership style, company culture, and customer interactions. Being authentic fosters trust and credibility, both of which are vital for achieving long-term success. For example, a founder who values community engagement might integrate social responsibility into their business model, attracting like-minded employees and customers who appreciate and support these efforts.

To align your personal and business aspirations, begin by reflecting on your core values, passions, and long-term dreams. Document them and consider how they can be integrated into your business goals. Regularly revisit and reassess these goals to ensure they remain aligned as both your personal life and business evolve.

Steps to Aligning Personal and Business Aspirations

Step 1: Understanding Personal Values and Goals

The first step in aligning personal and business aspirations is to understand your personal values and long-term goals. This involves taking a deep dive into what is most important to you in life. Reflect on whether you prioritize financial independence, work-life balance, making a social impact, or achieving industry recognition. These personal values and goals should serve as a foundation upon which your business aspirations are built.

Start by asking yourself some key questions. What drives you? What makes you excited to get out of bed every morning? Is it the desire to create something new, help others, or build a legacy? Your answers to these questions will help you identify your core values and long-term goals.

For instance, if financial independence is a major goal, you might be driven by the freedom to make choices without worrying about money. Your business goals could then include creating a scalable business model that generates significant revenue and allows you to reinvest in further growth. On the other hand, if work-life balance is a top priority, you might aim to build a business that allows flexible working hours or remote work options, ensuring you have time for family, hobbies, and personal well-being.

Understanding your personal values can also help you make more meaningful connections with your customers. When your business practices reflect what you truly care about, you attract like-minded individuals who share your values. This can lead to a loyal customer base that feels a genuine connection to your brand. For example, if making a social impact is important to you, incorporating social responsibility initiatives into your business can resonate with customers who value companies that give back to the community.

To make this step more actionable, take some time to write down your personal values and long-term goals. Be honest and specific. Think about what success looks like for you, not just in business but in life as a whole. Once you have a clear understanding of your personal values and goals, you can start to see how they might align with and inform your business aspirations.

Step 2: Defining the Business Vision

Once your personal values and goals are clear, the next step is to define a business vision that reflects these aspirations. This vision should outline what you want your business to achieve and how it aligns with your personal life goals. A well-defined vision acts as a guiding star, directing your business decisions and ensuring your entrepreneurial journey is fulfilling and aligned with what matters most to you.

Start by thinking about the big picture. What do you want your business to look like in five, ten, or even twenty years? What impact do you want to make on your industry, community, or even the world? Your business vision should encapsulate these ambitions and provide a clear direction for your future efforts.

Let us say you are an entrepreneur who values creativity and innovation. You might establish a business that focuses on developing cutting-edge products or services. This could mean starting a tech company that pioneers new software solutions or a design firm that pushes the boundaries of what is possible in architecture or fashion. By aligning your business with your creative passion, you make sure that your daily tasks remain engaging and satisfying.

When shaping your business vision, think about how it can act as a source of motivation, not just for yourself but also for your team and customers. A compelling vision can attract talent who share your values and motivate employees to work towards a common goal. It also helps in building a brand that resonates with your target audience. For instance, if your personal value is community service, your business vision might include being a leader in corporate social responsibility. This could involve initiatives like donating a portion of profits to local charities or implementing programs that encourage employees to volunteer. Such a vision can foster a strong sense of purpose and loyalty among both employees and customers.

Take some time to write down your business vision. Be ambitious yet realistic. Think about how this vision integrates with your personal values and goals. Ask yourself questions like "How does this business contribute to my personal aspirations?" and "What kind of legacy do I want to leave through this business?" By reflecting on these questions, you can develop a vision statement that is both inspiring and in harmony with your personal life goals.

Step 3: Setting Compatible Goals

Setting both personal and business goals that complement each other is essential for achieving a balanced and fulfilling life. When your goals are in harmony, it ensures that neither aspect is neglected and that both can flourish simultaneously. This approach enables you to build a life where your personal goals and professional ambitions complement and strengthen one another.

Start by identifying specific goals that align with both your personal values and business vision. Think about how your personal and professional life can coexist and even enrich each other. For instance, if your personal goal is to spend more quality time with your family, you might set business goals that allow for a more flexible work schedule. This could involve implementing remote work policies, creating a four-day work week, or delegating responsibilities to trusted team members. By doing so, you ensure your business operations continue smoothly while you also fulfill your personal desire for family time.

When setting compatible goals, it is crucial to be realistic and specific. For instance, if you aim to improve your health by exercising regularly, you might set a personal goal to work out for an hour each day. To ensure this goal is compatible with your business responsibilities, you could set a business goal to delegate certain tasks during your workout time or integrate fitness into your daily routine like holding walking meetings. This way, you make time for your personal health without compromising your business commitments.

Write down your personal and business goals and look for areas where they can complement each other. Create a plan that integrates these goals, ensuring they support and enhance one another. Regularly review and adjust your goals as needed to maintain this balance, considering both your personal aspirations and business objectives.

Step 4: Creating a Supportive Business Culture

Building a business culture that supports personal aspirations can significantly enhance the alignment between your personal and professional goals. This entails fostering an environment that prioritizes values such as work-life balance, ongoing learning, and personal development. A supportive culture not only helps in retaining and motivating employees but also ensures your personal values are reflected in the daily operations of the business.

Reflect on the type of workplace that would make you feel supported and fulfilled. By integrating these elements into your business culture, you can create a work environment that aligns with your personal goals and attracts like-minded individuals.

For instance, if health and wellness are important to you, consider implementing wellness programs, offering gym memberships, or hosting regular health workshops. By promoting these values within your company, you create an environment where both you and your employees can thrive.

A supportive business culture also involves recognizing and celebrating personal milestones and achievements. By acknowledging these individual successes, you show that you value your employees not just for their professional contributions but also for their personal growth and accomplishments. This recognition fosters a sense of belonging and appreciation, which can enhance employee morale and loyalty, leading to a more motivated and engaged workforce. Celebrating personal milestones also strengthens team bonds and promotes a positive work environment, ultimately contributing to the overall success of your organization.

To create a supportive business culture, start by clearly defining the values you want to promote within your organization. Communicate these values consistently and integrate them into your policies, practices, and daily operations. Encourage feedback from your team to ensure the culture you are building resonates with everyone involved. Consistently reassess and refine these values to ensure they remain in alignment with both your personal aspirations and business objectives.

Step 5: Regular Reflection and Adjustment

Aligning personal and business aspirations is not a one-time task but an ongoing process. Ongoing reflection and adjustments are essential to keep both in harmony as circumstances and priorities evolve. This continuous process helps you stay true to your values and adapt to new challenges and opportunities.

Start by scheduling regular times for reflection. This could be monthly, quarterly, or annually, depending on your preference and the nature of your business. During these reflection periods, take a step back and assess both your personal and business goals. Are they still aligned? Have any new priorities emerged? Is your current path still fulfilling and effective?

Regular reflection also involves being honest with yourself about what is and is not working. If you find that certain business strategies are causing stress or taking you away from your personal values, it is important to recognize this and make changes. For instance, if a business goal is demanding too much of your time and leaving little room for personal pursuits, consider ways to delegate or automate tasks. Alternatively, you might need to redefine your business goals to better fit your personal life.

Try creating a structured approach to reflection and adjustment. Use tools like journals, goal-tracking software, or regular meetings with a mentor or coach to review your progress. Set specific criteria for assessing alignment between your personal and business goals and do not be afraid to make bold changes if needed.

CHAPTER 2

PROS AND CONS OF GROWING BIG

Advantages of Scaling Up

Scaling up a business can unlock vast opportunities, fundamentally transforming the way a corporation operates and competes within the market. While it demands significant effort and investment, the potential advantages make expansion an attractive prospect for many entrepreneurs. By examining the key benefits of scaling up, it becomes evident how this strategic move can reshape the future of an organization and drive lasting success.

Advantage #1: Increased Revenue and Market Share

When businesses scale up, they gain the ability to offer a broader range of products and services, catering to diverse Tcustomer needs and preferences. This diversification often leads to higher sales volumes, as varied market segments are more effectively addressed. In addition, expanding operations allows businesses to enter new geographic markets, thereby increasing market share and solidifying their presence on a larger scale.

Moreover, the resources that accompany scaling up enable more aggressive investment in marketing and promotional activities. Enhanced marketing efforts can boost brand awareness and attract a wider customer base, driving significant revenue growth. With a larger budget, businesses are also able to leverage advanced marketing tools and strategies, such as data analytics and targeted advertising, to engage potential customers more effectively.

As market presence expands, stronger relationships with customers and partners are built, fostering loyalty and repeat business. This strengthened market position also facilitates better negotiation terms with suppliers and distributors, leading to cost savings and higher profitability. By scaling up, businesses create a virtuous cycle, where increased revenue and market share propel further growth and expansion, positioning the organization for long-term success.

Advantage #2: Economies of Scale

One of the most significant benefits of scaling up is the achievement of economies of scale, which can substantially reduce costs and enhance profitability. Economies of scale occur when an increase in production results in lower average costs over the long term. As businesses expand, the cost per unit of production typically decreases due to more efficient resource utilization, bulk purchasing, and optimized processes.

Access to advanced technologies also plays a crucial role in this process. For instance, investing in automated production equipment or sophisticated software for operations management can significantly boost efficiency and reduce labor costs. These technological advancements further decrease the per-unit cost of production, contributing to higher overall profitability.

Ultimately, economies of scale provide a competitive edge, enabling businesses to cut costs, increase profits, and strengthen their market position. By scaling up, businesses can fully leverage these cost efficiencies, creating opportunities for reinvestment in growth, innovation, and quality improvement—key components for sustained success in a competitive market.

Advantage #3: Enhanced Brand Recognition and Influence

Larger enterprises typically benefit from substantial marketing resources, enabling them to conduct comprehensive advertising campaigns with a broader reach. This increased visibility not only builds brand recognition but also fosters positive associations with reliability, quality, and value. As a result, the customer base expands, with consumers more likely to choose a familiar, trusted brand over lesser-known competitors, leading to greater loyalty and increased recommendations.

In addition, strong brand recognition opens doors to strategic partnerships and collaborations. Well-established brands are often seen as industry leaders, making them attractive partners for other businesses. These alliances can lead to co-branded products, joint marketing efforts, and shared resources, further enhancing the brand's influence and expanding the reach of the business within the market.

Advantage #4: Access to Better Resources and Talent

Scaling up provides businesses with access to superior resources and talent, both of which are essential for fostering innovation and sustaining growth. With increased financial resources, businesses can invest in advanced technology, research and development, and high-quality infrastructure—critical components for maintaining competitiveness and driving innovation forward.

Furthermore, larger businesses are better positioned to offer competitive salaries, comprehensive benefits, and professional development opportunities, which attract and retain top talent. Many employees are drawn to the stability, resources, and growth prospects that larger enterprises provide. This helps businesses build a strong talent pool that includes not only technical and managerial staff but also leaders and innovators who contribute fresh ideas and perspectives.

Accessing global talent is another key advantage. International expansion allows businesses to tap into diverse talent pools, bringing a wide range of skills and perspectives that can foster innovative solutions and improve operational efficiency. This global approach to talent acquisition helps businesses stay ahead in an increasingly competitive marketplace.

Advantage #5: Diversification and Risk Mitigation

Diversification is a powerful advantage of scaling up, enabling businesses to expand their products, services, and market presence while reducing dependence on a single revenue stream. This strategy is crucial for mitigating risks associated with market fluctuations, economic downturns, and shifting consumer preferences.

In addition to risk reduction, diversification fosters innovation and opens new growth opportunities. For instance, Amazon began as an online bookstore but rapidly diversified into electronics, clothing, cloud computing through Amazon Web Services (AWS), and streaming services with Amazon Prime Video. This broad range of services attracts different customer segments and reduces reliance on any one market, making the company more resilient to economic shifts and competitive pressures.

Moreover, expanding into different geographical markets helps protect businesses from regional economic downturns and regulatory changes. Operating across multiple regions offsets negative impacts in one area with stability or growth in another. For example, a global expansion strategy enables businesses to tap into new customer bases, diversify revenue streams, and mitigate the risk of being affected by localized events such as political instability or natural disasters.

In essence, diversification is not only about spreading risk but also about seizing growth opportunities and fostering innovation. This strategy can transform a business into a resilient, multi-faceted enterprise capable of navigating various challenges while capitalizing on emerging trends.

Advantage #6: Increased Bargaining Power

As businesses scale up, they often experience increased bargaining power, a significant advantage for operations and profitability. This leverage with suppliers, distributors, and other stakeholders can be transformative. Larger enterprises often have the ability to negotiate better terms, lower costs, and access key resources more effectively, which enhances their position in the market.

When larger volumes are involved in a deal, suppliers are more likely to offer discounts and improved terms, appreciating the steady and significant business. This exemplifies economies of scale, where higher order quantities justify lower per-unit costs.

Additionally, increased bargaining power enhances the ability to form strategic partnerships and alliances. As key players in their industries, larger businesses attract collaboration from others eager to benefit from shared opportunities and expanded market access. These alliances often result in mutual gains, driving innovation, broadening market reach, and creating synergies that smaller competitors may struggle to achieve.

Moreover, securing favorable long-term contracts with suppliers helps mitigate business risks. Larger enterprises can lock in prices and terms that protect against market volatility and price increases. This stability is vital for long-term planning and financial forecasting, offering a buffer against economic uncertainties.

Advantage #7: Enhanced Customer Experience

Another key benefit of scaling up is the ability to offer more comprehensive services and faster delivery times. Larger businesses can maintain extensive inventories and leverage advanced logistics to ensure products reach customers quickly and efficiently, fostering loyalty and repeat business.

Additionally, scaling up enables businesses to invest in sophisticated customer service tools and infrastructure, such as advanced customer relationship management (CRM) systems, AI-driven chatbots, and personalized marketing strategies. These tools allow businesses to tailor the customer journey to individual preferences, significantly improving satisfaction and retention. By understanding customer needs and implementing technology that enhances service delivery, businesses can achieve substantial improvements in customer loyalty.

Furthermore, scaling up provides the additional resources needed to enhance the human aspect of customer service. Investing in training for customer service representatives and creating dedicated customer success teams can make a notable difference. A well-trained team can resolve issues more efficiently, offer personalized assistance, and build stronger relationships with customers, ultimately leading to higher retention.

In addition, scaling allows for the implementation of effective loyalty programs that reward customers for their continued patronage. These programs might include discounts, exclusive offers, or points-based rewards that encourage repeat business. Companies such as Starbucks and Sephora have successfully utilized loyalty programs to elevate the customer experience, fostering a community of loyal customers who actively advocate for the brand.

Advantage #8: Competitive Advantage

Larger businesses often have the ability to establish multiple competitive advantages. One way this is achieved is through significant investments in marketing and research. With greater resources, companies can execute extensive marketing campaigns that reach a wider audience. High-quality advertisements across multiple platforms ensure that the brand remains top-of-mind for consumers, attracting more customers and strengthening brand recognition—both crucial in today's competitive market.

Additionally, larger budgets can be allocated to research and development, driving innovation that keeps companies ahead of the curve. This commitment to innovation leads to the creation of new products and services that set industry standards and create market trends.

Economies of scale are another critical factor that provides a competitive edge when businesses operate on a larger scale. The ability to reduce per-unit costs allows for more competitive pricing, a feat that smaller businesses often struggle to match. Suppliers are also more inclined to offer discounts to companies purchasing in bulk, further lowering the cost of goods sold. This capacity to undercut competitors on price while maintaining healthy profit margins is a significant advantage in dominating the market.

Larger enterprises also have the power to set industry standards and shape market direction. For instance, Amazon's innovations in fast shipping, customer service, and product variety have redefined consumer expectations, creating substantial barriers to entry for new competitors that may lack the resources to meet these established standards.

Moreover, larger businesses gain competitive advantages through the creation of barriers to entry, such as high initial investment requirements, exclusive access to distribution channels, and strong brand loyalty. With substantial resources, these companies can secure long-term contracts with suppliers, invest in proprietary technology, and build expansive networks that are difficult for new entrants to replicate. These strategies ensure that even if smaller competitors enter the market, they face significant challenges in scaling up and competing effectively.

Advantage #9: Opportunities for Innovation and Expansion

Expanding provides access to a broader range of resources that can drive innovation. Substantial research and development budgets enable the creation of new products and services, keeping companies at the forefront of their industries.

Expansion also opens the door to diversification of offerings and entry into new markets. This diversification not only reduces risk but also generates multiple revenue streams, making the business more resilient to market fluctuations.

Additionally, scaling up allows operational costs to be spread over a larger base, achieving economies of scale that smaller competitors cannot match. This reduction in per-unit costs enables competitive pricing, further reinforcing market position.

Leveraging existing infrastructure and customer bases to support new ventures is another strategic advantage. For instance, Amazon's extensive logistics network, initially built for retail operations, now powers its cloud computing services (AWS) and grocery business, Amazon Fresh. This strategic use of existing resources accelerates the growth of new business lines while minimizing the risks associated with initial investments.

As businesses grow, they become more capable of attracting and retaining top talent, which is essential for innovation. Larger companies are often able to offer competitive compensation packages and career development opportunities, making them more appealing to skilled professionals. This influx of talent introduces fresh ideas and expertise, which are crucial for ongoing innovation. Having more resources to invest in cross-cultural training and global talent acquisition further enhances the ability to innovate by fostering diverse perspectives and ideas—an essential element in the global market.

Market expansion strategies, such as geographical and sector expansion, also create new opportunities for growth. Entering new geographic markets provides access to untapped customer bases, reducing dependency on a single market. Expanding into different sectors by adapting products for various industries can drive additional growth. For example, a healthcare product repurposed for the education sector can create entirely new business opportunities.

However, expansion into new markets comes with its challenges. Navigating different regulatory environments, cultural nuances, and logistical complexities requires effective market research, strategic planning, and strong local partnerships to overcome these hurdles and ensure successful expansion.

By embracing innovation and expansion, businesses remain competitive and pave the way for sustained growth and market leadership. The ability to adapt, explore new markets, and continuously innovate distinguishes successful large companies from their smaller counterparts, positioning them for long-term success.

Advantage #10: Financial Strength and Stability

Larger companies benefit from having substantial assets and a solid balance sheet, which may include cash reserves, properties, and investments. These assets act as a buffer during economic downturns, enabling these companies to withstand financial crises that could devastate smaller businesses. For example, during the 2008 financial crisis, many large firms with robust financial foundations not only survived but also thrived, while smaller companies either struggled or went out of business.

Another key advantage is the ability to secure financing and attract investments. Strong financial health allows larger companies to obtain loans more easily and draw in investors who are reassured by the company's stability and track record. This access to capital is vital for funding new projects, expanding into new markets, and acquiring other companies. Microsoft's acquisition of LinkedIn in 2016 for $26.2 billion serves as an example of how financial strength can drive strategic growth opportunities.

Larger companies also benefit from economies of scale, further enhancing their financial stability. By producing goods and services at a larger scale, they can reduce per-unit costs, thereby increasing profit margins. This efficiency strengthens profitability and provides a competitive edge in pricing, making it challenging for smaller competitors to keep pace.

Financial strength often translates into the ability to pay dividends and deliver returns to shareholders. The capacity to generate consistent and attractive returns helps large companies maintain investor confidence and attract additional investment. For instance, technology giants such as Apple and Microsoft have consistently paid dividends and conducted share buybacks, enhancing shareholder value and solidifying their positions in the market.

Additionally, a strong financial position allows for significant investment in research and development, which is critical for innovation and staying ahead in competitive industries. Comprehensive financial statements and ratio analyses used by larger businesses provide a clear picture of their financial health, guiding management teams in making informed decisions, planning future investments, and managing risks effectively. This strategic approach ensures ongoing success and leadership in the marketplace.

Challenges and Risks Associated with Growth and Effective Coping Strategies

While scaling up offers numerous advantages, it also presents a variety of challenges and risks that must be navigated carefully. Recognizing these potential pitfalls is essential for any business considering whether to pursue expansion or maintain operations at a smaller scale in order to achieve sustainable growth and long-term success. Outlined below are some of the primary challenges and risks associated with business growth, along with strategies to address them effectively.

Challenge #1: Operational Complexity

Growth inevitably brings an increase in operational complexity. Managing larger inventories, expanded production, extended supply chains, and additional locations can place significant strain on existing systems and processes. If not managed effectively, this added complexity can lead to inefficiencies, errors, and higher costs.

Operational complexity can quickly become a barrier to growth. As businesses expand, operations become more intricate, encompassing logistics, supply chain management, production scheduling, and quality control. Each new layer of complexity introduces the potential for bottlenecks, miscommunication, and operational errors. For example, managing multiple locations requires a robust system to ensure consistency in operations, quality, and customer service across all sites.

There are, however, effective strategies to address these challenges and optimize operations throughout periods of growth. One of the most critical approaches is investing in advanced operational systems and infrastructure. Implementing software solutions such as enterprise resource planning (ERP) systems, which integrate various business processes and provide real-time data, can help manage resources efficiently. These systems streamline processes, improve accuracy in inventory management, and enhance overall productivity. For instance, ERP systems can automate inventory tracking, reducing the likelihood of costly stockouts or overstock situations.

Clear and consistent communication throughout the organization is also crucial. As operations become more complex, ensuring that every team member is aligned with the company's direction can mitigate uncertainty and maintain trust. Regular updates and transparent decision-making processes help employees understand their roles and the company's goals. Involving staff in decision-making, especially regarding their roles and responsibilities, fosters a sense of ownership and reduces resistance to change. This inclusive approach not only improves morale but also leverages the insights and expertise of the workforce to streamline operations.

Standardizing processes is another critical step. Developing standard operating procedures (SOPs) for routine tasks ensures consistency and reduces variability in operations. SOPs serve as guidelines, ensuring that tasks are performed efficiently and accurately, regardless of who is executing them. Additionally, using tools like process maps and project management systems can help visualize workflows, identify inefficiencies, and optimize processes for better performance.

Strategic resource allocation is also vital. As businesses grow, resources such as personnel, equipment, and capital must be allocated effectively to support expansion. This may involve hiring additional staff, investing in new technology, or restructuring the organization to better align with operational goals. For example, creating dedicated teams for specific functions, such as supply chain management or quality control, can help manage complexity more effectively and improve overall efficiency.

Continuous assessment and improvement are key to maintaining operational efficiency. Regularly reviewing operations through performance metrics and feedback can help identify areas for improvement and ensure processes remain efficient as the business evolves. This proactive approach allows for data-driven decision-making and enables businesses to swiftly adapt to new challenges, maintaining the agility and resilience needed to thrive in a complex environment.

Challenge #2: Quality Control

Maintaining consistent product or service quality becomes increasingly complex as a business expands. This complexity arises from higher production volumes, the need for additional suppliers, and a larger workforce, each introducing new variables that can impact quality.

One significant challenge is onboarding new employees. Rapid growth often necessitates quick hiring, which may result in bringing on staff who are unfamiliar with the company's standards and processes. This can lead to inconsistencies in task performance and output quality.

Expanding production also presents challenges. Increased reliance on new suppliers or higher output from existing ones introduces variability in quality control measures, potentially affecting the materials or components received. Without proper oversight, this can lead to fluctuations in the final product's quality.

Outsourcing tasks to meet increased demand further complicates quality control. External partners may have different standards and practices, which can affect the consistency and quality of the products or services provided.

Additionally, with a larger workforce and more production sites, maintaining oversight becomes more difficult. Managers and quality control teams may struggle to monitor and enforce standards across all areas of the business, particularly when stretched by growing operational demands.

The pressure to meet higher demand quickly can also lead to shortcuts or reduced focus on quality, as speed takes priority. This can result in products or services that fall below established standards, ultimately harming customer satisfaction and the brand's reputation.

To maintain quality during growth, it is essential to implement strict quality control measures. Establishing clear standards and ensuring they are communicated and adhered to across the organization is crucial. For products, this may involve setting specific criteria for materials, production processes, and final inspections. For services, it could mean defining delivery protocols and performance metrics.

Investing in continuous training programs is also key. As new employees are onboarded, thorough training on quality standards and processes is critical. Regular updates for existing staff help them stay current with changes in procedures or expectations, fostering a culture where quality is prioritized across the team.

Leveraging quality improvement tools such as Six Sigma and Lean Six Sigma can also be beneficial. These methodologies focus on reducing defects and variability in processes through data-driven approaches. Six Sigma, for instance, utilizes the DMAIC (define, measure, analyze, improve, control) framework to identify and eliminate the root causes of quality issues. Lean Six Sigma emphasizes efficiency by reducing waste and optimizing workflows. Both methods are valuable in maintaining quality during periods of rapid growth.

Regular audits and performance reviews are equally important. Conducting frequent quality audits helps identify potential issues before they escalate. These audits should be thorough, covering all aspects of the operation—from supplier performance to final product inspection. Regularly reviewing performance data allows businesses to spot trends and make informed decisions to improve quality control processes.

Fostering a culture of continuous improvement is also essential. Encouraging team members to provide feedback and suggest improvements helps identify areas for enhancement while empowering employees to take ownership of quality control. Continuously seeking ways to improve ensures that quality remains a priority as the business scales, safeguarding both reputation and customer satisfaction.

Challenge #3: Financial Strain

As businesses expand, the need for resources grows, leading to significant upfront costs that can put pressure on financial reserves. Expanding operations often requires substantial capital investment, such as purchasing new equipment or opening additional locations. Similarly, ramping up marketing efforts to reach a broader audience involves significant expenditure, while hiring additional staff to support increased production or service delivery adds to the financial burden. These expenses can quickly outpace revenue, creating cash flow challenges that, if not managed carefully, could jeopardize the financial health of the business.

Managing these financial pressures becomes more complex with the added burden of ongoing operational expenses. Day-to-day costs, including higher utility bills, increased inventory needs, and additional maintenance, can accumulate rapidly. Without careful planning, these incremental costs can erode profit margins and further strain the company's financial stability.

Another challenge is the potential delay in returns on investment. Many of the expenses associated with scaling, such as marketing campaigns or new hires, may not yield immediate returns. There can be a lag between when the investment is made and when it begins generating additional revenue. During this period, businesses must have sufficient cash flow to sustain operations without relying on anticipated future income.

Accessing the necessary funding to support growth can also present difficulties. Traditional financing options, such as bank loans, often require substantial collateral or come with stringent repayment terms, potentially putting further pressure on cash flow. Equity financing, while providing significant capital, may involve giving up a portion of ownership and control over the business. Navigating these funding challenges requires a strategic approach to ensure that the chosen financing method aligns with the company's long-term goals and operational needs.

Economic fluctuations and market uncertainties can exacerbate financial strain. Changes in consumer demand, shifts in market conditions, or economic downturns can impact revenue streams, making it harder to maintain financial stability. Businesses must be prepared to adapt to these external factors while managing growth-related expenses.

One strategy to mitigate financial strain is securing adequate funding through various means, including equity financing, debt financing, venture capital, and bootstrapping. Choosing the right mix of funding sources is crucial. For example, while venture capital can provide large sums quickly, it often involves relinquishing some control over the business. Debt financing allows businesses to maintain control but requires regular repayments, which can strain cash flow if not managed properly.

Effective cash flow management is essential for sustaining growth, requiring careful planning that balances both short-term and long-term financial needs. The foundation of this approach is developing a comprehensive financial plan that incorporates projections for income, expenses, and overall cash flow. However, planning alone is not enough; regularly reviewing and adjusting this plan based on actual performance and changing conditions is critical to mitigating financial risks. This process ensures that the business remains responsive to fluctuations in its financial landscape.

A well-structured financial plan must also include departmental budgets, with a clear focus on prioritizing expenditures that contribute directly to growth and profitability. Equally important is ensuring the timely collection of receivables, as delayed payments can disrupt cash flow. By keeping costs under control and directing resources toward areas that deliver the most impact, businesses can maintain healthier cash flow and, consequently, a more stable financial position.

Technology plays a crucial role in this financial management process. Modern financial management software provides real-time insights into a business's financial health, equipping decision-makers with the information needed to make informed choices. Besides, these tools can automate essential processes like invoicing, payroll, and expense tracking, reducing errors and saving valuable time. More advanced features, such as analytics, can help forecast future cash flow needs, identify potential financial bottlenecks, and offer actionable insights for refining financial strategies. For instance, cloud-based accounting software can adapt as the business scales, ensuring that financial systems evolve with growing operational complexity.

In addition to managing ongoing financial activities, it is vital to build a financial cushion that can buffer against unforeseen challenges. Maintaining a reserve fund serves as a safety net, allowing the business to cover unexpected expenses or manage temporary revenue shortfalls. This financial resilience ensures continued smooth operations, even during periods of financial strain, and provides peace of mind as the business navigates growth.

In summary, scaling a business presents significant financial challenges that require careful planning and strategic management. By securing adequate funding, managing cash flow effectively, leveraging technology, and building financial resilience, businesses can navigate these challenges and sustain their growth.

Challenge #4: Talent Acquisition and Retention

The need for a larger and more specialized workforce rises as companies continue to grow. Yet, attracting the right talent in a competitive market can prove difficult. Many companies face talent shortages, with employers often reporting a lack of qualified candidates, making it difficult to find suitable hires. This scarcity leads to increased competition among businesses, each striving to secure top professionals. As a result, salaries and benefits packages tend to rise, making it more costly to attract highly qualified individuals. Moreover, candidates with strong qualifications often receive multiple job offers, further complicating the recruitment process.

Another challenge stems from the evolving expectations of the modern workforce. Employees today often prioritize factors beyond salary, such as work-life balance, career development opportunities, and company culture. Businesses that fail to meet these expectations may find it difficult to attract and retain talent. Additionally, the rise of remote work has expanded the job market, enabling candidates to consider positions outside their immediate geographic area. While this broadens the talent pool, it also heightens competition for skilled workers.

High turnover rates present yet another obstacle. As companies grow, maintaining a stable workforce becomes essential. Frequent turnover can disrupt operations, lower employee morale, and increase recruitment and training costs. It can also damage a company's reputation, making it more difficult to attract new hires.

Retention challenges can arise from a lack of clear career progression. Employees are more likely to remain with a company if they see opportunities for growth and development. Without clear advancement pathways, employees may seek career growth elsewhere, contributing to higher turnover rates.

The recruitment process itself can be resource-intensive. Finding the right candidates often requires significant time and effort. Traditional recruitment methods may not be efficient enough to keep up with the rapid pace of business growth, resulting in prolonged vacancies and an increased workload for existing staff, further exacerbating the talent shortage.

One critical strategy for addressing these challenges is developing a strong employer brand. An employer brand represents a company's reputation as a workplace, attracting potential candidates and encouraging them to join the team. To build a compelling employer brand, businesses can highlight what makes them unique, whether it is an innovative work environment, opportunities for career advancement, or a strong commitment to work-life balance. Platforms like Glassdoor and LinkedIn are valuable tools for showcasing the brand and gathering reviews from current and former employees.

Offering competitive compensation is another key factor. Compensation encompasses not only salary but also benefits, bonuses, and other perks that make an offer attractive. In a competitive market, companies are increasingly offering unique benefits such as flexible work hours, remote work options, and even unconventional perks like pet insurance. These offerings enhance the overall value proposition, making the company more appealing to top talent.

Creating a positive work environment is essential for both attracting and retaining employees. This involves fostering a culture where employees feel valued, respected, and engaged. Regularly measuring employee satisfaction and acting on feedback can address critical areas such as workload balance, career development opportunities, and workplace inclusivity. Such efforts contribute to higher employee satisfaction and reduce turnover.

Retention strategies are equally important. High turnover can be costly and disruptive, so focusing on career development and continuous learning opportunities is crucial. Providing clear career paths, mentorship programs, and professional development resources helps employees envision a future with the company and fosters personal and professional growth.

Moreover, leveraging technology can streamline the recruitment process. Tools like applicant tracking systems can manage job postings, applications, and candidate communications more efficiently. Additionally, artificial intelligence and data analytics can help identify top candidates and predict hiring trends, allowing for more informed decision-making.

By implementing these strategies, businesses can not only attract top talent but also keep employees engaged and committed to the company's long-term success.

Challenge #5: Cultural Dilution

In the early stages of a business, the culture often directly reflects the founders' values and vision. Communication is straightforward, everyone knows one another, and the shared mission is clear. However, as the business grows, the introduction of new employees, the opening of additional locations, and the layering of organizational structures can weaken this closely-knit culture. The original values and practices may become lost in the process, leading to a diluted and inconsistent culture.

One significant challenge lies in onboarding new employees who may not be familiar with the company's foundational values and mission. As the workforce expands, ensuring that every new hire understands and aligns with the established culture becomes more difficult. This can result in inconsistencies in how work is approached and how values are upheld across different areas of the organization.

Geographic dispersion of the workforce presents another challenge. As businesses expand into new regions or countries, cultural differences and local practices can influence how company values are interpreted and applied. This geographic spread can make it harder to maintain a unified culture and consistent practices across all locations.

The layering of organizational structures further complicates matters. As more levels of management and departments are introduced, communication becomes less direct, potentially diluting the influence of the founders and early leaders. With more people involved in decision-making, there is a risk that the original cultural elements may be miscommunicated or lost altogether.

Rapid growth also creates pressure to prioritize short-term goals over preserving cultural integrity. In the rush to scale, important cultural practices and values may be overlooked or deprioritized, leading to their gradual erosion.

As the company evolves, cultural shifts are inevitable, which can lead to tension between long-time employees who are accustomed to the original culture and newer employees who are contributing to its evolution. Balancing these dynamics is essential to prevent a divide within the workforce.

One of the most effective strategies for combating cultural dilution is to clearly define the company's culture from the outset. This involves articulating core values, beliefs, and behaviors that define the organization. A well-defined culture allows for better communication across the company and ensures that these values are maintained during periods of growth. Input from employees at all levels is essential to ensure the culture resonates throughout the organization.

Integrating company culture into the onboarding process is another key strategy. New employees should understand and embrace the company's values from the beginning. Cultural orientation sessions, mentorship programs, and regular reinforcement of these values can help embed the culture deeply within the organization, ensuring alignment among new hires.

Hiring a dedicated Culture Manager can also be instrumental in maintaining a strong culture during rapid growth. This individual would be responsible for monitoring the health of the company culture, identifying potential issues, and implementing initiatives to reinforce cultural values. They can help ensure that culture remains a priority as the company navigates expansion.

Regular and transparent communication with employees is critical for preserving trust and maintaining alignment with the company's mission and values. Establishing consistent communication channels—such as town halls, internal newsletters, and feedback sessions—keeps everyone informed and engaged, fostering a culture of transparency and trust, particularly during times of change.

Celebrating and recognizing employees who exemplify the company's values can further reinforce the desired culture. Public recognition, awards, and informal acknowledgments motivate employees to uphold and promote the organization's core values. This positive reinforcement helps embed the culture deeply within the workforce, allowing it to endure even as the company grows.

Adapting strategies as the company evolves is also crucial. This involves regularly reassessing and refining core values to ensure they remain relevant as the organization grows. Additionally, creating a physical and digital workspace that reflects the company's cultural values helps foster a positive and cohesive work environment.

Through the prioritization of these strategies, organizations can maintain the core values that distinguish them and contribute to their success, even as they grow.

Challenge #6: Customer Experience

One of the initial challenges businesses face during growth is the potential weakening of the personal connection with customers. In smaller companies, it is often easier to engage directly with customers, understand their needs, and provide personalized service. However, with expansion comes an increased customer base and operational complexity, making it more difficult to maintain those close relationships.

The surge in customer interactions often leads to longer response times and a decline in service quality. As the customer base grows, the volume of inquiries, complaints, and support requests rises accordingly. Without adequate systems in place, this increased demand can overwhelm customer service teams, resulting in slower response times and a reduction in the quality of support.

Ensuring consistent service across various channels and touchpoints also becomes more challenging. Today's customers interact with businesses through multiple channels, including phone, email, social media, and live chat. As a business scales, maintaining a seamless and consistent experience across all these platforms becomes increasingly complex. Inconsistent service can lead to customer frustration and negatively impact the overall experience.

As businesses expand, maintaining personalized service becomes increasingly challenging. Smaller companies are often able to remember individual customer preferences and deliver tailored experiences with ease. However, as the customer base grows, replicating this level of personalization across a larger audience becomes more difficult. Customers still expect to be recognized and have their specific needs met, yet scaling personalized service demands sophisticated tools and strategies that are not easily implemented without the right resources.

This challenge is compounded by the need to instill and maintain a customer-centric culture within a growing team. As more employees are brought on board to support expansion, ensuring that each team member aligns with the company's commitment to exceptional customer service becomes crucial. New hires must undergo thorough training to understand the company's standards while existing employees need ongoing engagement to continue delivering high-quality service. Without sustained effort, inconsistencies in service delivery can arise, impacting the customer experience.

Operational complexity also increases as businesses grow, leading to additional challenges. Expanding product lines, services, or locations introduces more variables that can cause breakdowns in the customer experience. Miscommunications and inefficiencies between departments can further complicate efforts to maintain consistent service. When operations become fragmented, customers are more likely to encounter inconsistent experiences, which can damage satisfaction and loyalty.

A key solution for maintaining high customer satisfaction during growth is shifting from a reactive to a proactive customer service approach. While smaller businesses often handle customer issues as they occur, scaling operations necessitates anticipating customer needs and addressing potential problems before they escalate. By adopting a proactive strategy, businesses can improve satisfaction levels, even as their customer base and operational complexity increase. This shift requires investing in advanced tools, such as predictive analytics and automated customer service solutions, which enable businesses to identify trends, foresee potential issues, and offer solutions before customers even realize a problem exists. These tools not only enhance the customer experience but also streamline operations by reducing the need for reactive interventions.

Investing in the right tools and technologies is essential for monitoring and enhancing the customer experience as businesses grow. Tools such as behavior analytics and customer feedback systems provide valuable insights into customer interactions, enabling businesses to identify pain points and address them more effectively. This data-driven approach fosters continuous improvement, ensuring that customer needs are met as the company expands.

A crucial aspect of scaling customer experience is consolidating customer data to create a unified view across the organization. By tracking customer behavior through a centralized system, businesses can ensure that all departments have access to consistent information. This integration, often facilitated by customer relationship management (CRM) systems, enables more personalized and cohesive interactions across various touchpoints, enhancing the overall customer journey.

Employee training and engagement are equally important in maintaining high levels of customer satisfaction. Frontline employees have a direct impact on customer experiences, making it vital to equip them with the skills and knowledge required to deliver exceptional service. Regular training sessions and workshops can reinforce the importance of customer-centricity, encouraging employees to approach their roles from the customer's perspective, which helps build empathy and dedication to customer satisfaction.

Breaking down organizational silos is essential for creating a seamless customer experience. When departments operate independently, it often results in service inconsistencies and communication gaps that frustrate customers. By fostering interdepartmental collaboration and ensuring alignment with customer experience goals, businesses can develop a cohesive and effective strategy. Regular cross-functional meetings and shared performance metrics help bridge communication gaps, ensuring all teams work toward the same customer-centric objectives.

Personalization is another critical aspect of the customer experience that becomes increasingly important as customer expectations evolve. Today's customers expect businesses to recognize and cater to their individual needs. By leveraging data analytics to personalize interactions and regularly refining these strategies, companies can provide relevant, timely solutions that enhance customer satisfaction and build loyalty. Segmentation based on behavior and preferences further ensures that each interaction is tailored to the customer's unique requirements, making them feel valued and understood.

Maintaining transparent and regular communication is also essential in fostering strong customer relationships. Keeping customers informed about changes, promptly addressing their concerns, and actively seeking their feedback creates an environment of trust and reliability. Establishing multiple communication channels, such as email, social media, and customer portals, allows customers to access support and information easily, reinforcing positive engagement with the brand and contributing to a lasting sense of connection.

Challenge #7: Increased Competition

As businesses expand into new markets, they often encounter well-established competitors that can pose significant challenges. Established companies, with their ample resources, may launch aggressive marketing campaigns, making it difficult for emerging brands to gain visibility. Additionally, these competitors may engage in price wars, lowering prices to levels that are challenging for a growing business to match without sacrificing profitability. This dynamic can put considerable pressure on margins and overall market positioning.

Staying competitive requires businesses to focus on the speed of innovation. Larger, well-funded companies are often able to invest heavily in research and development, quickly introducing new and improved products to the market. For smaller or growing businesses, maintaining an innovation pipeline that can compete with these established players is essential but challenging. This involves not only financial investment but also a strong commitment to creative and strategic thinking.

Market saturation presents another significant hurdle. In new markets, businesses often face a customer base that is already loyal to existing brands. Convincing these customers to switch to a new product or service requires a compelling value proposition and substantial marketing efforts. Overcoming entrenched brand loyalty and customer relationships in saturated markets demands innovative approaches and sustained persistence.

Operational efficiency becomes increasingly critical as businesses grow. With expansion comes added complexity, and streamlining processes is essential to deliver products or services at competitive prices without compromising quality. Achieving this balance can be difficult, particularly when facing aggressive competition that may already have highly efficient operations.

Differentiating a brand in a crowded market is crucial yet challenging. With many competitors vying for attention, standing out requires a clear and compelling value proposition. Communicating what makes a product or service unique can be difficult, especially when competitors are quick to replicate successful strategies. This necessitates a strong focus on branding and messaging to ensure differentiation is effectively conveyed to the target audience.

Conducting continuous market analysis is essential for navigating competitive landscapes. Regularly gathering and analyzing data on market trends, competitor strategies, and customer preferences helps businesses remain informed about current conditions and competitor moves. This information allows for data-driven decision-making and quick adaptation to changing market dynamics.

Innovation is a key driver in staying ahead of the competition. This goes beyond developing new products; it also involves improving existing offerings and exploring new business models. Staying attuned to emerging technologies and customer feedback can guide innovation efforts, helping to maintain a competitive edge.

Strategic agility is another crucial factor. The ability to pivot quickly in response to market changes can be a significant advantage. Agile businesses can adjust their strategies, reallocate resources, and implement new plans faster than their competitors. This flexibility is particularly valuable in rapidly changing industries. Promoting a culture of continuous improvement, encouraging cross-functional collaboration, and utilizing project management tools that support quick decision-making are essential components of adopting an agile approach.

Lastly, focusing on differentiation is vital for standing out in a crowded market. Whether through superior customer service, unique product features, or a strong brand identity, businesses must ensure that their value proposition is clear and compelling to the target audience. Differentiation strategies can help attract and retain customers, even in the face of intense competition.

Challenge #8: Regulatory and Compliance Issues

Expanding into new territories introduces the significant challenge of understanding and adhering to local regulations, which can vary widely from one region to another. These regulations may encompass employment laws, environmental standards, tax obligations, data protection rules, and industry-specific requirements. For example, the European Union's General Data Protection Regulation (GDPR) imposes strict guidelines on data privacy, with broad implications for any business handling the personal data of EU citizens.

Navigating these diverse regulations can be complex and overwhelming. Different countries and regions often have their own sets of rules, which may conflict with one another. Successfully managing these discrepancies requires a deep understanding of each regulatory environment and the ability to reconcile these differences to ensure compliance across all jurisdictions. For growing enterprises, this challenge is particularly pronounced, as they may lack the resources available to larger corporations.

The dynamic nature of regulatory environments presents yet another challenge. Laws and regulations are constantly evolving, and staying informed about these changes requires ongoing monitoring. Tax regulations, for example, may shift annually, and new data protection laws are frequently introduced in response to advancements in technology and privacy concerns. Failing to keep up with these changes can result in inadvertent non-compliance, which could lead to serious consequences.

As businesses grow, they also face increased scrutiny from regulators and competitors. With expansion comes greater visibility, which often leads to more frequent and thorough inspections, audits, and compliance checks.

Managing these interactions requires robust internal controls and meticulous documentation to ensure preparedness and adherence to regulations.

Compliance efforts can be resource-intensive, demanding significant investments of time, money, and human resources. Developing a comprehensive compliance program may require hiring or training compliance officers, implementing management systems, and conducting regular audits and training sessions. For growing businesses, effectively balancing these demands with other operational priorities can be a complex challenge.

Cultural and language barriers further complicate compliance, especially for businesses expanding into international markets. Understanding and interpreting regulations across different languages and cultural contexts requires specialized expertise. Miscommunications or misunderstandings in this area can lead to non-compliance, which carries substantial risks.

The consequences of non-compliance extend beyond financial penalties. Legal actions, fines, and sanctions can have a detrimental impact on the financial health of a business. Additionally, non-compliance can severely damage a company's reputation, eroding customer trust and potentially resulting in the loss of business opportunities. The reputational harm can be particularly damaging, affecting customer loyalty and the brand's perception in the marketplace.

To navigate these challenges, businesses should invest in dedicated compliance resources. This may involve hiring legal experts who specialize in the regulatory frameworks of the markets being entered or partnering with compliance consultants. These professionals can provide guidance on specific regulatory requirements and help develop strategies for maintaining compliance. They can also assist in implementing compliance management systems that monitor regulatory changes and keep the business informed and up-to-date.

Establishing robust internal processes and controls is another crucial strategy. Developing comprehensive compliance policies and procedures, conducting regular audits, and providing employees with ongoing training ensures that the entire organization understands the importance of adhering to regulations. For example, regular training on data protection laws can equip employees with the knowledge needed to mitigate risks associated with data breaches.

Leveraging technology can significantly aid in managing compliance. Compliance management software can automate many of the tasks involved in monitoring and reporting, reducing the likelihood of human error and ensuring consistent compliance activities. These tools can track regulatory changes, manage documentation, and provide real-time insights into compliance status, enabling businesses to identify and address potential issues before they escalate.

Proactive compliance management is essential not only for avoiding fines but also for safeguarding the company's reputation and maintaining stakeholder confidence. Ensuring adherence to regulations helps protect the brand from legal and reputational risks while fostering trust with customers, partners, and regulators.

Challenge #9: Technological Challenges

As businesses grow, technological challenges often emerge as significant obstacles. One of the primary issues is ensuring that IT infrastructure can accommodate increased demand. Server capacity, data storage, network bandwidth, and processing power all come under pressure as customer bases expand and transaction volumes rise. For example, an e-commerce platform may experience a sudden traffic spike during peak shopping seasons, which can overwhelm systems if they are not prepared, resulting in lost sales and dissatisfied customers.

Scalability is another critical concern. Many businesses struggle to scale their technology efficiently without requiring substantial upfront investments. Physical hardware, while powerful, can be both costly and inflexible, making it difficult to adjust resources quickly in response to fluctuating demands.

Cybersecurity becomes increasingly complex with growth. As a business expands, its visibility increases, making it a more attractive target for cyber threats. Protecting against data breaches, ransomware, and other cyberattacks becomes essential, but developing a comprehensive security strategy can be both daunting and resource-intensive.

Keeping pace with technological advancements is also a challenge. The technology landscape evolves rapidly, and staying current is crucial to maintaining a competitive edge. Regularly reviewing and updating the technology stack can be time-consuming and costly but is necessary to ensure efficiency and competitiveness.

Another challenge arises in ensuring interoperability between various software solutions. As businesses adopt different systems for customer relationship management (CRM), enterprise resource planning (ERP), and human resource management (HRM), making these systems work together seamlessly can be difficult, often requiring custom solutions and specialized expertise.

Data management grows more complex as businesses expand. The increasing volume of data necessitates effective strategies for data storage, retrieval, analysis, and governance. Ensuring that data remains accurate, accessible, and secure can be challenging but is critical for informed decision-making and long-term success.

Finally, implementing new technologies involves training employees and managing the associated changes. Structured training programs and ongoing support are needed to ensure that staff are comfortable with new systems. Additionally, change management strategies must be in place to minimize resistance and facilitate a smooth transition.

Investing in scalable technology solutions, such as cloud computing, can help address many of these challenges. Cloud services like Amazon Web Services (AWS) and Microsoft Azure offer the flexibility to scale resources up or down based on demand, eliminating the need for substantial upfront investments in physical hardware.

To mitigate cybersecurity risks, a comprehensive strategy should include robust access controls, regular software updates and patches, security audits, and employee education on cyber hygiene. Advanced security measures, such as firewalls, intrusion detection systems, and encryption technologies, can also play a critical role in safeguarding business operations.

Staying up-to-date with technological advancements is crucial for maintaining a competitive edge. Regular assessments help businesses modernize systems, address inefficiencies, and prevent outdated tools from hindering growth. Adopting new software is a key strategy in this process. It provides businesses with the latest tools to streamline operations, improve collaboration, and enhance customer experiences.

Integrating artificial intelligence (AI) and machine learning (ML) is also becoming increasingly important for businesses looking to stay ahead of competitors. These technologies can automate routine tasks, allowing employees to focus on higher-value work, while also providing predictive insights based on data analysis. Big data analytics is another powerful tool for businesses seeking to enhance their decision-making capabilities. The vast amounts of data generated by modern businesses can be overwhelming, but with the right analytics tools, this data can be transformed into actionable insights. These insights allow businesses to better understand customer behaviors, optimize processes, and identify new opportunities for growth.

For system interoperability, engaging IT specialists or consultants can provide the expertise needed to assess current infrastructure, identify areas for improvement, and develop a strategic plan for technology integration and scaling.

Finally, structured training programs and ongoing support are key to successful technology adoption. Clear communication about the benefits and impact of new systems, alongside resources to address any concerns, can help employees embrace change and fully leverage the potential of new technologies.

By anticipating and addressing these technological challenges through thoughtful planning and investment, businesses can navigate growth seamlessly and continue to thrive.

Challenge #10: Strategic Alignment

Strategic alignment is often more easily achieved in smaller companies due to the simplicity of communication and the clarity of shared goals. With fewer people and departments involved, the company's direction is generally understood by everyone. However, as businesses grow, the number of employees, teams, and divisions increases, making it more difficult to maintain a unified strategic focus.

One of the primary challenges that emerges with growth is the increased complexity of communication. As more layers of management and additional teams are introduced, the direct lines of communication that exist in smaller organizations become fragmented. This fragmentation can result in misunderstandings, miscommunications, and a lack of clarity regarding the company's strategic objectives. In some cases, different departments may pursue goals that are not fully aligned with the overall direction of the organization.

Siloed operations present another significant challenge. As organizations expand, departments often become more focused on their own specific goals and metrics, sometimes at the expense of broader organizational objectives. This silo mentality can lead to duplicated efforts, where departments unknowingly work on similar projects without coordination, wasting valuable resources. Additionally, when departments fail to share information and insights, opportunities for collaboration and innovation may be missed, limiting the organization's overall potential.

Ensuring that employees understand how their roles contribute to the company's strategic goals becomes more challenging as organizations grow. In larger environments, individuals may struggle to see the connection between their day-to-day activities and the broader objectives of the company. This disconnect can lead to disengagement, as employees may feel less connected to the company's mission and vision, which in turn reduces motivation.

Leadership consistency is another critical factor in maintaining strategic alignment. As companies grow, new leaders may be brought in, or internal promotions may occur, leading to varying leadership styles and priorities. Inconsistent leadership can create confusion and undermine the effort to maintain alignment across the organization. It is essential that leaders at all levels are aligned in their messaging and behaviors to ensure that the entire organization moves in the same direction.

Resource allocation is another area where misalignment can arise. Different departments may compete for limited resources, such as budget, personnel, and technology, often prioritizing their individual goals over the company's strategic priorities. This misalignment can result in suboptimal use of resources and hinder the overall effectiveness of the organization.

The pace of growth itself can compound these challenges. Rapid expansion often requires that strategic plans be revisited and adjusted more frequently. Ensuring that all departments are aware of and aligned with these updated strategies demands ongoing coordination and attention.

One of the most effective strategies for maintaining strategic alignment is the establishment of a clear and compelling vision. This vision must be consistently communicated across the organization, with leaders ensuring that every team understands how their work contributes to the company's overall goals. Regular town hall meetings, internal newsletters, and clear documentation of strategic plans can help reinforce this message and keep the organization on track.

Effective communication channels are vital for maintaining alignment as the business grows. Fostering an environment where information flows freely between departments and hierarchical levels is essential. Tools such as Slack, Microsoft Teams, and project management software can facilitate better communication and collaboration. Regular interdepartmental meetings and updates ensure that all teams are aligned and working toward common objectives.

Coordination among departments is another key component in overcoming the challenges of strategic alignment. Cross-functional teams can help break down silos and ensure that different parts of the organization are working in sync. For example, bringing together representatives from marketing, sales, product development, and customer service for a new product launch ensures that all perspectives are considered and efforts are coordinated.

Leadership plays a critical role in reinforcing strategic alignment. Leaders must not only set the vision but also model the behaviors and attitudes necessary to achieve it. This includes transparency about goals and progress, listening to feedback from all levels of the organization, and making adjustments as needed to stay on track. Celebrating achievements that contribute to strategic goals also helps reinforce alignment and encourages continued focus on the company's objectives.

Finally, establishing clear metrics and performance indicators that align with strategic goals is essential for maintaining alignment. These metrics should be communicated to all employees so that everyone understands how their performance contributes to the company's success. Regularly reviewing these metrics and providing feedback keeps the organization focused and ensures that efforts remain aligned with the overall strategy.

Challenge #11: Risk Management

As businesses expand, the scope of potential risks broadens considerably. Managing financial risks, for instance, becomes increasingly complex as operations grow. Fluctuating cash flow may result from rising operational costs or delayed receivables, creating pressure on financial stability. Operational risks, such as supply chain disruptions, can significantly impact business continuity, making it essential to identify potential bottlenecks and vulnerabilities within the supply chain. Additionally, market risks—such as shifting consumer behavior and increased competition—demand constant vigilance and the ability to adapt quickly. Strategic risks, including poor decision-making or misalignment with market trends, can be particularly damaging to sustained growth.

To address these challenges, developing a robust risk management framework is a critical first step. This framework should outline clear processes for identifying potential risks, assessing their likelihood and impact, and implementing effective mitigation strategies. A proactive approach to identifying risks is essential, as it allows businesses to stay informed about industry trends, regulatory changes, and emerging threats. Regular risk assessments and audits help uncover vulnerabilities across operations, financial health, and strategic initiatives. Engaging with experts, such as risk management consultants or industry analysts, can offer valuable insights and provide a broader understanding of the risk landscape.

Effectively managing risk begins with understanding the potential consequences each risk can pose. This awareness allows for the development of targeted mitigation strategies that address financial, operational, market, and strategic risks in a focused manner. By tailoring these approaches, businesses are better equipped to navigate challenges as they emerge, ensuring they remain resilient in the face of uncertainty. Informed decision-making, backed by data analysis, helps steer the organization in the right direction, enabling leaders to make sound choices with confidence. A culture of strategic thinking embedded throughout the organization enhances the ability to anticipate risks before they escalate, fostering a more proactive and sustainable path toward growth.

Technology also plays an important role in risk management, as leveraging risk management software enables businesses to track risks in real time, analyze data, and generate actionable insights. Fostering a risk-aware culture within the organization further enhances risk management efforts. Ensuring that employees at all levels understand their role in managing risks and are vigilant in identifying and reporting potential threats creates a more resilient business environment.

Challenge #12: Managing Change

As businesses grow, they inevitably face the challenge of managing change, which often involves restructuring departments, introducing new processes, or adopting different strategies to support expansion. These transitions can be disruptive, leading to resistance, confusion, and a decline in productivity if not handled effectively.

A primary challenge is overcoming employee resistance. Changes in established routines and responsibilities can generate skepticism and fear among staff, who may worry about job security, increased workloads, or the need to learn new skills. These concerns often result in hesitation or refusal to embrace new processes, impeding successful implementation.

Ensuring clear communication and achieving widespread buy-in across the organization presents another challenge. Miscommunication or lack of clarity about the reasons for change can cause confusion and misalignment, leaving employees disengaged or uncertain about their roles in the new environment. Without clear understanding, change initiatives risk becoming ineffective due to a lack of proper execution.

Maintaining alignment with the organization's culture and values is also difficult during periods of change. When new processes or structures conflict with long-standing cultural norms, employees may feel disconnected or demoralized. For instance, changes perceived as undermining teamwork in a company that values collaboration can lead to increased resistance and reluctance to participate in the transition.

Managing the logistical aspects of change introduces further complications. Implementing new processes, technologies, or organizational structures requires careful coordination and planning. Neglecting the logistical details, such as training, documentation updates, or resource allocation, can create confusion and disrupt normal operations, further slowing progress.

Sustaining momentum and ensuring the long-term adoption of changes present significant challenges. Initial enthusiasm for change often diminishes over time, leading to a gradual return to old habits. This backsliding can weaken the impact of the change initiative and prevent it from taking root within the organization. Without continuous reinforcement and regular monitoring, it becomes difficult to fully embed new practices, making long-term success elusive.

Establishing a clear and compelling vision for the change is crucial in addressing the challenges that come with managing transitions. Employees need to understand not only why the changes are necessary but also how they will benefit both the organization and themselves. This understanding should be reinforced through transparent and consistent communication, which helps build trust and reduce uncertainty. For instance, regular updates can be delivered via town hall meetings, emails, and internal newsletters to ensure that everyone remains informed and aligned with the organization's goals throughout the process.

Early engagement of stakeholders is equally important for successful change management. Involving top management, employees at all levels, and, when appropriate, external stakeholders such as customers and suppliers, fosters a sense of ownership and commitment to the change. By creating cross-functional teams to provide input on new processes, organizations can ensure that changes are both practical and effective, with insights from various perspectives contributing to a well-rounded approach.

Equally important is recognizing and addressing the emotional impact of change. Employees may feel anxious about job security or their ability to meet new expectations, making it essential to acknowledge these feelings and provide reassurance. Regular check-ins with employees to discuss their concerns and offer feedback foster a supportive environment where employees feel valued and understood.

Finally, monitoring and measuring the progress of change initiatives is essential for ensuring that they remain on track and achieve the desired outcomes. Setting clear metrics and key performance indicators (KPIs) provides a framework for assessing the effectiveness of the changes. Regularly reviewing these metrics, along with gathering employee feedback, enables timely adjustments and interventions when challenges arise, ensuring that the change initiative remains successful.

CHAPTER 3

PROS AND CONS OF STAYING SMALL

Advantages of Remaining a Small Business

Although the prospect of scaling up can be appealing, there are distinct advantages to maintaining a small business. For many entrepreneurs, staying small aligns with their values and long-term objectives, allowing for greater control and flexibility in operations. The advantages of remaining small are varied and can offer unique opportunities that larger enterprises may find more challenging to achieve. In the following sections, we will explore these key advantages in greater detail.

Advantage #1: Greater Control and Flexibility

One of the primary advantages of remaining a small business is the ability to maintain greater control and flexibility in decision-making. Smaller businesses can navigate through both calm and turbulent conditions with agility, as decisions are made without the bureaucratic delays often faced by larger organizations. This streamlined approach allows for swift responses to market changes, customer preferences, and emerging opportunities.

For instance, when a shift in customer behavior is observed, small businesses can quickly adjust their product offerings or marketing strategies to align with new demands. This ability to pivot rapidly is particularly valuable in dynamic industries such as technology or fashion, where trends evolve rapidly. Innovation thrives in such environments, as smaller businesses are free to experiment with new ideas and introduce innovative products or services without the slow approval processes that can hinder creativity in larger companies.

Additionally, the flexibility afforded by small business ownership enables the creation of a work environment that reflects the values and vision of the leadership. Whether it involves cultivating a close-knit team culture, promoting sustainable practices, or delivering personalized customer service, a small business can more easily align its operations with its core principles. This alignment often leads to higher employee satisfaction and stronger customer loyalty, both of which are essential for sustained success.

Another significant benefit is the ability to build closer relationships with customers. Small businesses are uniquely positioned to engage directly with their clientele, gaining a deeper understanding of their needs and responding promptly to feedback. This level of personalized attention not only enhances the overall customer experience but also fosters loyalty and satisfaction. The ability to adapt services and products based on real-time feedback encourages repeat business, as customers value the tailored approach and feel appreciated by the attentiveness of the business.

Advantage #2: Personalized Customer Experience

The ability to offer a highly personalized customer experience is one of the major advantages of staying small. In a small, community-oriented setting, interactions can feel more intimate and meaningful, much like a neighborhood café where the barista remembers a regular customer's name and favorite coffee order. This personal touch helps create a welcoming atmosphere that makes customers feel valued and appreciated.

Because small businesses typically serve a more concentrated customer base, there is greater opportunity to build strong personal relationships with clientele. Familiar faces often greet customers, whether in-store or online, allowing businesses to remember preferences, anticipate needs, and provide individualized service. For example, a boutique owner may set aside items for a loyal customer based on their style preferences, or a local tailor may offer customized fittings and alterations that larger chains cannot easily replicate.

This deep understanding of customer preferences enables small businesses to tailor their offerings with precision, offering recommendations and services that make customers feel genuinely valued. Unlike interactions with larger businesses, which can sometimes feel transactional, small businesses are able to provide a level of personal attention that resonates with customers on a deeper level, fostering strong emotional connections and increasing the likelihood of repeat business.

Moreover, small businesses often exude a unique charm and character that larger corporations may struggle to achieve. Thoughtful gestures, such as personalized thank-you notes or a warm, inviting ambiance, enhance the overall customer experience, making each interaction memorable. The flexibility of small businesses also allows for a more responsive approach to customer service. When issues arise, they can be addressed directly and immediately, often with a level of care and attention that goes above and beyond customer expectations.

Satisfied customers are more likely to share their positive experiences, contributing to organic growth through word-of-mouth referrals. In the digital age, these experiences often extend to social media and online reviews, further amplifying the reach and impact of the business.

In a competitive marketplace, these personal connections serve as a powerful differentiator, setting small businesses apart from larger, more impersonal corporations.

Advantage #3: Enhanced Quality Control

Remaining small offers significant advantages in maintaining a high level of quality control over products and services. With fewer layers of management and a more streamlined team, it becomes easier to oversee operations and ensure adherence to the company's quality standards. This hands-on approach allows for the swift identification and resolution of potential issues before they escalate into larger problems.

For instance, consider a local bakery where the owner personally inspects each loaf of bread before it reaches the customer. This dedication to quality can result in a strong reputation and foster brand loyalty, as customers come to trust the consistent excellence of the bakery's offerings. In larger organizations, achieving this level of oversight is often more difficult due to the sheer volume of products and the distance between decision-makers and day-to-day operations.

Smaller businesses also have a unique ability to cultivate a culture of quality among employees. When team members work closely with leadership and witness a direct commitment to maintaining high standards, they are more likely to adopt the same mindset and take pride in their work. This shared dedication enhances overall performance, leading to better products and services for customers.

Moreover, the ability to provide personalized service contributes significantly to quality control. Smaller businesses often know their customers personally, which allows them to tailor offerings to meet specific needs and preferences, thereby improving the quality of the customer experience. For example, a local tailor might offer custom fittings and alterations that larger retail chains cannot match, leading to higher levels of customer satisfaction and loyalty. This individualized attention ensures that each product or service is crafted with care, directly aligning with customer expectations and preferences, thus elevating both perceived and actual quality.

A strong focus on quality helps build a solid reputation and cultivate long-term brand loyalty. Customers who consistently receive superior products and services are more likely to return and recommend the business to others. Positive word-of-mouth referrals and favorable online reviews can significantly boost visibility and credibility, attracting new customers who prioritize quality and reliability.

Maintaining high-quality standards also allows smaller businesses to justify premium pricing for their products and services. Customers are often willing to pay more for items they perceive as superior in quality, which can enhance profitability and ensure long-term sustainability. This premium positioning further differentiates small businesses from larger competitors that may prioritize price competition over quality.

Advantage #4: Strong Community Connections

Small businesses are uniquely positioned to cultivate deep relationships within their communities, resulting in a loyal customer base that prioritizes supporting local enterprises. These community connections can enhance a business's reputation and strengthen its presence within the local market, creating a sense of belonging that larger companies may struggle to replicate.

Active participation in community events is one way that small businesses can deepen their ties to the community. Whether through sponsoring local sports teams, participating in charity events, or hosting gatherings, such involvement demonstrates a commitment to the well-being of the community. For instance, a local bakery might sponsor a 5k run, providing snacks and beverages for participants. These activities not only promote the business but also position it as an integral part of the community, significantly enhancing visibility and reputation.

Collaborations with other local businesses and organizations further amplify this effect. Partnering on events, cross-promotions, or joint marketing efforts helps small businesses expand their reach while fostering a sense of community solidarity. For example, a local coffee shop might collaborate with a nearby bookstore to host book readings or signings. Such partnerships attract new customers to both businesses and build stronger connections within the community.

The support of the local community can also play a critical role in a small business's sustained success, particularly during challenging periods. During the COVID-19 pandemic, many communities rallied to support their local businesses by purchasing gift cards, ordering takeout, and promoting them on social media. This support helped numerous small businesses survive and even thrive despite the economic downturn, demonstrating the resilience that strong community ties can provide.

These connections also enhance a small business's brand identity. Being known as a community-oriented enterprise sets small businesses apart from larger, more impersonal corporations. This local identity can be a powerful marketing tool, appealing to consumers who prioritize supporting their local economy and sustainable practices. Many consumers are willing to pay a premium for businesses that demonstrate a commitment to sustainability, and small businesses often exemplify these values through locally sourced products and eco-friendly practices.

Ultimately, fostering strong community connections not only strengthens the business but also enriches the broader community, contributing to a thriving local economy where businesses and residents mutually benefit.

Advantage #5: Better Work-Life Balance

Remaining small can offer significant benefits for achieving a better work-life balance, particularly for business owners. Managing a smaller operation typically involves fewer demands and stresses than overseeing a large corporation, allowing for greater flexibility and well-being. Smaller businesses enable owners to design a work environment that aligns with their personal values and lifestyle, leading to enhanced satisfaction both professionally and personally.

For example, small business owners have the ability to structure their workday according to their preferences. In contrast to larger corporations, where decision-making is often slowed by multiple layers of approval, small business owners can make quick decisions and implement changes efficiently. This agility provides more time for personal activities and family life, contributing to a healthier work-life balance. A small business owner might, for instance, adjust business hours to prioritize time with family in the afternoons.

Additionally, the reduced scale of operations in a small business often translates to a lighter administrative burden. With fewer employees to manage, less paperwork, and simpler logistics, the workload becomes more manageable. This streamlined approach allows owners to focus on the aspects of the business they find most fulfilling, whether it be customer interactions, product development, or service improvement. By avoiding the burnout that can come with larger operations, small business owners can maintain their passion for their work.

An important advantage of staying small is the ability to foster a work environment that reflects personal values. Business owners can create a company culture that promotes work-life balance not only for themselves but also for their employees. This may involve offering flexible work hours, remote work options, and cultivating a supportive workplace atmosphere. A positive work environment has been shown to enhance employee satisfaction, reduce turnover, and boost overall productivity.

Maintaining a strong work-life balance can then contribute to greater creativity and innovation. When individuals are not overwhelmed by work, they have the mental clarity and space to think creatively, leading to new ideas and innovations. This advantage is particularly important in competitive markets, where innovation can lead to differentiation and success. Many successful entrepreneurs have attributed their best ideas to moments of relaxation and downtime, underscoring the importance of a balanced lifestyle.

Another benefit of a balanced work-life approach is increased productivity. When business owners and their employees are well-rested and content, they tend to be more efficient and effective in their roles. This heightened productivity can contribute to better business performance and growth, even without the scale of larger operations. Employees who experience a positive work-life balance are generally more engaged, less stressed, and more loyal to the company, further enhancing the overall success of the business.

Advantage #6: Financial Stability and Sustainability

Staying small allows businesses to maintain financial stability by steering clear of the large costs and risks that often come with aggressive growth. Expanding quickly typically requires significant capital investment in new facilities, equipment, and personnel, which can strain financial resources and increase the risk of overextension. Maintaining a smaller scale allows for more effective management of expenses and helps businesses avoid accumulating excessive debt.

By focusing on steady, sustainable growth, small businesses can make strategic investments that align with their financial capabilities. Instead of rushing to capture market share, businesses can prioritize building a loyal customer base and enhancing their products or services. This measured approach strengthens the financial foundation of the company and improves its market position. For instance, reinvesting profits into the business rather than relying heavily on external financing reduces dependency on loans and investors, fostering greater financial autonomy and long-term stability.

Aligning growth with a company's risk tolerance is another benefit of staying small. Every venture carries some level of risk, but smaller businesses are better positioned to manage and mitigate these risks. Experimenting with new ideas and strategies on a smaller scale allows for learning from setbacks without jeopardizing the entire business. This cautious approach helps minimize the impact of potential failures and supports incremental improvements that contribute to sustainable growth over time.

Financial stability provides businesses with the resilience needed to weather unforeseen challenges. Whether faced with economic downturns, sudden shifts in the market, or unexpected operational issues, financially stable businesses are better equipped to handle adversity. Maintaining a strong balance sheet and healthy reserves ensures that a business has the necessary resources to navigate difficult times without resorting to drastic measures such as layoffs or cutbacks. This stability not only protects the business but also boosts confidence among employees, customers, and investors.

Advantage #7: Niche Market Focus

The ability to cater to niche markets with specialized products or services, which larger corporations may miss, stands out as one of the main advantages of staying small. This targeted approach allows small businesses to become experts within their specific niches, fostering strong customer loyalty and the ability to command higher prices.

For example, a small business that specializes in organic, handmade skincare products can tailor its offerings to meet the exact demands of a niche audience, in contrast to larger companies that aim to cater to broader markets. This level of specialization often results in higher-quality products and a personal touch that mass-market brands may find difficult to replicate. Customers who are seeking organic skincare solutions tend to appreciate the detailed knowledge and dedication to quality that smaller businesses can provide. This focus on a specific market segment helps to build trust and loyalty, as customers feel understood and valued.

Mastering a particular niche also enables small businesses to command premium pricing. When customers recognize the superior quality and specialized nature of the products or services offered, they are often willing to pay more for them. This pricing advantage can contribute to enhanced profitability and long-term sustainability. Additionally, a strong reputation within the niche often leads to word-of-mouth referrals and positive reviews, further strengthening the business's position in the market.

Small businesses can also capitalize on their niche focus to establish a distinctive brand identity. Emphasizing what sets their products or services apart from competitors helps to create a unique presence in a crowded market. For instance, a local coffee shop that sources its beans from a specific region and roasts them in-house can differentiate itself from larger coffee chains. This unique selling proposition not only attracts customers but also fosters a deeper connection with them, as they become part of a community that shares similar values and interests.

Focusing on a niche market also offers resilience against competition from larger companies. Large corporations tend to prioritize high-volume markets and may overlook or under-serve niche segments, creating opportunities for smaller businesses to thrive. By maintaining strong customer relationships, having a deep understanding of the niche, and staying attuned to its evolving needs, small businesses remain agile and adaptable, allowing them to respond quickly to changes and maintain their competitive edge.

Advantage #8: Innovation and Agility

The inherent agility of small businesses fosters an environment that encourages innovation and adaptability. With fewer layers of bureaucracy, smaller businesses have the flexibility to make swift decisions and implement changes quickly. This speed is crucial in today's fast-paced market, where trends and consumer preferences shift rapidly. For instance, a small fashion boutique noticing a new trend among its customers can promptly adjust its inventory and marketing strategies to capitalize on it, whereas larger companies might face delays due to their more complex decision-making processes.

Moreover, the close-knit nature of small business teams enhances innovation. In a smaller organization, communication tends to be more direct, and employees can collaborate easily on new ideas and projects. This open and collaborative environment fosters creativity, as team members are often more empowered to share their thoughts and take risks, leading to innovative solutions and new product offerings.

Another advantage of staying small is the proximity to customers, which provides valuable insights into their needs and preferences. This closeness allows small businesses to tailor their products and services more precisely, ensuring offerings that resonate deeply with their target audiences. Understanding customer preferences firsthand gives smaller businesses the ability to pivot quickly and meet market demands effectively.

Smaller businesses also benefit from the ability to implement and test new ideas with relative ease. With fewer resources at stake, smaller operations can experiment and iterate more freely, refining products or services until the best approach is discovered. This iterative process is essential for innovation, as it allows for learning from failures and continuous improvement. Larger companies, facing higher stakes and slower processes, often find it more challenging to adopt such an agile approach.

The capacity to innovate and adapt swiftly not only differentiates small businesses from their larger competitors but also helps them remain competitive in rapidly changing markets. Being able to respond quickly to emerging opportunities or challenges is a significant advantage. Regularly introducing new and exciting products or services helps position small businesses as trendsetters in their industries. This reputation for innovation attracts customers seeking the latest, most unique offerings, further solidifying the business's market position. Additionally, this agility enables smaller enterprises to carve out niches and build loyal customer bases that value their unique and responsive offerings.

Advantage #9: Strong Team Dynamics

A major benefit of remaining small is the capacity to cultivate strong team dynamics within the company. Smaller businesses often have close-knit teams where employees feel more connected to the business's mission and values. The shorter, more direct lines of communication in small businesses enable better collaboration and quicker decision-making. Employees tend to work closely with upper management and leadership, giving them a clearer understanding of the company's goals and strategies. This transparency helps employees feel more valued and invested in the success of the organization.

The intimate nature of small businesses also cultivates a sense of camaraderie and teamwork that is often more difficult to achieve in larger organizations. When employees are familiar with one another, it strengthens trust and cooperation within the team. This environment encourages team members to support each other and collaborate effectively to overcome challenges. The result is enhanced problem-solving and innovation, as employees feel more comfortable sharing ideas and offering feedback.

In addition, employees in small businesses frequently take on a variety of roles and responsibilities, which can be more stimulating and rewarding compared to narrowly defined positions in larger companies. This diversity of tasks provides employees with the opportunity to develop a broader skill set, contributing to both personal and professional growth. The flexibility within small businesses benefits not only the employees but also the organization itself, as a versatile team is better equipped to adapt to changing circumstances.

Another significant motivator for employees in small businesses is the ability to see the direct impact of their work. When team members can witness firsthand how their efforts contribute to the success of the business, it instills a sense of accomplishment and purpose. This visibility of contribution fosters higher job satisfaction and strengthens employee loyalty.

Higher levels of employee engagement and satisfaction often translate into improved retention rates. When employees feel valued and see opportunities for growth within the company, they are less likely to seek employment elsewhere. This stability is advantageous for the business, as it reduces the costs and disruptions associated with turnover. A stable team that works well together helps maintain consistent quality and service, contributing to the long-term success of the business.

Advantage #10: Lower Overheads

One of the most evident advantages of operating a small business is the reduction in fixed costs. Large corporations often face significant expenses related to maintaining office spaces, warehouses, and manufacturing facilities. Additionally, they incur substantial costs in managing extensive IT infrastructure and other capital-intensive assets. In contrast, small businesses can operate from more modest setups, such as shared workspaces, smaller offices, or even home offices, leading to notable savings on rental and utility expenses.

For example, a small graphic design studio working out of a shared workspace can significantly reduce overhead costs. These savings can then be reinvested in other areas, such as upgrading equipment, investing in better software, or expanding marketing efforts. The ability to keep operating costs lower also allows small businesses to offer competitive pricing. With reduced overhead, small businesses can price their products and services attractively without sacrificing quality, making them more appealing to cost-conscious customers who might otherwise choose larger, well-established brands.

Payroll expenses are another area where small businesses benefit. While large organizations require numerous employees to manage various departments, such as human resources, IT, marketing, and compliance, small businesses tend to operate with leaner teams. Employees in smaller companies often take on multiple roles, reducing the need for extensive staff and cutting payroll costs.

Supply chain management is another domain where smaller businesses can achieve cost savings. Large enterprises often manage complex supply chains that span multiple regions or countries, increasing logistical costs and the risk of disruptions. Smaller businesses, however, can simplify their supply chains by sourcing from local suppliers or working with fewer intermediaries, which reduces transportation costs and minimizes potential supply chain interruptions.

Additionally, marketing and advertising expenses are typically lower for small businesses. While large corporations may spend substantial amounts on nationwide campaigns or sponsorships, small businesses can focus on more cost-effective strategies such as social media marketing, participation in local events, and word-of-mouth referrals. These approaches often resonate better with local customers and can be more personalized, further strengthening the business's connection to its community.

The savings generated from lower overheads can be reinvested back into the business, fueling growth and innovation. With these extra resources, small businesses can enhance their product or service offerings, improve customer experiences, or invest in new technologies. This reinvestment helps sustain competitive advantages and contributes to long-term success.

Challenges of Staying Small and The Coping Strategies

While remaining a small business offers many advantages, it also brings a distinct set of challenges and limitations that can affect growth potential, market reach, and operational efficiency. Navigating these hurdles requires careful planning and adaptability. Below are some of the key challenges that small businesses often face, along with strategies to effectively manage and overcome them.

Challenge #1: Limited Financial Resources

Operating a small business often involves managing tight budgets and limited financial resources. Unlike larger corporations with vast financial reserves, small businesses typically rely on funds generated from sales and modest initial investments. This scarcity of capital can make it challenging to invest in crucial areas such as technology upgrades, marketing campaigns, and product expansion. For instance, while a large company might easily allocate a substantial budget to a comprehensive digital marketing strategy, a small business may struggle to afford even basic online advertising.

Securing external financing further compounds this challenge. Banks and investors often perceive small businesses as higher-risk ventures due to their limited financial history and narrower profit margins. As a result, qualifying for loans or attracting significant investment can be difficult, making it harder to capitalize on growth opportunities such as entering new markets or increasing production capacity. This financial limitation can prevent small businesses from achieving economies of scale, placing them at a competitive disadvantage compared to larger firms.

Despite these obstacles, small businesses can adopt strategies to manage their financial constraints effectively. One approach is to explore financial technology (fintech) solutions, which offer alternative financing options such as peer-to-peer lending, crowdfunding, and microloans. These platforms can provide essential capital without the stringent requirements of traditional banks, helping small businesses access funds more easily.

Building strong relationships with local banks and credit unions is another viable strategy. These institutions may be more willing to provide financing based on personal relationships and a connection to the local community. Presenting a solid business plan, demonstrating consistent cash flow, and outlining a clear growth strategy can also increase the likelihood of securing loans and attracting potential investors.

Additionally, optimizing the use of available resources is key to navigating financial limitations. Careful cash flow management, reducing unnecessary expenses, and negotiating better terms with suppliers can help stretch limited budgets further. Small businesses can also leverage cost-effective marketing strategies, such as social media campaigns and community engagement, to reach new customers without the need for significant financial investment.

Challenge #2: Resource Constraints

Operating with limited resources, such as personnel, technology, and equipment, is a common challenge for small businesses. These constraints can lead to overworked employees, strained operations, and ultimately, a decline in productivity and service quality.

With a smaller workforce, employees often have to juggle multiple roles and responsibilities. This multitasking can lead to long hours and increased stress, which, in turn, may result in burnout and higher turnover rates. Overburdened employees are more likely to be less productive and prone to mistakes, which can negatively impact the overall quality of the products or services offered.

The lack of access to advanced technology and equipment further intensifies these difficulties. Small businesses may not have the capital to invest in state-of-the-art systems that streamline operations and boost efficiency. This technological gap can make it challenging to compete with larger firms that leverage cutting-edge tools for everything from customer relationship management to supply chain logistics. For instance, while large corporations may use sophisticated data analytics to guide their decisions, small businesses often rely on manual processes that are time-consuming and less accurate.

Resource constraints also hinder innovation, as developing new products or services requires both financial investment and specialized expertise. Small businesses often lack the resources needed for research and development, preventing new ideas from moving beyond the conceptual stage. This limitation can stifle growth and hinder the ability to seize emerging opportunities, making it difficult to remain competitive in a rapidly evolving market.

Moreover, the absence of specialized expertise in key areas such as IT, marketing, and finance can further impede the efficient operation and growth of small businesses. Without a dedicated IT team, for example, businesses may struggle to maintain their digital infrastructure, leaving them vulnerable to cyber threats. Similarly, a lack of marketing expertise can lead to ineffective promotional strategies that fail to attract and retain customers, while poor financial management can result in cash flow problems and limit the ability to secure necessary funding.

To overcome these challenges, small businesses can adopt several effective strategies. One approach is to prioritize resource allocation by focusing on core competencies and outsourcing non-core activities. For instance, hiring a third-party provider for IT support or accounting services can free up internal resources while ensuring that critical functions are managed by experts. This strategy can also be more cost-effective than hiring full-time staff for specialized roles.

Leveraging affordable technology is another key strategy for mitigating resource constraints. While small businesses may not have the budget for high-end systems, many scalable technological solutions are available at lower costs. Cloud-based software, for example, offers a range of tools for project management, customer relationship management, and financial planning—providing the same benefits as traditional systems but at a fraction of the cost. Adopting these tools can help small businesses streamline operations, improve efficiency, and reduce the workload on their employees.

Collaboration and partnerships can also provide small businesses with access to the resources and expertise they lack. By joining local business networks, participating in industry associations, and forming alliances with other small businesses, they can gain valuable support and tap into opportunities for growth. These connections foster knowledge sharing and innovation, helping small businesses stay competitive in their markets despite limited resources.

Challenge #3: Market Reach and Visibility

Expanding market reach and increasing visibility pose significant challenges for small businesses. With limited financial resources, smaller enterprises often struggle to compete with the extensive advertising campaigns used by larger corporations to dominate the market. Major companies have the ability to invest heavily in television, radio, and print advertising, creating a broad and pervasive presence that is difficult for small businesses to match.

In the digital space, the challenges are equally pressing. Competition for online visibility is intense, with search engine optimization (SEO) and pay-per-click (PPC) advertising often proving cost-prohibitive for small businesses. Larger firms with more substantial budgets are better positioned to secure top search engine rankings and prime ad placements, which drive significant traffic to their websites. This financial disparity can make it difficult for small businesses to achieve the online visibility necessary for growth.

Brand awareness is another area where small businesses can find themselves at a disadvantage. Large corporations often benefit from years of brand-building, leading to widespread customer trust and loyalty. These established brands dominate the market, making it harder for smaller businesses to carve out their own identity. Larger companies also tend to have dedicated teams focused on public relations and brand management, allowing them to maintain and enhance their brand image consistently over time.

Despite these challenges, small businesses can employ various strategies to improve their market reach and visibility. One highly effective approach is to leverage social media platforms, which offer cost-effective ways to engage potential customers and build brand awareness. Platforms like Facebook, Instagram, Twitter, and LinkedIn allow small businesses to reach a wide audience through targeted advertising and organic content. By creating compelling posts and actively engaging with followers, small businesses can foster a loyal online community and enhance their digital presence.

Another valuable strategy is to focus on local marketing. Small businesses can make a significant impact by prioritizing their local communities. Sponsoring events, participating in community activities, and collaborating with other local businesses not only boost visibility but also help establish a strong presence in the area. Additionally, optimizing for local SEO—such as targeting "near me" searches and getting listed in local business directories—can attract nearby customers and strengthen a business's local footprint.

Content marketing is another powerful tool that small businesses can use to their advantage. Producing high-quality, informative, and engaging content—such as blogs, videos, podcasts, and webinars—not only helps to attract and retain customers but also positions the business as an expert in its field. Consistently offering valuable content can improve SEO rankings and drive organic traffic to the business's website, further enhancing visibility.

Lastly, networking and building partnerships are critical for expanding market reach. By forming alliances with complementary businesses, small enterprises can tap into new customer bases and mutually benefit from each other's strengths. Networking at industry events, trade shows, and local business groups also creates opportunities for collaboration and support, helping to enhance both visibility and market presence.

Challenge #4: Vulnerability to Market Changes

Small businesses are often more vulnerable to market fluctuations and economic downturns due to their limited resources and lack of diversification. These factors make it more difficult for them to weather adverse conditions such as economic recessions, shifts in consumer preferences, or increased competition. The impact of these challenges can be far more pronounced for smaller enterprises, potentially threatening their survival.

One primary reason for this vulnerability is the limited financial cushion that small businesses tend to operate with. Unlike larger corporations that often have extensive reserves and cash flow buffers, smaller businesses usually run on tighter budgets with minimal savings to absorb financial shocks. For example, during the 2008 financial crisis, many small businesses struggled with cash flow problems, leading to widespread closures. Similarly, the COVID-19 pandemic exposed the fragility of small enterprises, with sudden revenue drops and rising operational costs pushing many to the brink.

A further challenge lies in the lack of diversification that often characterizes small businesses. These enterprises typically focus on a narrow range of products or services and serve a specific customer base. While this specialization can be advantageous in stable markets, it becomes a liability during times of market upheaval. For instance, if consumer preferences shift or a disruptive competitor enters the market, small businesses may struggle to adapt quickly. This concentration on a limited portfolio leaves them more exposed to risk than larger companies, which often have diversified product lines that can help absorb the impact of market changes.

The competitive landscape also poses significant threats to small businesses. Larger companies have the resources to invest heavily in marketing, innovation, and customer acquisition, making it difficult for smaller enterprises to keep pace. During economic downturns, this competitive pressure intensifies, as larger firms may lower prices or ramp up promotions to capture a greater share of the market. Small businesses, with their constrained budgets, may find it hard to match these efforts, leading to a decline in customer retention and revenue.

To mitigate these vulnerabilities, small businesses can adopt several proactive strategies. Building a financial buffer by setting aside a portion of profits as a reserve fund is essential for providing a safety net during challenging times. Securing flexible financing options, such as lines of credit, can also help ensure quick access to funds when needed.

Diversification is another critical strategy. While maintaining a core focus is important, exploring additional revenue streams through new products, services, or markets can spread risk and reduce reliance on a single source of income. For example, a restaurant might introduce delivery services or catering options to diversify its offerings. This adaptability allows small businesses to remain competitive and resilient in the face of changing market dynamics.

Staying attuned to consumer trends through regular market research is equally vital. By closely monitoring shifts in consumer preferences and identifying emerging market opportunities, small businesses can adjust their strategies proactively. Leveraging customer feedback, industry reports, and competitor analysis provides valuable insights that enable businesses to stay ahead of market changes.

Lastly, building strong relationships with customers can act as a buffer against market volatility. Loyal customers are more likely to support a business during difficult times. Implementing customer loyalty programs, providing exceptional service, and maintaining open lines of communication help foster these relationships and enhance customer retention, creating a foundation of support that can be crucial during periods of uncertainty.

Challenge #5: Limited Economies of Scale

Economies of scale provide large businesses with a significant cost advantage by allowing them to spread fixed costs over a greater number of units, thereby reducing the cost per item. For example, a large manufacturer producing thousands of units can distribute the expenses of machinery, labor, and overhead across a wider range of products, significantly lowering the cost of each. This efficiency enables large companies to offer lower prices to consumers, which can make it more difficult for small businesses to compete.

In contrast, small businesses often produce in smaller quantities, which limits their ability to achieve the same level of cost efficiency. Fixed costs—such as rent, utilities, and salaries—remain relatively high on a per-unit basis when production volumes are low. Additionally, small businesses typically have less leverage when negotiating with suppliers, resulting in higher prices for raw materials and other inputs. Large companies often receive bulk discounts that are inaccessible to smaller enterprises due to their limited order sizes.

The effects of limited economies of scale are evident across many industries. In retail, for example, large chains can secure more favorable terms with suppliers, allowing them to sell products at lower prices than independent stores. In manufacturing, larger firms can invest in advanced technologies and automation, reducing labor costs and boosting efficiency. Small manufacturers, on the other hand, may lack the capital needed for such investments, leaving them at a disadvantage.

Despite these challenges, small businesses can adopt several strategies to mitigate the impact of limited economies of scale. One effective approach is to focus on niche markets, where they can offer specialized products or services that larger companies may overlook. By catering to specific customer needs and delivering unique offerings, small businesses can differentiate themselves and command higher prices. For example, a local bakery specializing in organic artisanal bread can attract customers who are willing to pay a premium for quality and uniqueness.

Another strategy is to collaborate with other small businesses to increase collective bargaining power. Forming cooperatives or purchasing alliances allows small businesses to pool their resources and negotiate better terms with suppliers. This collective approach helps reduce costs and enhances competitiveness. For instance, independent grocery stores could join forces to purchase products in bulk, thereby securing lower prices and benefiting from shared cost savings.

Investing in technology and process improvements is also essential for overcoming the limitations of scale. While large-scale automation may be out of reach, small businesses can still benefit from affordable technological solutions that improve efficiency. Cloud-based software for inventory management, customer relationship management (CRM), and accounting can streamline operations and reduce expenses. Adopting lean manufacturing principles can also help small businesses minimize waste and optimize production processes, further improving cost efficiency.

Moreover, building strong relationships with customers can provide a valuable competitive advantage. Small businesses often excel at delivering personalized service and cultivating close community ties. By leveraging these strengths, they can create a loyal customer base that values personalized attention and is less driven by price. Implementing customer loyalty programs and engaging with the community through events and social media can reinforce these relationships, fostering repeat business and long-term success.

Challenge #6: Talent Acquisition and Retention

Attracting and retaining skilled employees presents a unique challenge for small businesses. One of the primary obstacles is limited financial resources. Larger companies can often provide higher salaries, comprehensive benefits packages, and a range of perks that smaller businesses may not be able to match. This financial disparity can make it difficult for small businesses to compete for top-tier candidates seeking competitive compensation.

Another challenge lies in brand recognition. Many job seekers are drawn to well-known companies, associating them with stability, prestige, and clear career growth opportunities. In contrast, small businesses—particularly new or niche enterprises—may struggle with visibility and public awareness. As a result, attracting talent can be more difficult, especially when candidates are unfamiliar with the company's brand or the unique benefits of working in a smaller, more intimate environment.

Opportunities for career advancement also play a pivotal role in attracting and retaining employees. Larger organizations often have well-structured career paths, mentorship programs, and extensive training resources that help employees progress within the company. In comparison, smaller businesses may offer fewer opportunities for upward mobility due to their size. This can deter ambitious individuals who are looking for clear and consistent career progression.

Despite these hurdles, small businesses can implement effective strategies to attract and retain talent. One key approach is to emphasize the distinct advantages of working in a small business environment. Smaller businesses often foster closer-knit work cultures, where employees have a more significant personal impact, take on varied responsibilities, and develop skills more rapidly. Highlighting these personal and professional growth opportunities can appeal to candidates who value a more personalized and dynamic work experience.

Offering flexible work arrangements is another powerful strategy. Today, many employees prioritize work-life balance and flexibility over higher salaries. By offering options such as remote work, flexible hours, and compressed workweeks, small businesses can broaden their appeal and attract candidates seeking a more adaptable work environment.

Investing in employee development is also essential. Small businesses can strengthen their value proposition by offering continuous learning opportunities, such as workshops, online courses, and professional development programs. Even if they cannot compete with the salaries of larger corporations, a strong commitment to employee growth and career progression can significantly boost retention rates and attract driven, growth-oriented candidates.

Building a strong employer brand is equally important. Small businesses should leverage platforms such as social media, their website, and other digital channels to showcase their company culture, values, and employee testimonials. By highlighting success stories and demonstrating the meaningful impact employees have within the organization, small businesses can create a positive image that resonates with prospective talent. This approach not only attracts candidates who align with the company's mission and culture but also reinforces the business's reputation as a place where employees can thrive and contribute to shared success.

Challenge #7: Operational Challenges

A significant operational challenge for small businesses is the over-reliance on a few key individuals. In many small enterprises, the owner or a select group of senior staff members are responsible for most critical decisions and day-to-day operations. This concentration of responsibilities can create bottlenecks, particularly when these key individuals are overwhelmed or unavailable. The entire business may experience delays or disruptions, especially when quick decisions are needed to address market changes or customer demands.

This heavy dependency not only heightens the risk of operational inefficiencies but also places immense pressure on these individuals, potentially leading to burnout. To reduce these risks, small businesses must develop a more robust organizational structure that distributes responsibilities more evenly across the team. Implementing a clear hierarchy and assigning specific roles and duties can ensure that tasks are managed efficiently, even when key individuals are not present. For example, delegating finance, operations, marketing, and customer service responsibilities to different team members helps prevent bottlenecks and ensures smoother business operations.

Delegation plays a crucial role in boosting operational efficiency. While small business owners may be hesitant to delegate out of fear of losing control or believing that tasks will not meet their standards, effective delegation can empower employees, enhance their skills, and improve overall productivity. By providing employees with the training, tools, and resources they need, small businesses can cultivate a more capable and self-reliant team that can handle a wide range of tasks with confidence.

Investing in technology can also help alleviate operational challenges. Tools such as project management software, customer relationship management (CRM) systems, and automated scheduling can streamline workflows and reduce the burden on key decision-makers. These technologies ensure that essential tasks are completed on time and with consistent quality, even when primary leaders are unavailable. For instance, a CRM system can automate customer follow-ups, ensuring that service remains seamless and uninterrupted.

Building a culture of collaboration and open communication is equally important. Encouraging regular team meetings and fostering an environment where information is shared freely helps keep everyone aligned with the business's goals, challenges, and progress. This collaborative approach ensures that all team members are on the same page and can step in to support one another when needed. Moreover, fostering a sense of collective responsibility and ownership among employees strengthens their commitment to the success of the business.

Challenge #8: Limited Market Influence

Small businesses often face the challenge of having limited influence over market trends and industry standards. Their smaller size can make it difficult to negotiate favorable terms with suppliers, distributors, and other key stakeholders. This lack of market sway can restrict their ability to secure advantageous deals and partnerships, further limiting their potential for growth and expansion.

One of the primary reasons for this limited market influence is the relatively low purchasing power of small businesses. Larger corporations, with their ability to place bulk orders, often receive significant discounts and more favorable payment terms from suppliers. In contrast, small businesses tend to place smaller orders, which reduces their bargaining power and affects their profit margins. The disparity in purchasing power puts small enterprises at a competitive disadvantage, making it harder for them to compete on price or access cost-saving deals.

Visibility and recognition within their respective industries is another area where small businesses often struggle. Established brands and large companies frequently dominate market share, using their significant marketing and research and development budgets to shape industry standards and influence trends. This imbalance makes it challenging for small businesses to break through the noise and establish themselves as key players in their field. As a result, they may miss opportunities to shape market direction or be excluded from influential industry events and networks that drive the sector forward.

The limitations of market influence also extend to forming strategic partnerships. Large companies benefit from established networks and often form alliances with other industry leaders to expand their reach and bolster their competitive advantage. Small businesses, however, may find it challenging to attract potential partners due to their smaller market presence and influence. This barrier can limit their ability to enhance their offerings, enter new markets, or improve their capabilities through collaboration.

Despite these challenges, small businesses can adopt strategies to enhance their market influence and improve their negotiating power. One effective approach is to focus on their unique value propositions. Small businesses often excel at offering specialized products or personalized services that larger corporations cannot easily replicate. By emphasizing their distinct strengths and cultivating a loyal customer base, small businesses can carve out a strong brand identity that sets them apart. For instance, a local organic food store might emphasize its commitment to sustainability and local sourcing, attracting customers who prioritize these values.

Building strong, long-term relationships with suppliers and distributors is another crucial strategy. While small businesses may not have the same purchasing power as larger firms, they can cultivate partnerships based on trust, reliability, and mutual benefit. Developing a reputation for timely payments, clear communication, and consistent orders can lead to better terms over time. Additionally, joining group purchasing organizations can help small businesses increase their collective bargaining power, enabling them to access discounts and favorable terms typically reserved for larger companies.

Active participation in industry associations and professional networks can also help small businesses increase their market influence. By attending industry events, joining trade organizations, and networking with other businesses, small business owners can stay informed about market trends, advocate for their interests, and form valuable connections. These activities can boost their visibility, open doors to collaboration, and help them remain competitive in the marketplace. For instance, being part of a local chamber of commerce can provide access to resources, advocacy, and networking opportunities that enhance market influence.

Investing in digital marketing and leveraging social media platforms offers another avenue for small businesses to amplify their reach. Effective use of content marketing, search engine optimization (SEO), and social media engagement can increase brand visibility and attract a wider audience. By creating engaging online content that resonates with their target market, small businesses can build an active online community, interact directly with customers, and increase their market presence and influence over time.

Challenge #9: Risk of Burnout

Running a small business can be incredibly demanding, especially when resources are stretched thin. Both business owners and employees often face long hours and heavy workloads, leading to burnout and a decline in productivity. Balancing the demands of work with personal well-being is essential for sustaining long-term success and maintaining a healthy work environment.

A major contributor to burnout in small businesses is the constant need for multitasking. Owners and employees frequently wear multiple hats, juggling roles such as customer service, marketing, and financial management all at once. This wide range of responsibilities can spread individuals too thin, leaving little room for rest or recovery. Over time, this pressure can take a significant toll on both physical and mental health.

The long hours that often accompany small business ownership further exacerbate the risk of burnout. Many business owners work well beyond the standard 40-hour workweek, often without taking regular breaks or vacations. This relentless pace can lead to physical fatigue, weakened immune systems, and more serious mental health challenges such as anxiety and depression. The World Health Organization now recognizes burnout as an occupational phenomenon, underscoring the importance of addressing this issue in the workplace.

To reduce the risk of burnout, it is crucial for small business owners and employees to prioritize work-life balance. One proven tactic is to set clear distinctions between work and personal life. Setting regular working hours, scheduling designated breaks, and respecting time off are essential practices that can foster a healthier work environment. Cultivating a workplace culture that values rest and discourages excessive overtime also plays a key role in preventing burnout.

Delegation is another important factor in managing stress and workload. Many small business owners feel the need to oversee every aspect of their operations, but this approach often leads to burnout. By delegating tasks to trusted employees, owners can lighten their load while also empowering their team and fostering a sense of shared responsibility. Hiring part-time help or outsourcing specific tasks, such as accounting or IT support, can further alleviate pressure and ensure that everyone's workload remains manageable.

Incorporating stress management techniques into daily routines can also help mitigate the effects of burnout. Practices such as mindfulness, meditation, and regular exercise have been shown to lower stress levels and improve overall well-being. Encouraging employees to adopt these practices can build a more resilient and productive workforce. Creating an open and supportive work culture, where employees feel comfortable discussing their stress levels and seeking help when needed, can significantly enhance morale and reduce the likelihood of burnout.

Regularly assessing workload distribution is equally important. Small businesses should periodically review their operations to identify inefficiencies and areas where employees may be overburdened. Streamlining processes and implementing productivity tools can help manage workloads more effectively, leading to a smoother workflow. By leveraging tools like project management software and automation systems, businesses can reduce the administrative burden on staff, freeing up valuable time and easing stress. Ultimately, these efforts contribute to a healthier work environment where both productivity and well-being can thrive.

Challenge #10: Innovation and Technological Advancements

Keeping pace with technological advancements presents a unique challenge for small businesses, largely due to limited budgets and expertise. While larger companies can invest significantly in cutting-edge technologies and research and development, smaller enterprises often struggle to implement and fully leverage these innovations. This can impact their ability to remain competitive and meet the evolving expectations of their customers.

One of the biggest hurdles is the high cost associated with adopting new technologies. Advanced tools like artificial intelligence (AI), machine learning, and sophisticated data analytics often come with substantial price tags. For large corporations, these investments are justified by economies of scale and the potential for significant returns. However, for small businesses, allocating funds for such technologies can strain their finances. This financial constraint may restrict their ability to modernize operations and improve efficiency, placing them at a disadvantage.

Adding to the challenge is the rapid pace of technological change, which can be overwhelming for small business owners who may lack the expertise to identify and integrate the right solutions. Unlike larger companies with dedicated IT teams or consultants, small businesses often rely on a few individuals to manage multiple roles, including technology adoption. This lack of specialized knowledge can lead to suboptimal decisions regarding technology, resulting in missed opportunities for innovation.

The inability to harness the latest technologies can leave small businesses at a competitive disadvantage. Larger companies that embrace digital transformation are often able to streamline their operations, reduce costs, and enhance customer experiences. For example, a large retailer might use AI to personalize marketing efforts and optimize inventory management, leading to improved customer satisfaction and lower operational costs. By contrast, a smaller retailer without access to these technologies may struggle to keep up in terms of both pricing and service quality.

Despite these obstacles, there are strategies small businesses can use to remain competitive in a rapidly advancing technological landscape. One approach is to leverage affordable, scalable solutions tailored specifically to smaller enterprises. Cloud computing, for instance, provides powerful tools for data storage, processing, and collaboration without the need for significant upfront investments. Software-as-a-service (SaaS) platforms allow businesses to access advanced functionalities on a subscription basis, paying only for what they need.

Prioritizing technology investments that directly impact performance and customer satisfaction is another key strategy. For example, investing in customer relationship management (CRM) systems can help businesses manage customer interactions more effectively, while e-commerce platforms can expand market reach. Similarly, using social media marketing tools can boost brand visibility and engagement. By focusing on technologies that provide immediate and measurable benefits, small businesses can maximize their return on investment.

Collaborating with technology partners and drawing on external expertise can also help small businesses navigate the complexities of technological adoption. Partnerships with tech firms, participation in local business networks, and involvement in industry associations can provide valuable resources, knowledge, and support. Outsourcing specific IT functions to managed service providers ensures that small businesses have access to the latest technologies and expertise without the need for a full in-house IT department.

Finally, investing in employee training and development is essential for fostering a culture of innovation. Upskilling staff and promoting continuous learning can equip employees with the knowledge and tools they need to embrace new technologies. By offering access to online courses, workshops, and industry certifications, small businesses can empower their teams to drive digital transformation and innovation from within.

Challenge #11: Compliance and Regulatory Challenges

Navigating the complex landscape of regulations and compliance requirements can be particularly demanding for small businesses. Ensuring adherence to local, state, and federal regulations often requires resources that smaller enterprises may struggle to allocate effectively.

Small businesses are expected to comply with a wide range of regulations that vary by industry, location, and size. These may include health and safety standards, environmental laws, labor laws, tax codes, and industry-specific regulations. The sheer volume and complexity of these requirements can quickly become overwhelming, especially for business owners who may lack the time or expertise to stay updated. For instance, businesses in the food industry must comply with the Food and Drug Administration's (FDA) stringent regulations, while workplace safety falls under the purview of the Occupational Safety and Health Administration (OSHA), each with its own detailed requirements.

Adhering to these regulations demands the dedication of time and resources to understand, implement, and monitor compliance. This task is particularly challenging for small businesses with limited budgets and personnel. Unlike larger companies that can allocate entire departments to manage compliance, small businesses often rely on the owner or a small team to handle these responsibilities. This additional burden can divert attention from core operations and limit the business's ability to focus on growth.

The impact of non-compliance should not be taken lightly. Legal issues, fines, and penalties can significantly strain a small business's financial resources, sometimes to the point of jeopardizing its survival. Moreover, non-compliance can erode customer trust and damage the business's reputation. For example, failure to comply with data protection laws such as the General Data Protection Regulation (GDPR) can result in hefty fines and undermine consumer confidence in the business. For small businesses, the financial and reputational damage from incidents like data breaches can be catastrophic, sometimes even leading to closure.

Despite these challenges, there are strategies small businesses can adopt to mitigate the risks of non-compliance. Education and training play a vital role. Both business owners and employees should be well-versed in the regulations relevant to their industry. Regular training sessions help ensure that everyone understands their responsibilities, which in turn promotes a culture of compliance. Resources offered by organizations like the Small Business Administration (SBA) can provide valuable guidance and training programs to support small businesses in staying compliant.

Although hiring a full-time compliance team may be out of reach for many small businesses, seeking the assistance of a consultant or part-time compliance officer can be a cost-effective solution. These professionals can conduct audits, offer guidance, and help implement the necessary changes to ensure compliance. Additionally, compliance management software can simplify the process. Tools such as ComplySci and Netwrix Auditor are tailored for small businesses, helping them track regulatory changes, manage documentation, and automate reporting processes, thereby reducing the burden on internal resources.

Cultivating a culture of compliance throughout the organization is just as essential. Making compliance a collective responsibility ensures that everyone is committed to maintaining the necessary standards. Regular communication about compliance issues, integrating compliance into the overall business strategy, and staying proactive about regulatory updates are key to ensuring long-term adherence. Subscribing to industry newsletters, joining professional associations, and attending seminars or workshops can keep businesses informed of new or evolving regulations.

Consider the example of a small business in the food industry. Ensuring compliance with health and safety regulations is critical for avoiding penalties and ensuring customer safety. By hiring a part-time health and safety consultant, utilizing compliance software to track and manage inspections, and regularly training staff on hygiene practices, the business can navigate regulatory requirements effectively. This proactive approach minimizes the risk of non-compliance while also building a reputation for quality and safety among customers.

CHAPTER 4

SELF-ASSESSMENT TOOLS

Questionnaires to Evaluate Business Goals and Personal Preferences

Understanding your business goals and personal preferences is essential for making informed decisions about the direction of your business. Questionnaires can be a valuable tool in this process, helping you to clarify your vision, set priorities, and align your business strategies with your personal values and lifestyle.

By gaining a deeper understanding of what you want to achieve and how you want to live your life, you can make more informed decisions that align with both your business objectives and personal values. This alignment is key to achieving long-term success and fulfillment in your entrepreneurial journey. Here are some comprehensive questionnaires designed to evaluate both your business goals and personal preferences.

Business Goals Evaluation

Vision and Mission:

- What is the long-term vision for your business?
- What mission statement best describes the purpose and core values of your business?
- How do you see your business evolving over the next 5-10 years?
- What impact do you wantt your business to have on your customers, industry, and community?

Growth and Scale:

- What are your primary goals for business growth (e.g., revenue targets, market expansion, product development)?
- How quickly do you want to achieve these growth milestones?

- Are you interested in expanding your business nationally or internationally?
- What resources (financial, human, technological) will you need to achieve your growth goals?

Financial Objectives:

- What are your short-term and long-term financial goals for your business?
- What level of profitability do you aim to achieve within the next year? Five years?
- How much capital are you willing to invest in your business for growth?
- Are you comfortable taking on debt or seeking external investors to fund your expansion?

Market Position and Competition:

- How do you currently position your business in the market?
- Who are your main competitors, and what differentiates your business from theirs?
- What strategies do you plan to implement to increase your market share?
- How do you plan to innovate and stay ahead of the competition?

Customer Focus:

- Who is your target customer, and what are their needs and preferences?
- How do you plan to attract and retain customers?
- What customer service standards do you want to uphold?
- How will you gather and respond to customer feedback to improve your offerings?

Personal Preferences Evaluation

Work-Life Balance:

- How important is work-life balance to you?
- How many hours per week are you willing to dedicate to your business?
- What personal commitments (family, hobbies, health) do you need to balance with your business responsibilities?
- How do you plan to manage stress and avoid burnout?

Risk Tolerance:

- How comfortable are you with taking financial risks for the potential of higher rewards?
- What level of financial stability do you need to feel secure?
- How do you handle uncertainty and potential setbacks in business?
- Are you prepared to face the challenges and sacrifices that come with scaling a business?

Personal Values and Ethics:

- What personal values do you want your business to reflect?
- How important is it for your business to contribute to social, environmental, or community causes?
- How do you handle ethical dilemmas in business?
- What kind of company culture do you want to create and maintain?

Leadership and Management Style:

- What type of leadership style do you prefer (e.g., hands-on, delegative, collaborative)?
- How do you handle decision-making and problem-solving?
- What are your strengths and weaknesses as a leader?
- How do you plan to develop and support your team?

Long-Term Aspirations:

- What are your long-term career goals?
- How do you envision your personal life in 10-20 years?
- How does your business fit into your long-term personal and professional aspirations?
- What legacy do you want to leave through your business?

Combining Insights

Alignment Assessment:

- How well do your business goals align with your personal values and lifestyle preferences?
- Are there any conflicts between your business aspirations and personal commitments?

- What adjustments can you make to ensure better alignment between your business and personal life?

Prioritization:

- Based on your evaluations, what are your top three business priorities?
- What personal goals are most important to you, and how can your business support them?
- What immediate actions can you take to move closer to your business and personal goals?

Action Plan:

- Create a detailed action plan outlining steps to achieve your top business and personal goals.
- Set specific, measurable, achievable, relevant, and time-bound (SMART) goals for both your business and personal life.
- Regularly review and adjust your action plan to stay on track and adapt to any changes in your circumstances or goals.

Checklists for Assessing Readiness for Growth

Determining whether your business is ready to grow involves evaluating various aspects of your operations, finances, and strategic planning. The following checklists provide a comprehensive guide to assess your business's preparedness for expansion, ensuring that you have the necessary foundations in place to support successful growth.

By using these checklists to assess your readiness for growth, you can identify areas that need improvement and ensure that your business is well-prepared for expansion. Addressing any gaps and strengthening your foundations will help you navigate the challenges of growth more effectively and position your business for long-term success.

Operational Readiness

Infrastructure:

- Do you have the physical space and facilities needed to support increased production or services?
- Is your current technology infrastructure capable of handling higher volumes of transactions and data?
- Are your supply chain and logistics networks robust and scalable?

Processes and Systems:

- Have you documented and optimized your business processes to ensure efficiency?

- Are your inventory management and distribution systems capable of handling higher demand?

- Do you have reliable systems in place for quality control and compliance?

Human Resources:

- Do you have a strong, skilled team that can manage increased workloads and responsibilities?

- Are your hiring and onboarding processes efficient and scalable?

- Do you offer training and development programs to support employee growth and retention?

Customer Service:

- Is your customer service infrastructure capable of handling an increase in customer inquiries and support requests?

- Do you have systems in place to gather and respond to customer feedback?

- Are you prepared to maintain high levels of customer satisfaction as you grow?

Financial Readiness

Financial Health:

- Do you have a strong balance sheet with healthy cash reserves?

- Are your profit margins sufficient to support expansion?

- Have you demonstrated consistent revenue growth over time?

Funding:

- Have you identified and secured the necessary funding for growth, whether through internal cash flow, loans, or investors?

- Do you have a clear plan for managing debt and financing costs?

- Are you prepared to meet the financial obligations associated with growth, such as increased payroll, inventory, and marketing expenses?

Financial Planning and Forecasting:

- Have you developed detailed financial projections and budgets for your growth plans?

- Do you regularly review and adjust your financial plans based on performance and market conditions?

- Are you using financial metrics and key performance indicators (KPIs) to track your progress?

Market and Customer Readiness

Market Analysis:

- Have you conducted thorough market research to identify growth opportunities and potential risks?

- Do you understand the competitive landscape and how your business will differentiate itself?

- Are you aware of market trends and customer preferences that could impact your growth plans?

Customer Demand:

- Is there a demonstrated demand for your products or services in new or existing markets?

- Have you identified your target customer segments and developed strategies to reach them?

- Are your marketing and sales strategies aligned with your growth objectives?

Brand and Reputation:

- Is your brand strong and well-recognized in your current market?

- Do you have a positive reputation and customer loyalty that will support your expansion?

- Are you prepared to maintain and enhance your brand reputation as you grow?

Strategic Readiness

Strategic Planning:

- Have you developed a comprehensive growth strategy that outlines your objectives, target markets, and key initiatives?

- Do you have a clear roadmap with timelines, milestones, and performance metrics?
- Are your growth plans aligned with your overall business vision and mission?

Risk Management:

- Have you identified potential risks associated with growth and developed mitigation strategies?
- Do you have contingency plans in place for unforeseen challenges or setbacks?
- Are you prepared to manage the increased complexity and potential disruptions that come with growth?

Leadership and Governance:

- Do you have a strong leadership team with the skills and experience to guide your business through growth?
- Are your organizational structure and governance practices scalable and adaptable?
- Do you have advisory boards or mentors to provide guidance and support during your growth journey?

Technology Readiness

IT Infrastructure:

- Is your current IT infrastructure scalable to support growth?
- Do you have robust cybersecurity measures in place to protect your data and systems?
- Are your software and hardware systems up-to-date and capable of handling increased workloads?

Innovation and research and development:

- Are you investing in research and development to drive innovation and stay competitive?
- Do you have processes in place to bring new products or services to market efficiently?
- Are you leveraging technology to improve efficiency and enhance customer experience?

Digital Marketing and E-Commerce:

• Are your digital marketing strategies and platforms optimized for growth?

• Do you have a strong online presence and e-commerce capabilities?

• Are you utilizing data analytics to drive decision-making and improve performance?

Tools to Identify Risk Tolerance and Management Skills

Understanding your risk tolerance and developing strong risk management skills are critical for navigating the uncertainties that come with running and growing a business. There are various tools that can help entrepreneurs assess their risk tolerance, identify potential risks, and develop effective risk management strategies. By utilizing these tools to assess your risk tolerance and enhance your risk management skills, you can make more informed decisions and better navigate the uncertainties. Effective risk management helps protect your business from potential threats, ensuring long-term stability and success. Below are some tools and methods to help you evaluate your risk tolerance and enhance your risk management skills.

Risk Tolerance Assessment Tools

Risk Tolerance Questionnaires:

• **Personal Risk Tolerance Questionnaire:** These questionnaires help you evaluate your comfort level with taking risks in both personal and professional contexts. They typically include questions about your financial goals, investment preferences, past experiences with risk, and emotional responses to uncertainty. By understanding your personal risk tolerance, you can make informed decisions that align with your comfort level.

• **Business Risk Tolerance Assessment:** This assessment focuses on your business-related risk preferences. It includes questions about your willingness to invest in new projects, tolerance for financial volatility, and readiness to pivot strategies in response to market changes. This tool helps identify how much risk your business can handle and informs your growth strategies.

Scenario Analysis:

- **Best-Case/Worst-Case Scenarios:** Scenario analysis involves envisioning various outcomes based on different risk factors. By considering best-case, worst-case, and most-likely scenarios, you can better understand the potential impacts of your decisions. This helps you prepare for a range of possibilities and develop contingency plans.

- **Stress Testing:** Stress testing involves simulating extreme conditions to evaluate how your business would perform under significant stress. This can include financial downturns, supply chain disruptions, or sudden loss of key customers. Stress testing helps you identify vulnerabilities and areas where additional safeguards are needed.

Financial Ratios and Metrics:

- **Liquidity Ratios:** Liquidity ratios, such as the current ratio and quick ratio, measure your business's ability to meet short-term obligations. These metrics help assess your financial stability and risk exposure.

- **Debt-to-Equity Ratio:** This ratio evaluates your business's financial leverage and risk associated with debt. A higher debt-to-equity ratio indicates higher financial risk, while a lower ratio suggests more conservative financial management.

Risk Management Tools

Risk Identification Tools:

- **SWOT Analysis:** SWOT (strengths, weaknesses, opportunities, threats) analysis helps identify internal and external risks that could impact your business. By understanding your business's strengths and weaknesses, as well as external opportunities and threats, you can develop strategies to mitigate risks.

- **PESTLE Analysis:** PESTLE (political, economic, social, technological, legal, environmental) analysis helps identify external factors that could pose risks to your business. This tool allows you to systematically analyze how different external forces may affect your operations and plan accordingly.

Risk Assessment Tools:

- **Risk Matrix:** A risk matrix helps prioritize risks based on their likelihood and potential impact. By plotting risks on a matrix, you can visually identify which risks require immediate attention and which are less critical. This tool helps in prioritizing risk management efforts.

- **Risk Register:** A risk register is a comprehensive document that lists all identified risks, their potential impacts, likelihood, mitigation strategies, and responsible parties. It serves as a central repository for tracking and managing risks over time.

Risk Mitigation Strategies:

- **Diversification:** Diversification involves spreading investments and resources across different areas to reduce exposure to any single risk. This can include diversifying product lines, customer bases, suppliers, and markets.

- **Insurance:** Obtaining appropriate insurance coverage can protect your business from various risks, such as property damage, liability, and business interruption. Insurance serves as a financial safeguard against unexpected events.

Risk Monitoring and Review:

- **Key Risk Indicators (KRIs):** KRIs are metrics used to monitor the levels of risk in different areas of your business. Regularly reviewing KRIs helps you stay informed about potential risks and take proactive measures to address them.

- **Regular Risk Audits:** Conducting periodic risk audits involves systematically reviewing your risk management processes and controls. This helps ensure that your risk management strategies remain effective and up-to-date.

Training and Development:

- **Risk Management Training:** Providing training for yourself and your team on risk management principles and practices enhances the ability to identify, assess, and mitigate risks. Training can include workshops, seminars, and online courses on topics such as risk assessment, financial management, and crisis response.

- **Leadership Development Programs:** Developing strong leadership skills is essential for effective risk management. Leadership programs can help you build decision-making, problem-solving, and strategic planning skills, which are crucial for navigating risks.

Technology and Software Solutions:

- **Risk Management Software:** Specialized software solutions can help streamline risk management processes by automating risk identification, assessment, and monitoring. These tools provide real-time insights and analytics, making it easier to manage risks effectively.

- **Project Management Tools:** Project management tools, such as Trello, Asana, and Microsoft Project, can help you plan, execute, and monitor projects while identifying and mitigating risks. These tools facilitate collaboration and ensure that risk management is integrated into project workflows.

CHAPTER 5
STRATEGIC PLANNING FOR GROWTH

Creating a Scalable Business Model

Creating a scalable business model is essential for any enterprise aspiring to achieve sustainable growth and long-term success. Scalability is the capacity of your business to grow and manage increased demand without compromising quality or efficiency. A scalable model ensures that as your business expands, you maintain the same level of service and operational effectiveness. This involves designing your systems, processes, and strategies to adapt and grow alongside your business. Let us explore the key steps to developing a scalable business model, laying a solid foundation for continuous and effective growth.

Define a Clear Vision and Mission

A scalable business model begins with a well-defined vision and mission. Your vision acts as the ultimate destination for your business, serving as a guiding star that shapes every decision and action. This vision should be more than just a statement; it should be an inspiring, long-term goal that reflects your aspirations and the impact you want to make on your industry or community.

Complementing this vision is your mission, which serves as the roadmap that guides your journey. The mission outlines the core values, principles, and strategies that will drive your business forward. It provides a clear direction for your team, ensuring that everyone understands the overarching goals and their role in achieving them.t

When your vision and mission are clearly defined, they set the stage for your business's growth story. This clarity fosters consistency as your business expands, allowing every new team, project, or market to seamlessly integrate into the bigger picture. By anchoring your business in a strong vision and mission, you establish a framework that not only guides your current operations but also supports sustainable and scalable growth for the future.

Understand Your Market and Customer Needs

A deep understanding of your market and customer needs is essential to building a scalable business model. It begins with thorough market research, where you dive into the preferences, behaviors, and challenges of your target audience. By identifying market trends, uncovering customer pain points, and spotting opportunities for innovation, you can design products or services that not only meet current demands but also have the potential for widespread appeal.

Market research is your gateway to understanding the world of your customers. It provides invaluable insights into their purchasing decisions, the problems they encounter, and the gaps in the market that your business can fill. Through surveys, focus groups, and customer interviews, you gain qualitative insights, while data analytics and social media monitoring offer quantitative data that reveal patterns and trends. With this comprehensive understanding, you can create offerings that resonate deeply with your customers, ensuring they are both relevant and desirable.

However, market research is just the starting point. To effectively leverage the information you gather, segment your market into distinct groups based on demographics, behaviors, and preferences. Market segmentation involves dividing your broader audience into smaller, more manageable segments that share common characteristics. This targeted approach allows you to tailor your offerings and marketing strategies to meet the specific needs of each segment more effectively.

For instance, a skincare company might segment its market by factors such as age, skin type, and specific skincare concerns like acne or aging. By understanding the unique needs of each segment, the company can develop targeted products and marketing campaigns that speak directly to these customers. This level of personalization not only enhances customer satisfaction but also increases the likelihood of building customer loyalty and securing repeat business.

Focusing on your most promising market segments ensures efficient use of resources and maximizes growth opportunities. Instead of spreading efforts thinly across a broad audience, concentrate on segments that are likely to yield the highest returns. This targeted strategy leads to more effective marketing, stronger customer engagement, and ultimately higher sales and profitability.

Remaining attuned to market trends and customer feedback keeps your business agile and responsive. The business landscape is constantly evolving, and customer preferences can shift quickly. Regular market research and ongoing customer engagement enable you to adapt swiftly to changes and seize new opportunities as they arise. This proactive approach ensures your business stays relevant and competitive in an ever-changing market.

Develop a Value Proposition

Crafting a compelling value proposition is pivotal in creating a scalable business model. Picture your value proposition as the promise of value delivered to customers, the primary reason they should choose your product or service over competitors. It should clearly articulate the unique benefits of your offerings, addressing the specific needs and pain points of your target market. A strong value proposition attracts and retains customers, vital for scaling your business.

Start by identifying what sets your business apart. Reflect on the distinctive qualities of your products or services and how they solve customer problems more effectively than other market options. Whether it is superior quality, innovative features, exceptional customer service, or competitive pricing, your value proposition should highlight these unique aspects, making it clear why customers should choose your offerings.

Crafting a compelling value proposition goes beyond listing benefits. It requires communicating these benefits in a way that resonates with your audience. To make your value proposition stand out, focus on clarity, relevance, differentiation, and credibility:

- **Clarity:** Ensure your value proposition is straightforward and easy to understand. Avoid jargon and be concise. Customers should immediately grasp the key benefits without needing to decipher the message.

- **Relevance:** Address the specific needs and desires of your target market. Focus on what matters most to them, tailoring your message based on market research findings.

- **Differentiation:** Clearly communicate what distinguishes your product or service from competitors. Emphasize the unique features, advantages, or strategies that make your offering stand out as the preferred choice.

- **Credibility:** Support your claims with evidence. Use customer testimonials, case studies, industry awards, or measurable results to build trust and reinforce the value of your proposition.

Refining your value proposition is an ongoing process. As your business grows and market conditions evolve, continuously gather feedback from customers and stay attuned to industry trends. This ensures your value proposition remains compelling and aligned with your audience's changing needs.

Standardize Processes and Operations

Standardizing your business processes is a key step in preparing for effective scaling. Consistent and efficient operations form the backbone of sustainable growth, allowing your business to expand without losing control or compromising quality.

The journey begins with precisely documenting your business operations. By creating clear, detailed records of how tasks are performed within your company, you provide a valuable reference that ensures everyone knows exactly how to execute their responsibilities. This documentation should outline step-by-step procedures, identify responsible parties, and list the necessary tools or resources. With this foundation, you reduce variability, increase reliability, and create a cohesive understanding across your organization.

However, documentation is just the start. Regularly reviewing and refining these processes is crucial to maintaining efficiency as your business grows. As you analyze your workflows, you may find opportunities to streamline operations by eliminating redundant steps or adopting more efficient approaches. This continuous improvement not only enhances operational efficiency but also prepares your business to handle increased volumes seamlessly, ensuring that growth does not come at the expense of quality.

Technology plays a pivotal role in this process. Leveraging automation and digital tools can significantly streamline your operations. Implementing software solutions for key functions such as inventory management, customer relationship management (CRM), and accounting can transform how your business operates. Automation reduces manual effort, minimizes errors, and frees up your team to focus on more strategic, value-added tasks rather than repetitive, time-consuming activities.

Businesses that embrace automation and digital tools often see substantial improvements in both efficiency and accuracy. These gains are critical for scalability, as they allow your operations to expand smoothly without overwhelming your resources. By investing in technology, you not only enhance your current processes but also build a robust infrastructure capable of supporting your future growth.

Build a Strong Team

A skilled and capable team is the backbone of any growing business. However, building such a team is not just about hiring people with the right skills—it is about finding individuals who align with your business values and share your vision. This alignment ensures that everyone is working toward the same goals and upholding the same standards, creating a cohesive and motivated workforce. When your team members believe in your vision and are committed to helping you achieve it, they become more than employees—they become partners in your success.

Once you have assembled your team, it is crucial to invest in their ongoing development. The business landscape is constantly evolving, and staying current with industry trends and best practices is essential. Regular training sessions, workshops, and access to online courses help your team develop new skills and stay ahead of the curve. By investing in your employees' growth, you not only enhance productivity and innovation but also increase job satisfaction, which can lead to lower turnover rates and a more stable team.

As your business grows, the ability to delegate responsibilities becomes increasingly important. Delegation is not just about assigning tasks—it is about entrusting your team with meaningful responsibilities that contribute to the overall success of the business. This strategy not only helps to distribute the workload but also promotes a sense of ownership and accountability within the team. When employees are empowered to make decisions and take charge of their roles, it boosts their confidence and engagement, leading to higher performance and job satisfaction.

Effective delegation and empowerment are crucial to scaling your business without overburdening the leadership team. By entrusting capable team members with key responsibilities, leaders can focus on strategic planning and high-level decision-making rather than getting bogged down in daily operations. Moreover, empowering your employees brings fresh perspectives and innovative solutions, driving the business forward and ensuring that it remains competitive and adaptable.

To support delegation and empowerment, establish a framework that includes clear communication channels, regular check-ins, and feedback mechanisms. Encourage your team to take initiative, and provide them with the resources and support they need to succeed. Celebrate their successes and learn from setbacks together. By building a culture of trust and empowerment, you create a dynamic and resilient organization capable of sustained growth and success.

Focus on Customer Experience

Focusing on customer experience is essential for achieving long-term success and sustainable growth. When you prioritize customer satisfaction and actively seek to improve based on their feedback, you build strong relationships that foster loyalty and drive repeat business and referrals.

Delivering outstanding customer service is at the heart of this approach. Every interaction, whether it is a prompt response to an inquiry, a personalized conversation, or a swift resolution to an issue, plays a critical role in shaping the customer's experience. When you consistently exceed expectations at each touchpoint, you transform ordinary encounters into memorable experiences that naturally encourage customers to return and spread the word about your business.

Customer feedback is a powerful tool for guiding these efforts. Actively gathering and acting on feedback provides valuable insights into what your customers value, what frustrates them, and where improvements can be made. Whether through regular surveys, monitoring reviews, or engaging on social media, maintaining an ongoing dialogue with your customers demonstrates that you care about their experiences and are committed to meeting their needs. This not only strengthens your relationship with them but also provides a continuous stream of information that can be used to refine your offerings.

By leveraging the insights gained from customer feedback, you can make informed adjustments to your products, services, and interactions. For instance, if customers frequently mention a challenge with a specific feature, prioritizing its improvement shows that you are responsive to their concerns. On the other hand, if a particular aspect of your service is highly praised, finding ways to enhance it further can amplify customer satisfaction. This kind of responsiveness helps you stay relevant and competitive while building trust and loyalty among your customers.

Personalizing the customer experience adds another layer of engagement. Today's customers expect more than just a transaction; they want to feel understood and valued as individuals. Whether it is addressing them by name in communications or offering tailored recommendations based on their previous interactions, personalization shows that you recognize their unique needs and preferences. This approach deepens the connection between your business and your customers, making them more likely to return and advocate for your brand.

Finally, creating a seamless and enjoyable customer journey is crucial. Every interaction, whether online or offline, should be smooth and hassle-free. Streamlining processes, optimizing your website for ease of use, and ensuring your staff is well-trained to deliver consistent, high-quality service are all vital components. By focusing on the entire customer journey, you can identify and eliminate any potential pain points, ultimately enhancing customer satisfaction and laying a strong foundation for scalable growth.

Develop Scalable Marketing Strategies

Expanding your business reach and driving sustainable growth requires marketing strategies that can scale with your ambitions. To achieve this, digital marketing channels offer unparalleled opportunities. Unlike traditional marketing methods, which often come with limitations and high costs, digital platforms like social media, email marketing, content marketing, and search engine optimization (SEO) allow you to connect with a broader audience more efficiently.

Social media platforms such as Facebook, Instagram, Twitter, and LinkedIn have become essential tools for building a community around your brand. These platforms offer powerful features that enable you to craft targeted ads, reaching specific demographics, interests, and behaviors, ensuring your message resonates with the right audience. Moreover, social media provides a space for real-time engagement, allowing you to interact directly with followers, fostering stronger relationships, and cultivating customer loyalty.

Email marketing continues to stand out as one of the most cost-effective digital marketing strategies available. By building a mailing list and sending personalized, value-driven emails, you keep your audience informed and engaged. Newsletters, promotional offers, and tailored recommendations based on past interactions are just a few ways to drive repeat business and enhance customer lifetime value.

Content marketing is another cornerstone of a scalable digital marketing strategy. Creating high-quality, informative, and engaging content—such as blog posts, videos, infographics, and podcasts—helps attract and retain a clearly defined audience. This content not only establishes your brand as an authority in your industry but also drives organic traffic to your website, further expanding your reach.

SEO plays a critical role in enhancing your online visibility by improving your website's ranking on search engines like Google. Through strategic optimization of your website's content, structure, and technical aspects, you attract more organic traffic from users searching for relevant information. Effective SEO practices, such as keyword research, on-page optimization, link building, and regular content updates, ensure that your website remains competitive and visible.

Data-driven marketing is the key to making informed decisions and optimizing your strategies for maximum impact. By leveraging data analytics, you can track the performance of your marketing efforts, gaining insights into what works and what needs improvement. Analyzing customer data, campaign results, and market trends reveals patterns that guide your marketing decisions. Tools like Google Analytics, HubSpot, and Marketo provide valuable insights into customer behavior, conversion rates, and overall campaign effectiveness.

By combining digital marketing with data-driven insights, you create scalable marketing strategies that evolve with your business. These approaches allow you to reach a larger audience, engage customers more effectively, and allocate resources where they will have the greatest impact. As you scale your marketing efforts, remaining adaptable and continuously monitoring performance is crucial to ensuring sustained success. Investing in these strategies builds a strong foundation for business growth and keeps you competitive in a rapidly changing market.

Ensure Financial Health

Maintaining strong financial health is the backbone of your business's sustainable growth and stability. The journey begins with securing the right funding, which fuels expansion, covers operational costs, and opens doors to new opportunities. Whether you choose to bootstrap, take out loans, seek venture capital, or explore crowdfunding, each option carries its own set of advantages and challenges. Carefully weighing these options against your business goals and financial situation is crucial to setting the stage for success.

Bootstrapping, for example, allows you to grow your business using your savings or by reinvesting profits. This approach gives you full control over your business decisions without external influence, but it can also limit growth if your financial resources are stretched thin. On the other hand, loans from banks or financial institutions can provide the capital needed to scale, but they come with the responsibility of repayment, often with interest. To avoid cash flow issues that could threaten your business's stability, a solid repayment plan is essential.

For startups with high growth potential, venture capital can be an attractive option. Venture capitalists bring not only funding but also strategic guidance and valuable connections. However, this option requires giving up a portion of your company's equity and potentially some control over decision-making. Crowdfunding offers a different approach, allowing you to raise small amounts of money from a large number of people through online platforms. Beyond raising capital, crowdfunding can also serve as a powerful marketing tool, generating buzz and validating your business idea in the marketplace.

Regardless of how you secure funding, disciplined financial management is key to sustaining your business's health. Regularly reviewing your financial performance keeps you in tune with your company's pulse. By closely monitoring key financial metrics such as revenue, expenses, profit margins, and cash flow, you can spot trends, identify potential issues early, and make data-driven decisions. These financial metrics, along with key performance indicators (KPIs), offer a clear snapshot of your business's performance and progress toward your goals.

Revenue and profit margins are vital indicators of profitability. Keeping a close eye on these metrics helps you understand how much money your business is making and retaining after covering all expenses. Monitoring expenses, in turn, reveals areas where cost-cutting or efficiency improvements can be made. Effective cash flow management ensures that you have the liquidity needed to meet your obligations and seize growth opportunities. A positive cash flow, where you consistently bring in more money than you spend, is critical to maintaining financial stability.

To streamline your financial management, consider using specialized tools and software that automate tracking and reporting. These tools can generate accurate financial statements, forecasts, and analyses, offering valuable insights into your business's financial health. Additionally, consulting with a financial advisor or accountant can provide expert guidance and help you develop effective financial strategies tailored to your business's unique needs.

Sound financial management goes beyond just balancing the books; it empowers you to make informed decisions that drive long-term success and resilience in an ever-competitive market.

Create Scalable Infrastructure

Building a scalable infrastructure is vital for ensuring that your business can handle increased demand and grow seamlessly without significant disruptions. The foundation of this process lies in investing in systems that can expand alongside your business. For example, scalable IT systems enable you to manage larger volumes of data, transactions, and users without sacrificing performance. Cloud computing solutions like Amazon Web Services (AWS) or Microsoft Azure offer flexible, scalable resources that can be adjusted as your needs evolve. This flexibility ensures that you pay only for what you use, with the ability to scale up quickly during peak times.

In addition to IT systems, a flexible supply chain is a vital component of scalable infrastructure. Building strong relationships with multiple suppliers and integrating advanced supply chain management systems ensures that your business can meet rising demand and swiftly adapt to market changes. This flexibility helps prevent bottlenecks, maintaining a steady flow of products as your business expands. Technologies such as radio-frequency identification (RFID) tracking and Internet of Things (IoT) sensors further enhance supply chain visibility and efficiency, allowing for real-time monitoring and quick responses to any issues that arise.

Adaptable physical spaces also play a critical role in scalability. Whether it is your office, warehouse, or retail space, having environments that can be reconfigured and expanded as needed is essential. Modular office designs, flexible lease agreements, and scalable warehousing solutions allow you to adjust your physical footprint based on business requirements. This adaptability not only saves costs but also reduces downtime that could otherwise occur from moving or renovating spaces to accommodate growth.

Planning for expansion involves developing a strategic roadmap that outlines your growth objectives and the steps required to achieve them. This includes identifying potential new markets, selecting the best geographic locations for expansion, and making the necessary operational adjustments to support growth. A well-crafted market entry strategy helps you navigate the complexities of entering new regions or customer segments, while operational planning ensures that resources and processes are in place to scale efficiently.

Anticipating potential challenges and creating contingency plans is another integral part of building scalable infrastructure. Growth often brings unforeseen hurdles, such as supply chain disruptions, regulatory changes, or shifts in customer demand. By proactively identifying these risks and developing strategies to mitigate them, you can ensure that your business remains resilient and adaptable. For instance, diversifying your supplier base can protect against disruptions, while staying informed about regulatory changes allows you to adapt quickly and maintain compliance.

Creating a scalable infrastructure requires a proactive approach: investing in systems that can grow with your business, planning strategically for expansion, and anticipating potential challenges. This approach not only prepares your business to handle increased demand but also positions it to capitalize on new opportunities and navigate the complexities of a dynamic market environment.

Foster a Culture of Innovation

In a competitive and rapidly changing market, innovation is the engine that drives growth and success. Fostering a culture of innovation means creating an environment where new ideas are not just welcomed but actively encouraged, and where experimentation is part of the everyday workflow. It is about empowering employees at all levels to share their insights, try out new approaches, and learn from both their successes and failures.

The foundation of this culture begins with open communication and collaboration. Encourage your team to brainstorm and discuss their ideas regularly, whether through dedicated innovation meetings, idea-sharing platforms, or even informal gatherings. When employees know their contributions are valued, they are more likely to engage actively and think creatively. Consider the example of Google, which allows employees to dedicate 20 percent of their time to passion projects—a policy that has led to the creation of successful products like Gmail and Google News.

Providing the right resources and tools is equally important. Your team needs access to the latest technologies and training that can help them innovate. This might include software for prototyping, access to industry research, or workshops on cutting-edge methodologies. By investing in these resources, you demonstrate your commitment to innovation and equip your team with the means to transform their ideas into tangible outcomes.

Embracing risk and failure is another critical aspect of fostering innovation. Not every idea will succeed, but every failure offers a chance to learn and improve. Cultivate a mindset that views setbacks as integral to the innovation process rather than as endpoints. Celebrate your team's efforts and the lessons learned from unsuccessful attempts, thereby fostering resilience and a culture of continuous improvement.

Investing in research and development (R&D) is essential for driving product innovation and enhancing existing offerings. Allocating resources specifically for R&D activities can help you develop new revenue streams and strengthen your competitive edge. Companies like Apple and Amazon have made significant investments in R&D, enabling them to consistently bring groundbreaking products and services to market and maintain their leadership positions.

Forming partnerships with universities, research institutions, or other businesses can further expand your R&D capabilities. These collaborations provide access to new knowledge, technologies, and talent, helping you stay at the forefront of your industry. For example, partnering with a university might give you access to cutting-edge research and a pool of talented students and researchers eager to contribute to real-world projects.

To sustain the momentum of innovation, implement a system for tracking and evaluating new ideas. This could be an idea management platform where employees can submit their proposals and receive feedback. Regularly review these ideas, pilot the most promising ones, and scale those that show potential. This systematic approach ensures that valuable ideas are not overlooked and that innovation efforts remain aligned with your strategic goals.

By fostering a culture of innovation, you create a dynamic environment where creativity thrives, leading to continuous growth and a strong competitive advantage in the marketplace.

Developing a Growth Strategy

For any business aiming to expand and achieve long-term success, developing a growth strategy is essential. Think of it as your business's roadmap to the future, guiding how you will increase revenue, expand market share, and enhance overall business value. A well-defined growth strategy does more than just set goals; it provides clear direction and aligns your entire team toward a common vision, ensuring that everyone is working in sync to achieve shared objectives. This strategic plan must be flexible, allowing your business to adapt to changing market conditions and seize new opportunities as they arise. Here are the key steps to creating an effective growth strategy.

Set Clear Objectives

The journey toward growth begins with setting clear, actionable objectives. Start by defining specific, measurable, achievable, relevant, and time-bound (SMART) goals that align seamlessly with your overall business vision and mission. These objectives serve as your business's guiding light, ensuring that every effort contributes directly to your broader ambitions. Common growth objectives might include increasing sales, expanding into new markets, launching innovative products, and enhancing customer retention. For example, if your vision is to become a leader in eco-friendly products, your growth objectives might focus on launching a new line of sustainable goods and capturing a larger share of the eco-conscious consumer market.

Once your objectives are in place, establish key performance indicators (KPIs) to measure progress. KPIs are quantifiable metrics that gauge the effectiveness of your strategies in achieving your goals. Essential KPIs might include revenue growth, market share, customer acquisition cost, and customer lifetime value. Revenue growth reflects how well your sales strategies are performing, while market share indicates your competitiveness within the industry. Customer acquisition cost helps you assess the efficiency of your marketing efforts, and customer lifetime value provides insight into the long-term profitability of your customer relationships.

Regularly monitoring these KPIs is crucial. By keeping a close eye on these metrics, you can quickly identify what is working and where adjustments are needed, allowing you to make informed, data-driven decisions. For instance, if you notice that your customer acquisition cost is increasing, it might be time to reevaluate your marketing strategies or channels. Conversely, a steady rise in customer lifetime value could signal that your customer retention efforts are yielding positive results. Tools like Google Analytics, customer relationship management (CRM) systems, and business intelligence platforms are invaluable for tracking these KPIs effectively.

In summary, setting clear objectives and establishing KPIs are vital components of a successful growth strategy. They provide a clear roadmap and a framework for measuring progress, guiding your business toward its growth goals. By aligning your objectives with your vision and mission and consistently monitoring your KPIs, you can ensure that your growth strategy remains focused, effective, and adaptable to changing market conditions. This strategic approach not only drives growth but also fosters a culture of continuous improvement and accountability within your organization.

Conduct Market Research

Understanding the landscape in which your business operates is essential for identifying growth opportunities and staying ahead of the competition. Start by thoroughly analyzing market trends, delving into the current shifts in customer preferences, emerging demands, and potential opportunities within your industry. Keeping a pulse on these trends allows you to anticipate changes that could impact your business and strategically leverage them to your advantage. For example, the increasing demand for sustainable products offers a substantial opportunity. Providing eco-friendly options or implementing sustainable practices can help a business attract a growing base of environmentally conscious consumers.

Conducting a thorough analysis of competitors is also an essential part of effective market research. By examining your competitors, you can gain insights into their strengths, weaknesses, and strategies, which can inform your own growth plans. Look closely at the products or services they offer, their pricing strategies, marketing tactics, and customer feedback. Identifying gaps in the market that your business can fill, or areas where you can differentiate yourself, is key. For example, if your competitors are strong in digital marketing but lack customer service, you could set your business apart by providing exceptional support. This type of competitive analysis not only uncovers opportunities but also prepares you to counter potential threats from existing or emerging competitors.

Beyond analyzing competitors, it is essential to understand the broader dynamics of your industry. Consider factors such as regulatory changes, technological advancements, and economic conditions that could influence your business. For example, the rise of technologies like artificial intelligence and machine learning is revolutionizing many industries, enhancing efficiency, and enabling new product offerings. Staying ahead of such advancements can give your business a significant competitive edge.

Directly engaging with customers can also offer valuable insights. Conducting surveys, focus groups, and interviews allows you to gather feedback on their needs, preferences, and pain points. This direct engagement helps you understand what your customers value most and how your products or services can better meet their needs. Platforms like SurveyMonkey or Google Forms can streamline the process of collecting and analyzing this feedback, making it easier to turn customer insights into actionable strategies.

By combining these research efforts, you gain a comprehensive view of your market, equipping you to make informed decisions and develop a robust growth strategy. For example, after conducting thorough market research, you might identify a rising trend, discover an underserved customer segment, and pinpoint a market gap that aligns with your business's strengths. Armed with this knowledge, you can tailor your growth strategy to capitalize on these insights, positioning your business for sustainable success.

Identify Growth Opportunities

Taking your business to the next level begins with identifying and capitalizing on growth opportunities. One powerful approach is to expand your product or service offerings to better meet the evolving needs of your target market. This could involve developing new products, enhancing existing ones, or bundling services to provide greater value to your customers. For example, if you run a tech company that offers a popular software tool, consider adding new features or complementary services that enhance the overall user experience. By continually improving your offerings, you not only meet the changing demands of your customers but also increase the perceived value of your products, leading to higher satisfaction and loyalty.

Expanding into new markets is another strategic way to drive growth. This might mean entering new geographic regions or targeting new customer segments within your existing market. Conducting a thorough market entry analysis is vital to assess the potential of different regions and to develop strategies tailored to each one. For instance, if you own a retail business, exploring opportunities in international markets or underserved local markets could open up significant avenues for growth. Understanding the cultural, economic, and regulatory environments of these new markets is key to tailoring your approach and increasing your chances of success.

Increasing market penetration in your current markets is also an effective growth strategy. Capturing a larger share of the market involves attracting new customers while retaining existing ones. This can be achieved through targeted marketing campaigns, enhanced customer service, and promotions or incentives. For example, offering limited-time discounts, loyalty programs, or referral bonuses can draw in new customers and encourage repeat business. Enhancing customer service by providing personalized experiences, quick responses, and efficient issue resolution can further boost customer satisfaction and retention.

Leveraging digital marketing can significantly amplify your market penetration efforts. Utilizing social media platforms, email marketing, and content marketing helps you reach a broader audience and engage with potential customers more effectively. Search engine optimization (SEO) and pay-per-click (PPC) campaigns increase your online visibility, driving more traffic to your website and converting more visitors into loyal customers.

Staying updated with industry trends and technological advancements is equally important. The rise of e-commerce and mobile shopping, for example, has created new opportunities for retailers to reach customers through online platforms and mobile apps. Adapting to these trends can help you capture new market segments and enhance your competitive edge, positioning your business for sustained growth in an ever-evolving marketplace.

Develop a Marketing and Sales Strategy

Driving business growth and reaching your objectives begins with a well-crafted marketing and sales strategy. Start by developing a comprehensive marketing plan that outlines how you will engage with your target audience. This plan should integrate digital marketing, content marketing, social media, email marketing, and traditional advertising to maximize both reach and impact. By connecting with your audience across multiple channels, you ensure that your message is seen and heard by a broader spectrum of potential customers.

Digital marketing plays a pivotal role in enhancing your online presence and attracting new customers. Search engine optimization (SEO) involves optimizing your website content to rank higher in search engine results, which drives organic traffic to your site. Pay-per-click (PPC) advertising, on the other hand, allows you to place targeted ads in search engine results and across various websites. By focusing on specific keywords and demographics, PPC enables you to reach your ideal customers more effectively.

Content marketing is about creating valuable and relevant content that resonates with your target audience. This might include blog posts, videos, infographics, and ebooks designed to provide useful information and address the challenges your audience faces. Consistently producing high-quality content not only establishes your brand as an industry authority but also builds trust with your audience and drives more traffic to your website.

Social media marketing is another powerful tool for reaching your audience and building brand awareness. Platforms like Facebook, Instagram, Twitter, and LinkedIn offer diverse advertising options and analytics tools to help you target specific demographics, track engagement, and measure campaign success. Social media also facilitates direct interaction with your audience, fostering a sense of community and loyalty that can translate into long-term business success.

Email marketing continues to be one of the most effective methods for nurturing leads and sustaining relationships with current customers. By segmenting your email list and sending personalized, relevant content, you can significantly boost engagement and conversion rates. Email newsletters, promotional offers, and automated drip campaigns keep your audience informed and encourage repeat business, making email marketing a vital component of your strategy.

Traditional advertising, including print ads, radio spots, and TV commercials, still has its place, especially when targeting local audiences or specific demographics less engaged with digital channels. Combining traditional and digital marketing efforts creates a more comprehensive and impactful strategy, ensuring you reach your audience wherever they are.

Optimizing your sales processes is equally crucial for driving growth. Equip your sales team with the best practices, tools, and resources they need to succeed. Implementing customer relationship management (CRM) systems can streamline sales operations, improve customer interactions, and provide valuable insights into customer behavior and preferences. CRM systems help manage and analyze customer data, track sales interactions, and automate follow-ups, making your sales processes more efficient and effective.

Developing sales scripts and materials that resonate with your target audience is also essential. Ensure your sales team has access to well-crafted presentations, brochures, and case studies that highlight the benefits of your products or services. Tailoring your sales approach to address specific customer needs and pain points increases your chances of closing deals and building long-term relationships.

By combining a robust marketing strategy with an optimized sales process, you position your business to achieve sustained growth and long-term success.

Strengthen Your Brand

Building recognition, trust, and loyalty among your customers is essential for long-term success. Prioritize building brand awareness as your first step. Launch branding campaigns that consistently communicate your brand's message, values, and unique selling points. Utilize a mix of platforms such as social media, content marketing, and traditional advertising to reach a wider audience. Public relations efforts, like press releases, media engagements, and event sponsorships, can further enhance your visibility and credibility. Additionally, partnering with influencers or complementary businesses can open doors to new audiences and build trust through association. Influencer marketing, in particular, is powerful because consumers often trust recommendations from the people they follow and admire.

However, creating a strong brand goes beyond just being visible—it is about being memorable and trusted. This requires maintaining a consistent brand voice and visual identity across all touchpoints. From your website and social media profiles to your packaging and customer service interactions, every element of your brand should reflect a cohesive image and message. Consistency helps reinforce your brand in the minds of consumers, building a sense of reliability and professionalism.

Enhancing the customer experience is another essential aspect of strengthening your brand. Deliver exceptional experiences at every stage of the customer journey, beginning with top-notch customer service. This is because prompt, friendly, and solution-oriented interactions leave a lasting positive impression. Equip your customer service team with the tools and training they need to resolve issues effectively and exceed customer expectations.

A seamless and intuitive user experience on your website and apps is equally important. Ensure your digital platforms are easy to navigate, visually appealing, and optimized for mobile devices. A well-designed user interface significantly boosts customer satisfaction and retention. Personalizing interactions based on customer preferences can further elevate their experience. Use data and analytics to understand customer behavior, tailoring communications and offers accordingly. Personalization can range from addressing customers by name in emails to recommending products based on their past purchases.

Building customer loyalty requires ongoing engagement. Regularly interact with your customers through various channels—social media, email newsletters, and loyalty programs. Share valuable content, updates, and exclusive offers to keep them interested and connected to your brand. Encourage and reward loyalty through programs that offer points, discounts, or special privileges, making customers feel valued and appreciated. By focusing on these elements, you ensure that your brand remains strong, trusted, and capable of fostering long-term relationships with your customers.

Optimize Operations

Streamlining operations is crucial for boosting productivity and cutting costs, allowing your business to thrive in a competitive market. Start by identifying inefficiencies in your current processes. Conduct a detailed analysis to pinpoint bottlenecks, areas of wasted resources, and opportunities for improvement. One effective approach is implementing lean management techniques, which focus on maximizing customer value while minimizing resource use. Lean methodologies such as 5S (sort, set in order, shine, standardize, sustain) and Kaizen (continuous improvement) help refine workflows, eliminate waste, and encourage ongoing improvements in efficiency.

Automation is another powerful tool for optimizing your operations. By automating repetitive, time-consuming tasks, you free up employees to concentrate on higher-value, strategic activities. For example, using automation software for invoicing, inventory management, or customer service not only reduces errors but also increases efficiency across the board. Upgrading your technology systems—such as implementing advanced software for project management or customer relationship management (CRM)—can enhance productivity by improving data insights and streamlining workflows.

Scalable infrastructure is equally important to support long-term growth. Investing in technology systems that can handle increased volumes of data and transactions without compromising performance is essential. Cloud-based solutions, like Amazon Web Services (AWS) or Microsoft Azure, offer the flexibility and scalability to adjust resources as your business grows. These platforms allow you to scale up or down seamlessly based on demand, ensuring that your infrastructure evolves alongside your business.

As your business expands, scaling physical facilities may also be necessary. Whether it means moving to a larger office, opening new retail locations, or increasing warehouse capacity, ensuring that your physical infrastructure can accommodate growth is key. Expanding in line with demand prevents bottlenecks and keeps operations running smoothly during periods of rapid growth.

Optimizing supply chain management is another critical aspect of streamlining operations. A well-managed supply chain allows your business to efficiently handle increased demand and respond quickly to changes in the market. Strengthen supplier relationships, diversify your supplier base to mitigate risks, and adopt supply chain management software to enhance visibility and coordination across the entire supply chain.

These efforts create a foundation of smooth, efficient operations that position your company for long-term success in an ever-evolving and competitive market.

Invest in Talent and Leadership

Building a strong team is the cornerstone of executing a successful growth strategy. The first step is attracting and retaining skilled employees who not only possess the right expertise but also align with your company's values and culture. This can be achieved through targeted recruitment efforts, offering competitive compensation packages, and providing clear opportunities for career advancement. The more aligned your employees are with your mission, the more they contribute to the overall success of the business.

Once you have the right talent in place, the next crucial step is investing in their ongoing training and development. Continuous learning not only helps employees stay up-to-date with industry trends but also enhances their skill sets, making them more effective in their roles. In fact, LinkedIn's 2020 Workplace Learning Report revealed that 94 percent of employees would stay longer at a company if it invested in their career development. Offering professional development programs, access to online courses, and cross-functional training significantly boost both employee satisfaction and retention, creating a more engaged and skilled workforce.

Equally important is fostering a positive work environment where employees feel valued and empowered to contribute their ideas. A culture of innovation and collaboration encourages creativity and drives productivity. Promote open communication, recognize and reward achievements, and prioritize a healthy work-life balance. These factors help elevate employee morale and nurture a workplace where creativity and innovation thrive.

Leadership development within your organization is another critical component for sustained growth. Strong leaders provide the guidance needed to navigate periods of growth and change. It is essential to equip your leadership team with the skills and experience necessary to tackle challenges and seize new opportunities. Investing in leadership development programs, such as formal training sessions, workshops, and executive coaching, helps build these capabilities. Mentoring programs are also effective, allowing seasoned leaders to offer support and guidance to less experienced managers.

Executive coaching can take leadership development a step further by offering personalized guidance for refining management skills, improving decision-making, and inspiring and motivating teams. By prioritizing the development of both your talent and leadership, you create a resilient, forward-thinking team capable of driving your business toward sustained success.

Secure Financing

Executing a successful growth strategy depends on securing the necessary financing. Start by evaluating your funding options, assessing your financial needs, and exploring various methods that can support your growth initiatives. Some of the most common options include reinvesting profits, securing loans, attracting investors, or seeking grants. Each approach has its benefits and challenges, so it is important to choose the one that aligns best with your business goals and financial situation.

Reinvesting profits is a straightforward and low-risk option, allowing you to fund growth using the capital generated by your business. This approach avoids taking on debt or giving up equity, but it may limit the speed of your expansion depending on the profitability of your operations. For many small businesses, securing loans from banks or financial institutions is a viable alternative. Loans provide the capital needed for expansion while allowing you to retain full ownership of your company. However, it is essential to establish a solid repayment plan to manage debt responsibly and avoid potential cash flow issues.

Attracting investors is another effective way to secure financing for growth. This could involve seeking venture capital, angel investors, or equity crowdfunding. Investors often provide significant funding along with valuable expertise and networking opportunities. However, they will expect a return on their investment, which usually means giving up a portion of their equity and, in some cases, relinquishing some control over key business decisions.

Grants are another funding source worth exploring, particularly for businesses in sectors like technology, healthcare, or renewable energy. Grants do not require repayment, making them an appealing option, but they often come with stringent eligibility requirements and highly competitive application processes. Websites like Grants.gov offer information on federal grants available to small businesses.

Once you have determined the appropriate funding method, it is essential to create a detailed financial plan. This plan should outline the costs associated with your growth strategy, as well as how you will manage cash flow throughout the expansion process. Include projections for revenue, expenses, and profitability to ensure financial sustainability during growth. Accurate financial forecasting will help you anticipate potential shortfalls and enable you to make informed decisions about resource allocation. Tools like QuickBooks or other financial planning software can streamline this process by providing templates and automated calculations.

In addition to financial planning, your strategy should include risk management measures. Growth often brings uncertainty, and having a plan to mitigate financial risks is critical. This might involve setting aside reserves, diversifying your revenue streams, or purchasing insurance to protect against unforeseen events. Proactively managing these risks will help safeguard your business as it expands, allowing you to focus on driving long-term success.

Implement Risk Management Strategies

To ensure your business can navigate challenges and achieve long-term success, it is essential to implement robust risk management strategies. Start by identifying potential risks tied to your growth strategy, which may include market risks, operational risks, and financial risks. Conducting a comprehensive risk assessment helps you evaluate the likelihood and impact of each risk, allowing you to prioritize those that require immediate attention. Market risks, for example, might involve shifts in consumer preferences, heightened competition, or economic downturns. Operational risks could include supply chain disruptions, technological failures, or staffing shortages, while financial risks range from cash flow issues to unexpected expenses or funding gaps.

Once risks are identified, developing targeted mitigation plans is the next step. Diversifying revenue streams is a powerful strategy for reducing dependence on a single income source, thus making your business more resilient to market fluctuations. For instance, if your primary sales channel is a physical store, expanding into e-commerce or offering complementary services can provide additional revenue streams. Businesses with diversified incomes are better equipped to endure economic downturns and market volatility.

Securing appropriate insurance coverage is another crucial element of risk management. Insurance helps protect your business from risks such as property damage, liability claims, and business interruptions. Collaborating with an insurance advisor will ensure you have the right coverage in place to shield your company from potential threats. Additionally, implementing strong internal controls is vital. This includes establishing clear policies and procedures, conducting regular audits, and leveraging technology to monitor and manage risks. Well-executed internal controls can prevent fraud, ensure compliance with regulations, and enhance overall operational efficiency.

Developing contingency plans for potential disruptions is critical to maintaining business continuity. These plans should detail the steps your business will take in response to various emergencies or unexpected events. For example, a contingency plan for supply chain disruption might involve identifying alternative suppliers, increasing inventory reserves, or adjusting production schedules to minimize impact.

Regularly reviewing and updating your risk management strategies is equally important. As your business evolves and external conditions shift, new risks may arise while existing ones may change in scope or severity. Continuously assessing and refining your risk management approach ensures that it remains relevant and effective. Engaging your team in this process can provide fresh perspectives and foster a culture of risk awareness and preparedness throughout your organization.

By proactively identifying risks, creating mitigation plans, and remaining adaptable, you can safeguard your business against uncertainties and position it for sustained success.

Monitor and Adjust

Maintaining the effectiveness and sustainability of your growth strategy requires ongoing monitoring and adjustments. Track the progress of your initiatives using the key performance indicators (KPIs) you established earlier. Metrics such as revenue growth, customer acquisition cost, and market share offer valuable insights into how well your strategies are performing. Leverage data and analytics to assess these indicators, using advanced tools like Google Analytics, HubSpot, and Tableau to visualize trends, identify patterns, and make informed decisions. By consistently monitoring these KPIs, you can quickly determine what is working and where improvements are needed.

Flexibility is crucial to a successful growth strategy. The business environment is ever-changing, and your ability to adapt to these shifts can determine your long-term success. Be ready to adjust your strategy based on performance data, market conditions, and feedback from customers and stakeholders. For example, if a marketing campaign is underperforming, do not hesitate to pivot—this might mean reallocating resources to more effective channels or refining your messaging to better connect with your target audience.

Listening to customer feedback is also important. Customers provide invaluable insights into their needs, preferences, and pain points. Regularly collecting and analyzing feedback through surveys, social media, and direct communication can help you understand how your products or services are perceived, revealing areas for improvement. Engaging with customers and demonstrating that their input is valued not only enhances customer satisfaction but also fosters loyalty.

Stakeholder feedback offers another critical perspective. Engaging with employees, investors, and business partners can provide a wealth of insights that inform your growth strategy. These stakeholders have a vested interest in your success and can offer advice based on their unique experiences and expertise.

Adapting to changing market conditions is also vital. Economic shifts, technological advancements, and competitive dynamics can all impact your business. Staying informed about these external factors and being ready to adjust your strategy can help you navigate challenges and seize new opportunities. For instance, if a new technology emerges that could enhance your operations or product offerings, being an early adopter could provide a significant competitive advantage.

By consistently monitoring and adjusting your growth strategy, you ensure it remains relevant and effective. This proactive approach enables you to stay ahead of the competition, meet customer needs, and maintain sustainable growth while navigating the ever-evolving business landscape.

Planning for Infrastructure, Technology, and Team Expansion

Planning for infrastructure, technology, and team expansion is fundamental to sustaining business growth and securing long-term success. As your business scales, building a strong foundation becomes increasingly important to manage growing demand, improve operational efficiency, and uphold high service standards. Effective planning requires anticipating future needs and strategically investing in scalable systems, advanced technologies, and skilled personnel. This forward-thinking approach not only helps your business handle the complexities of growth but also positions your company to seize new opportunities and stay competitive. Below are the key steps to successfully planning for infrastructure, technology, and team expansion.

Infrastructure Expansion

Key Step #1: Assess Current Infrastructure

The first crucial step in preparing for business growth is to conduct a thorough assessment of your current infrastructure. Begin by auditing your existing facilities, production capacities, office spaces, and technological systems. This comprehensive evaluation will help you identify any limitations or bottlenecks that could obstruct your expansion efforts. For example, you might find that your production capacity is approaching its limit, your facilities are becoming outdated, or your office space is growing too cramped for an expanding team. Addressing these issues early allows you to plan strategically and ensures that your scaling efforts are smooth and efficient.

Once you have a clear picture of your current infrastructure, the next step is to forecast future needs based on your growth projections. Consider how increasing production volumes, expanding your team, or upgrading technology will impact your setup. Will you need additional machinery, more storage space, or an expanded distribution network? Think about whether expanding your team will require larger office spaces or advanced technological systems to support operations. Accurately forecasting these needs will help you make informed decisions about where to invest in upgrades or acquisitions. For instance, if you anticipate a 50% increase in production within the next two years, you might need to invest in new manufacturing equipment or lease additional warehouse space.

By assessing your current infrastructure and planning for future requirements, you create a solid foundation that aligns with your growth objectives. This proactive approach not only prepares your business for upcoming demands but also positions you to seize new opportunities as they arise.

Key Step #2: Develop an Infrastructure Plan

Creating a comprehensive infrastructure plan is essential for supporting your business as it grows. The key is to prioritize investments that will have the most significant impact on your expansion efforts. This could include expanding or upgrading your facilities to handle higher production volumes, investing in new equipment to boost efficiency and output, or enhancing your logistics and distribution capabilities to ensure smooth operations as demand increases. For example, if your current warehouse is nearing capacity, you may need to consider expanding it or implementing automated storage solutions. Similarly, if your production equipment is outdated, upgrading to modern machinery could improve productivity and reduce costly downtime.

Once your priorities are clear, develop a detailed budget and timeline for your infrastructure expansion plan. Outline all costs associated with the planned investments, such as construction, equipment purchases, and additional operational expenses. Being thorough during this stage helps you avoid unexpected financial shortfalls that could derail your expansion efforts. Establish realistic deadlines for each phase of the project, considering factors like lead times for equipment, construction schedules, and potential delays. This ensures that infrastructure upgrades are completed on time and with minimal disruption to your current operations. A structured timeline also enables you to monitor progress effectively and make necessary adjustments along the way.

It is also important to build flexibility into your infrastructure plan to account for unforeseen challenges or shifts in your growth trajectory. Regularly review and adjust your budget and timeline to remain agile, allowing you to adapt to new opportunities or challenges as they arise. Engage with key stakeholders throughout the process—including team members, suppliers, and financial advisors—to gather valuable insights and secure buy-in for your expansion initiatives. This collaborative approach will help strengthen your infrastructure plan and ensure it stays aligned with your business goals.

Key Step #3: Implement Scalable Solutions

To support sustainable growth, implementing scalable solutions within your infrastructure is essential. Designing your infrastructure to be flexible and adaptable ensures that your business can expand without significant disruption. For example, modular facility designs allow for easy expansion of physical space as needed, eliminating the need for major overhauls. This flexibility is particularly advantageous for manufacturing plants or warehouses, where the ability to add or reconfigure space can dramatically improve operational efficiency. Similarly, scalable storage solutions, such as cloud-based data storage, provide additional capacity on demand, ensuring your technology infrastructure can seamlessly accommodate increasing volumes of data and transactions.

Incorporating sustainability into your infrastructure planning not only benefits the environment but also reduces costs and enhances your brand's reputation. Energy-efficient buildings, for example, can significantly lower utility expenses over time, while waste reduction initiatives—such as recycling programs or using materials that generate less waste—can streamline operations and cut costs. Embracing environmentally friendly materials can further elevate your company's image as a responsible and forward-thinking organization, appealing to consumers who value sustainability. Moreover, many governments offer incentives, such as tax credits or rebates, for businesses that adopt green practices like installing energy-efficient systems or renewable energy sources such as solar panels. These incentives can help offset the initial costs of sustainable infrastructure and lead to long-term savings.

Integrating smart technology and automation into your infrastructure planning is another key factor in optimizing scalability. Smart systems that monitor and manage energy usage, climate control, and security can improve operational efficiency and minimize waste. For example, smart lighting systems that adjust based on occupancy and natural light availability can significantly reduce energy consumption. Automated systems for inventory management can streamline operations and reduce human error, helping your business run smoothly even as it scales.

By focusing on scalable, sustainable, and smart solutions, you ensure that your infrastructure grows with your business while maintaining efficiency, reducing costs, and enhancing your brand's reputation in an increasingly eco-conscious market.

Technology Expansion

Key Step #1: Evaluate Technology Needs

A thorough evaluation of your technology infrastructure is key to supporting your business's growth. Begin by reviewing your existing hardware, software, and network systems to identify any limitations or weaknesses that may impede your ability to scale. Perhaps your servers are nearing their capacity, your software is outdated, or your network is struggling to manage increasing demands. Recognizing these issues early on allows you to address them proactively, ensuring that your technology can effectively support your growth strategy.

Once you have a comprehensive understanding of your current technology landscape, the next step is to identify the technology requirements necessary to achieve your growth goals. Research new hardware, software, and network solutions that can fill the gaps you have identified and support your expansion efforts. When evaluating new technologies, consider factors such as scalability, cost, compatibility, and future-proofing to ensure your choices align with both your immediate needs and long-term objectives. By thoughtfully upgrading your technology infrastructure, you build a strong foundation that facilitates seamless growth and enhances overall operational efficiency.

Key Step #2: Invest in Scalable Technology

Investing in scalable technology is a strategic move that can empower your business to grow seamlessly and adapt to evolving demands. Cloud-based solutions are at the heart of this approach, offering a range of benefits such as scalability, flexibility, and cost-efficiency. Unlike traditional IT infrastructure, cloud services allow for quick adjustments to meet increased demand, providing the capacity you need without the delays and costs associated with upgrading physical hardware. Platforms like Amazon Web Services (AWS), Microsoft Azure, and Google Cloud not only offer scalable solutions but also give you access to the latest tools and software, keeping your business on the cutting edge of technology.

Incorporating automation and integration technologies is another essential step in scaling your operations. Automation streamlines business processes, reduces manual tasks, and enhances overall efficiency. For example, automated inventory management systems can monitor stock levels in real time, trigger reorders, and even automate purchase orders, ensuring that you are always stocked with critical items. Integrated customer relationship management (CRM) platforms like Salesforce or HubSpot unify your sales, marketing, and customer service functions, offering a comprehensive view of customer interactions that improves customer experience and loyalty. AI-driven analytics tools can further transform your operations by analyzing vast data sets to reveal patterns and insights that drive better decision-making. Predictive analytics, for instance, can forecast customer behavior, optimize marketing efforts, and improve demand planning.

Investing in scalable technologies like these not only enhances operational efficiency but also gives your business a competitive edge. Automation and integration reduce errors, accelerate processes, and free your team to focus on strategic initiatives. This, in turn, boosts productivity and ensures that resources are used more effectively. Moreover, by leveraging AI and cloud computing, your business becomes better positioned to scale quickly, adapt to market changes, and continuously innovate in a rapidly evolving landscape.

Key Step #3: Strengthen Cybersecurity

Protecting your business from cyber threats and ensuring the integrity and confidentiality of your data requires a strong cybersecurity strategy. Start by conducting a comprehensive cybersecurity risk assessment to evaluate your current systems and identify potential vulnerabilities. This assessment should consider both external and internal risks, including malware attacks, phishing schemes, and insider threats. By thoroughly understanding where your weaknesses lie, you can better prepare your defenses.

After identifying these risks, implement robust security measures to safeguard your data and systems. This might include deploying firewalls, antivirus software, and intrusion detection systems to block malicious activity. Ensure all software remains up-to-date with the latest security patches, and use encryption to protect sensitive data both during transmission and while at rest. Adding multi-factor authentication (MFA) is another essential step to strengthen security, requiring users to provide multiple verification factors before accessing critical systems, making unauthorized access significantly more difficult.

Employee education is a critical component of any effective cybersecurity strategy. Many cyberattacks target human vulnerabilities, such as falling victim to phishing schemes or accidentally clicking on malicious links. Regular cybersecurity training helps ensure that your team is aware of the latest threats and understands best practices for protecting company data. Teach employees how to recognize suspicious emails, create strong passwords, and adhere to security protocols. Interactive training, such as phishing simulations, can make the learning experience engaging and practical. Foster a culture of security where everyone takes responsibility for safeguarding the company's data and stays vigilant in their daily activities. Additionally, establish clear protocols for reporting potential security incidents so employees know exactly how to respond when they encounter a threat.

It is also vital to regularly review and update your cybersecurity policies and procedures. Cyber threats are constantly evolving, and staying ahead of them requires a proactive approach. Engage with cybersecurity experts to conduct periodic audits and assessments, giving you an external perspective on your security posture. By regularly adapting your defenses to new threats and technological advancements, you ensure that your security measures remain effective and aligned with industry best practices, providing your business with a stronger shield against potential cyberattacks.

Team Expansion

Key Step #1: Assess Workforce Needs

Evaluating your workforce needs is a critical step in preparing your business for growth. Start with a thorough analysis of your current team, examining the skills you already have, identifying gaps or capacity challenges, and assessing how these factors might impact your expansion plans. Review current roles and responsibilities to determine whether your existing team can handle the demands of your growth objectives. For example, you may realize that you need more expertise in areas like digital marketing or data analysis to support your entry into new markets. Understanding your workforce's strengths and weaknesses will allow you to pinpoint areas where additional training or new hires may be necessary.

After assessing your current situation, shift your focus to future workforce planning by forecasting your needs based on your growth projections. Consider the additional roles, skills, and headcount required to meet your business goals. For instance, launching a new product line might call for expanding your research and development team, hiring specialized marketing professionals, and adding sales representatives. Similarly, entering a new geographic region may necessitate bringing in local staff with a deep understanding of the market and its cultural nuances. It is equally important to consider the evolving nature of work and anticipate which skills will be in demand. According to the World Economic Forum's Future of Jobs Report, technological advancements are driving the need for expertise in areas such as artificial intelligence, cloud computing, and cybersecurity. By anticipating these trends, you can ensure your workforce is equipped to tackle future challenges and seize new opportunities.

In addition to identifying the specific skills and roles you will need, it is essential to consider the overall headcount required to support your growth. This may involve not only hiring new employees but also developing the talent you already have. Investing in training and professional development programs can help upskill your existing team, making them more adaptable and capable of taking on new responsibilities as your business evolves. This approach not only fills skill gaps but also boosts employee morale and retention by demonstrating your commitment to their career growth.

Finally, as you expand your team, it is crucial to maintain the values and cultural elements that define your organization. Bringing in new talent offers an opportunity to enhance your company culture, but it also requires intentionality to ensure that your core values are preserved. Clearly communicate your company's mission and values during the hiring process, and foster an inclusive environment where all employees feel valued and engaged. This focus on culture will help you build a cohesive, motivated team that is aligned with your growth strategy.

Key Step #2: Develop a Recruitment Strategy

Developing a robust recruitment strategy is vital for attracting and retaining the top talent needed to fuel your business growth. Start by strengthening your employer brand—this means clearly showcasing your company's culture, values, and mission to potential candidates. Highlight what sets your organization apart as a great place to work, such as career development opportunities, a positive and collaborative work environment, and unique benefits. Use your company website, social media platforms, and employee testimonials to effectively communicate your brand and connect with prospective employees.

Offering competitive compensation packages is another crucial aspect of your recruitment strategy. Ensure that your salaries and benefits align with or exceed industry standards. Beyond salary, consider offering perks such as flexible work arrangements, health and wellness programs, and opportunities for career progression. These added benefits make your organization more appealing to high-quality candidates and help differentiate you from competitors in the job market.

To reach a broader and more diverse pool of candidates, leverage multiple recruitment channels. Use job boards, social media platforms, and industry-specific networks to connect with potential hires. LinkedIn, in particular, is a powerful tool for professional networking and job postings. In addition to online efforts, engage with potential candidates by participating in industry events, job fairs, and university recruiting programs. A combination of traditional and digital recruitment methods expands your reach and increases your chances of attracting the right talent.

Once you have attracted new talent, implementing a structured onboarding process is critical to ensuring they are integrated smoothly into your organization. A comprehensive onboarding program helps new employees understand their roles, familiarize themselves with company policies and culture, and feel supported from the start. This can enhance job satisfaction while simultaneously lowering turnover rates. Furthermore, offering ongoing training and development opportunities is essential. Regular training sessions, workshops, and access to online learning platforms enable employees to build the skills needed for their roles and stay ahead of industry trends.

Investing in continuous learning and professional development enhances individual performance and drives overall organizational growth. By fostering a culture of improvement and innovation, you encourage your team to grow alongside your business, ensuring long-term success and adaptability in a competitive marketplace.

Key Step #3: Foster a Positive Workplace Culture

Cultivating a positive workplace culture is crucial for creating an environment where employees feel engaged, satisfied, and motivated to stay with the company. Begin by prioritizing employee engagement through open communication across all levels of the organization. Encourage a culture where employees feel comfortable sharing their ideas and providing feedback. Recognize and reward achievements regularly to show your appreciation for hard work and dedication. This could involve acknowledging accomplishments during team meetings, offering bonuses or incentives, or celebrating key milestones and successes.

Providing opportunities for career growth is another essential component of a positive culture. Employees are more inclined to stay with a company that prioritizes their professional growth. This could mean offering training programs, creating mentorship opportunities, or establishing clear pathways for advancement. By prioritizing the growth of your employees, you enhance their skills while simultaneously increasing their loyalty and commitment to the organization.

Additionally, investing in leadership development is key to building a strong leadership team capable of guiding your business through growth. Effective leaders are essential for managing change, inspiring teams, and driving strategic initiatives. Leadership development programs—whether through formal training, workshops, coaching, or mentoring—help leaders sharpen vital skills such as communication, decision-making, and strategic thinking.

Fostering a positive workplace culture also requires creating an inclusive and supportive environment. Encourage collaboration and teamwork, ensuring that every employee feels valued and included. Act promptly to address any issues of discrimination or bias, and implement policies that actively promote diversity and inclusion. A diverse workforce brings varied perspectives, drives innovation, and improves problem-solving.

Promoting work-life balance is another vital aspect of a healthy culture. Offering flexible working arrangements, such as remote work options or flexible hours, allows employees to manage their personal and professional lives more effectively, which in turn boosts overall satisfaction and productivity.

By focusing on employee engagement, growth opportunities, leadership development, inclusion, and work-life balance, you create a positive workplace culture that not only attracts top talent but also retains and motivates your current team to drive your business forward.

Key Step #4: Implement Scalable HR Systems

Implementing scalable HR systems supports your business as it grows. Begin by adopting HR technology solutions that can evolve alongside your expanding needs. These may include HR management systems (HRMS), payroll software, and performance management tools that streamline HR processes and enhance efficiency. HRMS platforms such as Workday, ADP, or BambooHR automate routine tasks like employee record-keeping, benefits administration, and attendance tracking. These systems not only save time and reduce the risk of errors but also ensure consistency across the organization.

Payroll software is another vital component, helping to ensure that employees are paid accurately and on time. Automated payroll systems handle complexities such as tax deductions, benefits contributions, and compliance with local labor laws, making the entire payroll process more efficient and reliable. Similarly, performance management tools play an important role in fostering a culture of continuous improvement. Platforms like 15Five and Lattice offer comprehensive solutions for tracking employee performance, setting goals, and providing regular feedback, empowering managers to support their teams effectively and ensure alignment with business objectives.

Compliance with labor laws and regulations becomes more complex as your business scales, particularly if you operate in multiple regions with varying legal requirements. Regularly review and update your HR policies to stay in line with the latest changes in labor laws, health and safety regulations, and anti-discrimination legislation. Ensuring that your HR practices are compliant not only protects your business but also supports the creation of a fair and inclusive workplace.

Fostering diversity and inclusion is another key element of scalable HR systems. Make sure your policies promote equal opportunities for all employees, regardless of background. Implementing training programs on unconscious bias, developing mentorship opportunities for underrepresented groups, and creating channels for reporting and addressing workplace discrimination are critical steps in building an inclusive culture. A diverse and inclusive workplace leads to greater innovation, improved problem-solving, and enhanced employee satisfaction.

By investing in scalable HR systems, you prepare your business to handle the complexities of growth while maintaining efficiency, compliance, and a positive workplace culture.

CHAPTER 6

OPTIMIZING SMALL BUSINESS OPERATIONS

Improving Efficiency and Productivity

For small businesses, maximizing efficiency and productivity is paramount to maintaining manageable growth while optimizing performance and profitability. Every resource matters, and making the most of it can create a significant impact on the business's success. Streamlining operations, leveraging assets to their fullest potential, and fostering a culture of continuous improvement are all vital strategies that can drive substantial gains. These methods not only enhance overall performance but also contribute to long-term sustainability and resilience in a competitive marketplace. The following tailored strategies will help small businesses elevate their efficiency and productivity to new heights.

Streamline Processes

For small businesses aiming to enhance efficiency and productivity, refining processes is indispensable. Begin by engaging in process mapping, a technique that involves identifying and documenting key workflows. Focus on the core processes that drive your business, such as production, sales, customer service, and inventory management. Creating detailed process maps for these areas helps you visualize workflows, making it easier to identify inefficiencies or bottlenecks. This step is crucial in gaining a clear understanding of how work is carried out and where improvements can be implemented.

Once your processes are mapped out, the next phase is process improvement. Analyze the process maps to pinpoint redundancies or unnecessary steps that complicate workflows and consume valuable time without adding any real benefit. Streamlining these processes can significantly boost efficiency. For example, if a task requires multiple approvals that slow progress, consider simplifying or eliminating some of those steps to accelerate completion.

Standardizing procedures is another key component of process improvement. Develop standardized operating procedures (SOPs) to ensure that tasks are performed consistently and efficiently across your team. SOPs offer clear, structured guidelines for employees, reducing variability and minimizing errors. This consistency not only improves productivity but also ensures smoother operations when new team members are brought on board.

Incorporating automation can further streamline processes by taking over repetitive tasks, allowing your employees to concentrate on higher-value activities. For instance, customer relationship management (CRM) software can automate tasks like follow-up emails and tracking customer interactions, while inventory management systems can automate stock tracking and reorder alerts, ensuring that your business runs smoothly with minimal manual intervention.

Investing in the right technology can make a substantial difference in optimizing your operations. Tools like Trello or Asana can help streamline project management, keeping tasks organized and ensuring they are completed efficiently and on time. Similarly, accounting software such as QuickBooks can automate financial tasks, reducing the time spent on manual bookkeeping and allowing you to focus on growing your business.

With optimized processes and automation in place, your business can achieve greater efficiency and remain well-equipped to handle future expansion.

Leverage Technology

Harnessing technology is a powerful method to enhance efficiency and productivity in your small business. Implementing productivity tools that streamline operations and foster better collaboration is a good starting point. Project management software like Trello, Asana, or Monday.com can help you plan, track, and manage tasks with ease. These platforms offer a clear overview of ongoing work, ensuring that team members stay aligned and focused. Trello's intuitive board and card system allows for the visual organization of tasks, making it simple to assign responsibilities and track progress. Asana goes a step further with advanced features like task dependencies and timelines, ideal for managing more complex projects.

Communication platforms such as Slack or Microsoft Teams are indispensable for facilitating seamless communication among your team. These tools enable instant messaging, file sharing, and video conferencing, reducing the risk of miscommunication and improving overall workflow. Slack, for instance, allows you to create specific channels for different projects or departments, keeping conversations organized and focused. Meanwhile, Microsoft Teams integrates with other Microsoft

Office applications, making real-time collaboration on documents, spreadsheets, and presentations a breeze.

Another key component of leveraging technology is utilizing data analytics and business intelligence tools. Data-driven decision-making provides valuable insights into your business by analyzing trends, identifying inefficiencies, and uncovering new opportunities. Tools like Google Analytics, Tableau, and Power BI allow you to collect and visualize data from multiple sources, offering a comprehensive view of your business performance. For example, Google Analytics can track website traffic and user behavior, helping you better understand customer interactions with your online presence.

Establishing key performance indicators (KPIs) is equally important for measuring and monitoring productivity and efficiency. KPIs like sales growth, customer acquisition costs, and employee productivity offer quantifiable metrics to assess your progress toward business goals. Regularly reviewing these metrics allows you to make informed decisions and adjust your strategies when necessary. For instance, by tracking customer acquisition costs, you can evaluate the effectiveness of your marketing efforts and allocate resources more efficiently.

With the right technology in place, your business gains the agility to operate more efficiently, make smarter decisions, and foster stronger communication and collaboration across teams. Embracing these tools sets a solid foundation for long-term productivity and success.

Optimize Resource Management

Enhancing efficiency and productivity in your small business hinges on effective resource management. Start with thorough resource planning, utilizing tools like Microsoft Project, Resource Guru, or Smartsheet to better manage your staff, inventory, equipment, and facilities. These tools allow you to visualize resource allocation, track utilization rates, and ensure everything is being used effectively. By properly scheduling staff and resources, you can prevent issues such as overstaffing or understaffing, resulting in a more balanced workload and potential cost savings.

Another essential component of resource management is task prioritization. Employing techniques like the Eisenhower Matrix helps focus your team's efforts on tasks that have the greatest impact on your business. This method divides tasks into four categories based on their urgency and importance, allowing you to prioritize more effectively. Urgent and important tasks are addressed immediately, while important but less urgent tasks are scheduled for later. This approach ensures that your team's time and energy are directed toward activities that drive business growth and efficiency.

Managing your inventory effectively is also crucial for optimizing resources. Implementing just-in-time (JIT) inventory practices can help you significantly reduce holding costs and minimize waste. JIT ensures that you order inventory only as needed based on demand forecasts, which reduces storage costs and limits the risk of obsolescence.

Accurate inventory tracking is vital to avoid stockouts or overstock situations. Tools like TradeGecko or Zoho Inventory offer real-time visibility into your inventory, allowing you to monitor stock levels, set reorder points, and manage turnover efficiently. With these systems in place, you can make smarter decisions about when and how much inventory to reorder, ensuring that you maintain optimal stock levels without overextending resources.

Enhance Employee Productivity

Boosting employee productivity requires a holistic approach that incorporates continuous learning, cross-training, motivation, recognition, and a strong emphasis on work-life balance. Investing in training and development programs is a key factor in driving productivity. Well-trained employees not only work more efficiently but also contribute to higher overall performance. Regular workshops, courses, and professional development opportunities keep their skills sharp and introduce new methodologies and technologies that can help them streamline their tasks.

Another powerful strategy is implementing cross-training programs. Cross-training enables employees to take on multiple roles within the organization, increasing operational flexibility. This is especially valuable during staff absences, as other team members can seamlessly step in, ensuring that operations run smoothly without disruption. Additionally, cross-training broadens employees' understanding of the business, allowing them to gain insights into different functions and processes, which enhances their versatility and value to the company.

Employee engagement plays a critical role in enhancing productivity. Creating a positive work environment where employees feel motivated and appreciated leads to improved performance. Recognition programs that celebrate employee achievements, whether through formal awards, bonuses, or simple acknowledgments, significantly boost morale and foster a culture of excellence. When employees feel valued for their contributions, they are more likely to remain committed and dedicated to their work.

Equally important is promoting work-life balance. Offering flexible work arrangements, such as remote work options or adjustable hours, allows employees to better manage their personal and professional responsibilities. Encouraging regular breaks and ensuring that employees take vacation time helps prevent burnout, ensuring that productivity is sustained over the long term.

Implementing these strategies cultivates a work environment that boosts employee productivity while simultaneously prioritizing their overall well-being. As a result, your teams become more engaged and resilient, fostering a stronger and more cohesive organization.

Foster a Culture of Continuous Improvement

Building a culture of continuous improvement is essential for staying competitive and achieving long-term success. One of the most impactful ways you can encourage innovation is by providing your team with opportunities to share their ideas for improving processes and operations. Whether you host regular brainstorming sessions, set up suggestion boxes, or use digital platforms, giving your employees a voice in the process can lead to valuable insights and small, meaningful changes. Since your employees are the ones on the front lines, they have unique perspectives on what works and what could be better.

Another effective approach is to start with pilot programs. Testing new ideas or processes on a smaller scale first helps you identify potential issues and fine-tune your strategy before rolling it out to the entire organization. For example, if you are considering a new workflow, try implementing it in just one department to gauge its effectiveness. Companies like Google have used this method for years, testing new products and services in limited releases to gather feedback, make adjustments, and ensure their success when they go live.

Lean management principles can also play a pivotal role in cultivating continuous improvement. By focusing on eliminating waste and streamlining processes, you can deliver more value while using fewer resources. Lean methodologies, such as identifying unnecessary steps in your production processes, can help you speed up delivery times and improve overall quality. These principles, originally developed by Toyota, emphasize efficiency without sacrificing excellence.

The Kaizen approach, central to lean management, promotes ongoing, incremental improvements. You can implement this by encouraging regular reflection within your team—perhaps through weekly meetings where employees discuss what went well and what could be improved. By fostering a mindset of continuous progression, you empower everyone in your organization to contribute to a culture of improvement.

To keep your efforts on track, regular reviews and feedback loops are essential. Conduct performance reviews and process audits to identify areas where your business can grow. These should be constructive and aimed at helping both your processes and your people evolve. Involving your employees in these assessments not only gives you practical insights from those who are engaged in the day-to-day operations but also strengthens their engagement. For instance, holding quarterly reviews with input from various departments can help you spot inefficiencies across teams and ensure that your best practices are up to date.

When you prioritize continuous improvement, you create an environment where progress becomes a collective effort. Your team stays engaged, your operations become more efficient, and your business is constantly evolving to stay ahead of the competition. It is not just about making incremental gains—it is about creating a culture where every step forward drives lasting success.

Improve Time Management

Improving time management is key to boosting productivity and ensuring that tasks are completed efficiently. One technique worth exploring is the Pomodoro Technique, which involves working in focused intervals—typically 25 minutes—followed by a short 5-minute break. After four intervals, take a longer break of 15 to 30 minutes. Encouraging your team to use the Pomodoro Technique can significantly enhance focus and help maintain consistent productivity throughout the day. By breaking tasks into manageable chunks, this approach reduces the risk of burnout and makes long projects feel less overwhelming. Research supports the idea that regular breaks during extended work periods help sustain optimal performance and reduce mental fatigue.

Another highly effective time management strategy is time blocking. This method involves scheduling specific blocks of time for different tasks throughout the day. By designating time for particular activities, employees can avoid the pitfalls of multitasking and ensure that they focus on high-priority tasks. Time blocking not only helps structure the workday but also makes it easier to manage workloads and meet deadlines with greater ease.

Creating an environment that minimizes distractions is also essential for improving concentration. You might consider setting up quiet zones where employees can work uninterrupted or providing ergonomic workspaces that promote comfort and focus. Implementing policies that limit non-essential interruptions, such as discouraging non-urgent meetings during peak productivity hours, can further help your team stay on task. A well-organized and distraction-free workspace significantly enhances employees' ability to concentrate and complete their work efficiently.

Additionally, leveraging digital tools to limit distractions can have a meaningful impact on productivity. Browser extensions like StayFocusd or apps like Freedom can block access to distracting websites and apps during work hours, helping employees stay focused on their tasks. Reducing the temptation of social media and other non-work-related sites ensures that more time is spent on productive activities. Studies have shown that managing digital distractions can lead to significant increases in productivity and a notable reduction in wasted time.

Integrating effective time management strategies with a focus-friendly environment enables your team to enhance efficiency, produce stronger outcomes, and cultivate a workplace that is both productive and fulfilling.

Leveraging Technology to Streamline Processes

In today's fast-paced business landscape, effectively leveraging technology can be a game-changer, transforming operations and driving productivity. The right technological solutions not only improve efficiency but also help reduce costs and keep your business competitive. By automating routine tasks, improving communication, and optimizing how you manage resources, technology can give your business a significant edge. Whether it is through project management tools that keep your teams in sync, automation systems that handle repetitive tasks, or advanced data analytics that guide informed decision-making, adopting the right technology can accelerate your growth. Below are key strategies for integrating technology into your processes to keep your business ahead in a rapidly evolving market.

Automate Routine Tasks

Imagine a workplace where technology seamlessly handles repetitive tasks, freeing up time for you and your team to focus on more strategic initiatives. This is the power of automation. Robotic process automation (RPA) is a key tool that can take over tasks such as data entry, invoice processing, and report generation. With RPA software, your business can manage high-volume, routine tasks with remarkable precision, significantly reducing the risk of human error and speeding up processes. For example, RPA can streamline invoice processing by automatically extracting information, validating it, and inputting it into your accounting system—all without any manual effort.

Another essential technology for optimizing and automating workflows is business process management (BPM) software. BPM tools enable you to design, visualize, and automate business processes, helping you identify and eliminate bottlenecks. With a clear visual representation of your workflows, you gain the insight needed to improve operations and ensure that everything runs smoothly and efficiently. Tools like Appian and Bizagi help map out and automate even the most complex workflows, fostering better coordination between departments and enhancing overall productivity.

Automation also plays a critical role in communication. Platforms like Mailchimp and HubSpot allow you to automate email campaigns, segment your audience, and track performance metrics with ease. This level of automation ensures that your communications are both timely and personalized, which in turn improves customer engagement and boosts conversion rates. For example, you can create automated email sequences to welcome new subscribers, nurture leads, or re-engage inactive customers, each tailored to specific behaviors and preferences.

Customer relationship management (CRM) systems, such as Salesforce or Zoho CRM, take automation a step further by enhancing your interactions with customers. These systems automate a variety of customer management tasks, from tracking sales leads to managing customer data and automating follow-up communications. With CRM automation, you ensure that no sales lead is forgotten, and customer relationships are managed more efficiently. For instance, automated follow-up emails can be sent to prospects after a sales call, or reminders can be set for sales representatives to check in with clients, ultimately improving both sales performance and customer satisfaction.

Incorporating automation tools into your business helps minimize time spent on routine tasks, enhances accuracy, and frees up your team to concentrate on efforts that foster growth and spark innovation.

Enhance Communication and Collaboration

Strong communication and collaboration are essential for smooth operations and a productive work environment. By adopting unified communication platforms like Slack, Microsoft Teams, and Zoom, you can significantly improve real-time interactions among team members. These platforms offer a variety of features—instant messaging, video conferencing, and file sharing—that simplify and streamline internal communication. Slack, for example, allows you to create specific channels for different projects or departments, promoting focused discussions and easy access to important information. Microsoft Teams seamlessly integrates with other Microsoft Office applications, enabling real-time collaboration on documents and projects. Meanwhile, Zoom excels in video conferencing, allowing you to conduct high-quality virtual meetings that bridge the gap between remote team members and clients.

In addition to communication tools, project management software is a vital resource for enhancing team collaboration. Tools like Trello, Asana, and Monday.com organize tasks, set deadlines, and track progress visually, ensuring everyone is aligned on what needs to be done and by when. These platforms provide clear project timelines and task assignments, helping your team stay organized and focused on meeting goals.

Cloud storage solutions further enhance collaboration by improving document management. Platforms such as Google Drive, Dropbox, and OneDrive enable teams to store, share, and collaborate on documents in real time. With cloud storage, all team members have access to the latest versions of documents, eliminating the confusion that often comes with version control. For example, Google Drive enables multiple users to work on the same document simultaneously, with updates reflecting in real time. Dropbox offers flexible file-sharing options and integrates with a range of productivity tools, making it an adaptable solution for any business. OneDrive, as part of the Microsoft ecosystem, provides seamless integration with Microsoft Office applications, allowing for enhanced collaboration on documents, spreadsheets, and presentations.

Document automation tools also streamline workflows, from creation and approval to electronic signatures and storage. Solutions like DocuSign and PandaDoc make managing documents more efficient by reducing the time and effort required to handle paperwork. DocuSign allows for the secure and seamless sending, signing, and managing of documents, which is particularly valuable for contracts and legal paperwork. PandaDoc goes a step further with features such as document templates, tracking, and eSignatures, enabling you to create professional documents and obtain necessary approvals quickly. These tools not only boost efficiency but also ensure that critical documents are handled securely and in compliance with legal standards.

Utilizing these technologies helps create a more cohesive and collaborative workplace, allowing your team to operate more efficiently and effectively. This enhanced communication and streamlined workflow will propel your business forward, ensuring smoother operations and greater productivity.

Optimize Resource Management

Effective resource management is vital for driving operational efficiency and ensuring the sustainability of your business. Implementing advanced inventory management systems such as TradeGecko, Fishbowl, or Cin7 can automate tracking, manage stock levels, and generate real-time reports, significantly reducing the risk of stockouts and overstock situations. Automating inventory processes saves time and boosts accuracy by reducing human error.

In addition to inventory management systems, adopting just-in-time (JIT) inventory practices is an excellent strategy to optimize stock levels and minimize holding costs. JIT systems ensure that inventory arrives exactly when needed for production and sales, reducing storage requirements and waste. This approach enhances overall efficiency and can result in significant cost savings by preventing overstocking and minimizing the risk of outdated inventory.

Another powerful tool for optimizing resource management is enterprise resource planning (ERP) systems, such as SAP, Oracle, or Microsoft Dynamics. ERP platforms consolidate core business processes, including finance, human resources, procurement, and supply chain management, into one integrated system. This centralization enhances data visibility across the organization, leading to better decision-making and more streamlined workflows. These systems eliminate data silos, increase accuracy, and improve responsiveness to market shifts. For example, integrating procurement with inventory management ensures that orders are placed based on real-time sales data, which helps businesses avoid overstocking and reduce associated costs.

Through the use of automated systems and advanced resource management practices, you can significantly enhance your business's efficiency, reduce waste, and position yourself for long-term growth and success.

Improve Data Management and Analytics

In today's data-driven business world, taking control of your data management and analytics can unlock new opportunities for your business. By leveraging powerful platforms like Tableau, Power BI, or Looker, you can turn vast amounts of data into actionable insights, helping you make smarter, data-driven decisions. These tools provide interactive dashboards, real-time reporting, and data visualization that make it easier to identify trends, measure performance, and uncover areas for improvement.

Predictive analytics is another powerful tool that can help you anticipate future trends based on historical data. By using predictive models, you can forecast sales, manage inventory more efficiently, and even predict customer behavior. Imagine being able to foresee product demand more accurately—this could help you keep the right inventory levels, reducing the risk of stockouts or overstocking. In sales, predictive analytics can help you identify which leads are most likely to convert, allowing your team to focus their energy on the prospects that matter most.

To further enhance your data strategy, consider using customer data platforms (CDPs) like Segment, Tealium, or Salesforce CDP. These platforms collect and unify customer data from multiple sources—your website, apps, email campaigns, and social media—into a single, cohesive profile for each customer. This unified view enables you to personalize your marketing efforts, improve customer segmentation, and create more meaningful customer experiences.

By improving how you manage and analyze your data, you will not only gain a clearer understanding of your business but also streamline operations and deliver more impactful, personalized experiences for your customers. Embracing these strategies will allow you to move forward with confidence, knowing your decisions are grounded in accurate, insightful data.

Enhance Customer Service

Delivering outstanding customer service is key to maintaining a loyal customer base and building lasting relationships. One effective way to elevate your customer support is by incorporating chatbots and AI-powered tools. These technologies can handle common inquiries, provide instant assistance, and significantly improve response times. Tools like Intercom, Drift, and Zendesk Answer Bot excel in this area, offering quick resolutions to frequent issues while freeing up your customer service team to focus on more complex problems. For example, Zendesk Answer Bot uses machine learning to deliver accurate responses to customer queries, while Intercom's chatbot not only supports customer engagement but also assists with lead generation.

Another powerful strategy for enhancing customer satisfaction is implementing self-service portals. These platforms allow customers to find answers to their questions, track orders, and manage their accounts on their own. By empowering customers to resolve their issues independently, you lighten the load on your support team while increasing overall efficiency. Self-service options also align with the growing demand for quick and convenient solutions, leading to higher satisfaction rates.

Automating the collection and analysis of customer feedback is crucial for driving continuous improvement. Tools like SurveyMonkey, Qualtrics, and Typeform enable businesses to easily gather insights through automated surveys. By regularly collecting feedback, you can identify areas where your customer service or product offerings need enhancement, allowing you to make informed, data-driven decisions. Qualtrics, for instance, provides advanced survey logic and analytical tools that help uncover deeper insights from customer responses, giving you a clear picture of what needs improvement.

Sentiment analysis tools add another dimension of insight by tracking and evaluating customer feedback across social media, reviews, and surveys. These tools allow you to monitor overall customer sentiment—whether positive, negative, or neutral—and act accordingly. Sentiment analysis empowers you to address concerns proactively while celebrating positive feedback. Platforms like Hootsuite Insights and Brandwatch offer robust sentiment analysis capabilities, enabling you to stay in tune with how your customers feel and respond to their needs in real time.

Embracing these customer service strategies allows you to improve satisfaction, optimize your support systems, and build a more responsive, customer-centric experience. This approach not only boosts your brand's reputation but also cultivates long-term customer loyalty.

Strengthen Cybersecurity

As the world becomes more digital, defending your business from cyber threats is paramount. Strengthening cybersecurity starts with implementing advanced protection measures, such as multi-factor authentication (MFA). MFA adds an extra layer of security by requiring users to provide multiple forms of verification, greatly reducing the risk of unauthorized access and keeping your systems and data more secure.

Ensuring that all devices connected to your network are protected is equally critical. Solutions like Norton, McAfee, and CrowdStrike provide comprehensive defense against a variety of cyber threats, including malware, ransomware, and phishing attacks. These tools detect and neutralize threats in real time, helping to prevent breaches before they can cause damage. For instance, CrowdStrike's Falcon platform leverages artificial intelligence and machine learning to identify and respond to threats quickly, keeping your devices and network secure.

Regular security audits and vulnerability assessments are key components of maintaining a strong security posture. These audits help identify potential weaknesses in your systems that could be exploited by cybercriminals. By addressing vulnerabilities proactively, you can prevent data breaches and safeguard sensitive information. Tools like Nessus and Qualys are effective at scanning your systems for vulnerabilities and providing actionable insights on how to fix them.

In addition to technological solutions, employee training is a vital part of a robust cybersecurity strategy. Regularly educating your team on cybersecurity best practices helps ensure that they can recognize and respond to potential threats. Training should cover topics such as spotting phishing emails, creating strong passwords, and properly handling sensitive data. Since human error often plays a major role in security breaches, equipping your employees with the knowledge to stay vigilant is crucial for maintaining a secure technology environment.

Incorporating these cybersecurity measures into your operations strengthens your business's defense against evolving threats, ensuring both your data and reputation remain secure.

Strategies for Maximizing Profits Without Scaling Up

There is a common misconception that scaling up is the only way to boost profits, but that is not always the case. You can see significant growth in your earnings without expanding your business. By honing in on what you already have and making strategic adjustments, you can increase profitability while maintaining a smaller, more manageable operation. Start by optimizing your pricing strategy, streamlining operations to boost efficiency, and focusing on retaining your existing customers. These simple but powerful tactics can lead to impressive gains without the need for major expansion. In the following sections, we will explore some practical strategies to help you maximize profits while keeping your business at its current size.

Optimize Pricing Strategies

Optimizing your pricing strategies can significantly boost your business's profitability without the need to scale up. One powerful approach is value-based pricing, where you set your prices according to the perceived value of your products or services to your customers. By understanding what matters most to them—whether it is quality, unique features, or exceptional service—you can justify charging higher prices. For example, if your product saves customers time, they may be willing to pay a premium for that convenience.

Segment pricing is another effective strategy that allows you to attract a wider range of customers. By offering different pricing tiers or packages that cater to various customer segments, you can appeal to different needs and budgets. This might involve creating basic, premium, and deluxe versions of your product, each with distinct features and benefits. In doing so, you can maximize revenue by capturing customers across multiple price points. A software company, for instance, could offer a free basic version, a standard version with enhanced features, and a premium version with advanced capabilities.

Dynamic pricing is another way to increase revenue by adjusting your prices based on demand, time of day, or other relevant factors. This approach allows you to capitalize on peak demand periods while remaining competitive during slower times. For example, ride-sharing companies like Uber use dynamic pricing models where fares increase during high-demand periods such as rush hour or bad weather, effectively balancing supply and demand.

Keeping an eye on competitor pricing is also crucial for staying competitive while maximizing profits. By regularly monitoring what your competitors are charging, you can adjust your pricing strategies as needed. If a competitor lowers their prices, you may need to consider a similar move to stay attractive to budget-conscious customers. On the other hand, if your competitors raise their prices, you might find an opportunity to increase yours slightly while still offering superior value.

These pricing strategies allow you to fine-tune your revenue without requiring significant expansion, helping you increase profitability while keeping your business at a manageable size.

Improve Operational Efficiency

Enhancing operational efficiency is essential for boosting profits and ensuring your business operates smoothly. A key step in achieving this is streamlining processes to eliminate waste. Conduct regular process audits to pinpoint inefficiencies and apply lean management principles like the 5S methodology and Kaizen. The 5S methodology—sort, set in order, shine, standardize, sustain—creates a more organized and efficient workspace, reducing the time and effort needed to locate and use tools and materials. Meanwhile, Kaizen promotes continuous incremental improvements, encouraging employees at all levels to suggest and implement small, manageable changes that collectively lead to substantial efficiency gains.

Automation is another powerful way to improve operational efficiency by taking over repetitive tasks such as data entry, invoicing, and inventory management. Implementing software to automate invoicing ensures timely billing and minimizes errors, while inventory management systems automatically update stock levels and trigger reorders when supplies run low. This approach not only reduces labor costs but also frees up employees to focus on higher-value tasks that require creativity and human judgment.

Optimizing your supply chain is also vital for maintaining efficiency. Start by fine-tuning your inventory levels through inventory management software. These tools provide real-time tracking and allow you to set optimal reorder points, ensuring you have enough stock to meet demand without overstocking. This minimizes holding costs, enhances cash flow, and enables you to invest more in other critical areas of your business. Platforms like TradeGecko and Fishbowl offer comprehensive inventory management solutions that help small businesses maintain optimal stock levels and improve overall efficiency.

Building strong, reliable relationships with suppliers is just as important for streamlining operations. By negotiating better terms—such as bulk discounts or extended payment timelines—you can reduce costs and increase your profit margins. Establishing solid rapport with suppliers can also lead to more reliable service, preferential treatment, and priority during stock shortages, all of which contribute to a smoother, more efficient operation.

Improving operational efficiency through these strategies not only cuts costs but also helps your business run more effectively, positioning it for sustainable growth and long-term success.

Focus on Customer Retention

Prioritizing customer retention is one of the most effective ways to boost profitability while fostering a loyal customer base. A great starting point is implementing loyalty programs that reward repeat customers with perks such as discounts, points, or exclusive offers. These programs incentivize customers to return, increasing both their lifetime value and repeat business. Take Starbucks, for example, whose rewards program offers free drinks and personalized deals to members, a strategy that has significantly strengthened their customer loyalty and fueled repeat sales.

Personalized marketing also plays a critical role in customer retention. By harnessing customer data, you can create tailored marketing campaigns that align with individual preferences and behaviors. This targeted approach not only deepens customer engagement but also encourages repeat purchases. For instance, Amazon leverages browsing and purchase histories to recommend products, creating a personalized shopping experience that keeps customers coming back for more.

Another cornerstone of customer retention is delivering exceptional customer service. Investing in training for your customer service team ensures they are equipped to provide outstanding support, which directly impacts customer satisfaction and loyalty. When customers receive exceptional service, they are more likely to return and recommend your business to others, sparking a cycle of repeat business and attracting new customers through positive word-of-mouth.

Additionally, gathering and acting on customer feedback is essential for maintaining strong relationships. Regularly collecting feedback through surveys, reviews, or direct interactions helps you gain valuable insights into your customers' needs and preferences. Use this feedback to make thoughtful improvements to your products, services, and overall customer experience. Companies that actively listen to and implement customer suggestions tend to see improved satisfaction and higher retention rates.

By focusing on customer retention, you can create lasting relationships that not only increase profitability but also turn customers into loyal advocates for your business.

Diversify Revenue Streams

Diversifying your revenue streams is a powerful strategy for increasing profitability and building resilience in your business. One effective approach is through upselling and cross-selling. Train your sales team to identify opportunities where they can offer customers a higher-end product (upselling) or suggest complementary products (cross-selling). These techniques not only boost the average order value but also enhance the overall customer experience. For instance, if a customer purchases a smartphone, they might also benefit from accessories like cases, screen protectors, or even an extended warranty. By presenting these additional options, you not only add value for the customer but also drive more sales.

Another way to increase revenue is by creating product or service bundles. Offering multiple products or services at a discounted price when bought together encourages customers to purchase more than they initially planned. For example, a beauty salon might offer a discounted package that includes a haircut, manicure, and facial. This approach not only increases sales but also gives customers a sense of added value, enhancing their satisfaction.

Expanding your product or service lineup is also crucial for attracting new customers and generating more revenue from existing ones. Look for gaps in your current offerings and develop new products or services to fill those needs. This could mean expanding into complementary areas. For example, a coffee shop might introduce specialty teas or homemade pastries to appeal to a broader audience. By diversifying your offerings, you cater to a wider range of customers while keeping your business innovative and responsive to market trends.

Leveraging intellectual property can open new revenue opportunities as well. If you have developed unique products, processes, or technologies, consider licensing or franchising them. This allows you to generate additional income without directly expanding your operations. For example, a tech company with proprietary software could license it to other businesses, generating steady revenue from licensing fees while continuing to focus on its core services. Licensing and franchising enable you to extend your market reach with minimal overhead, creating new income streams with relatively low effort.

Exploring these strategies allows you to diversify your revenue streams, enhance financial stability, and better position your business for long-term growth and success.

Control Costs and Expenses

A key step in controlling costs and expenses is to monitor them closely. Utilizing accounting software such as QuickBooks or Xero enables you to track spending in real time and regularly review financial reports. This approach allows you to identify areas where you can cut costs more effectively. For example, if you notice operational costs are higher than expected, you can take action by renegotiating supplier contracts or switching to more cost-effective options. Keeping a close watch on your expenses empowers you to make informed financial decisions that directly improve your profitability.

Implementing cost-saving initiatives is another important strategy. Explore ways to reduce expenses without sacrificing quality. This could involve negotiating better rates with vendors, sourcing more affordable suppliers, or initiating energy-saving measures. For instance, switching to energy-efficient lighting or starting a recycling program can significantly lower utility and waste disposal costs. Consistently seeking out these opportunities helps you reduce overhead and boost your overall profitability.

Outsourcing non-core functions is another effective way for small businesses to manage expenses. By outsourcing tasks such as IT support, payroll processing, and marketing to specialized service providers, you can reduce overhead costs associated with salaries and benefits. This allows you to allocate more resources toward activities that directly contribute to your bottom line, ensuring that your efforts are focused on what matters most to your business growth.

Increase Employee Productivity

Enhancing employee productivity is crucial for small businesses striving to maximize profitability without the need for expansion. A great place to start is by investing in training and development. Providing ongoing learning opportunities not only sharpens your employees' skills but also improves overall efficiency. By equipping your team with up-to-date knowledge and techniques, they can perform their tasks more effectively. Regular workshops, online courses, and industry conferences keep your workforce informed about new trends and technologies, ensuring they remain competent and competitive. This continuous development elevates individual performance and strengthens the productivity of the entire team.

Equally important is fostering a positive work environment. A workplace that encourages collaboration, recognizes achievements, and promotes well-being can significantly boost employee engagement and satisfaction. When employees feel appreciated and happy, they are more likely to be committed to their work and perform at their best. Small but meaningful initiatives—like team-building activities, regular feedback sessions, and celebrating achievements—can have a powerful impact on morale and productivity.

Implementing performance incentives is another powerful way to increase productivity. Rewarding high-performing employees with bonuses, commissions, or profit-sharing schemes motivates them to go the extra mile. These incentives align employees' personal goals with the overall objectives of the business, encouraging them to push for better results. For instance, a sales team may be more driven to surpass their targets if they know higher commissions await them. Similarly, profit-sharing programs foster a sense of ownership, as employees directly benefit from the company's success, which in turn promotes a stronger commitment to excellence.

By focusing on employee development, fostering a supportive work culture, and incentivizing performance, you can significantly increase productivity and drive your business toward greater success without having to scale up.

Leverage Technology

Harnessing the power of technology can revolutionize your small business, enhancing efficiency and profitability without the need for significant expansion. A key strategy is to implement data analytics tools that provide valuable insights into customer behavior, market trends, and operational performance. By analyzing this data, you can make informed decisions that lead to improvement and growth. For example, data analytics can reveal which products resonate most with different customer segments, enabling you to target your marketing efforts more effectively. It can also pinpoint inefficiencies within your operations, allowing you to streamline processes and cut costs.

Optimizing your marketing campaigns through analytics is another game-changing approach. Tracking campaign performance gives you the ability to identify what works and what does not, allowing you to refine your strategies in real time. This ensures that your marketing efforts are consistently impactful. Targeted marketing, driven by data insights, can significantly improve your return on investment (ROI) and drive more sales. For instance, analyzing customer data might uncover that a specific demographic responds well to email marketing, encouraging you to allocate more resources to that channel for better results.

Strengthening your digital presence is equally vital. Your website often serves as the first point of contact for potential customers, so it should be user-friendly, mobile-responsive, and optimized for search engines. A well-designed, optimized website can attract more visitors and convert them into customers by offering a seamless user experience. Ensuring quick load times, easy navigation, and relevant, high-quality content will not only improve search engine rankings but also increase organic traffic and engagement.

Leveraging social media platforms is another essential strategy. Engaging with your audience on social media helps you build stronger relationships, promote your products, and foster brand loyalty. Social media allows for personal interaction with customers, enabling you to respond to their questions and feedback quickly while creating a sense of community around your brand. When done effectively, social media marketing can enhance your visibility, drive traffic to your website, and ultimately boost sales.

Embracing technology in these areas allows you to drive your business forward, enhancing its competitiveness and success without requiring substantial scaling efforts.

CHAPTER 7

RESOURCE MANAGEMENT

Managing Financial Resources for Growth or Stability

In the world of business, mastering the management of financial resources is essential, whether you are aiming for growth or striving to maintain stability. Effective financial management forms the foundation for achieving both goals, ensuring that every resource is used wisely, risks are mitigated, and returns are maximized. This requires a thoughtful approach to budgeting, investing, and controlling costs, all with the aim of advancing your business objectives. By keeping a close eye on cash flow, leveraging financial data to inform your decisions, and constantly searching for ways to improve financial efficiency, you create a solid framework for long-term success. In the following sections, we will explore key strategies to help you manage your financial resources effectively, whether you are focused on expanding your business or maintaining its current trajectory.

Develop a Comprehensive Financial Plan

Crafting a comprehensive financial plan is an essential step in steering your business toward either growth or stability. Begin by establishing clear financial objectives. If growth is your aim, your goals might include increasing revenue, expanding market share, or investing in new product development. These objectives should be SMART—specific, measurable, achievable, relevant, and time-bound. For example, you could aim to increase revenue by twenty percent within the next year by entering new markets and launching two new products. Having a defined direction helps you focus your efforts and measure progress effectively.

If your priority is maintaining stability, shift your focus to securing steady cash flow, reducing debt, or building financial reserves. These goals are crucial for protecting your business from economic fluctuations and unforeseen challenges. For instance, you might set a goal to reduce debt by fifteen percent over the next two years or build a reserve fund that covers six months of operating expenses. Achieving these stability targets provides a financial cushion that fosters long-term sustainability.

The next vital step is to create detailed budgets. An operating budget outlines expected revenues and expenses, enabling you to manage daily operations and ensure spending aligns with your business objectives. By forecasting sales and expenses accurately, you can allocate resources wisely, prevent overspending, and ensure sufficient funds are available for essential needs.

If growth is your focus, a capital budget is indispensable. This budget covers significant investments such as infrastructure, technology, or new product development. It details funding sources and projects the returns on these investments, helping you make informed decisions about resource allocation. For instance, if you plan to invest in a new manufacturing facility, your capital budget should outline the costs, financing options, and expected boosts in production capacity and revenue.

By setting clear financial goals and establishing detailed budgets, you create a roadmap that guides your business forward. This structured approach optimizes resource allocation, reduces risk, and maximizes returns, ensuring your business remains financially sound whether you are pursuing growth or focusing on stability.

Monitor Cash Flow

Maintaining a vigilant focus on cash flow is fundamental for the financial health of any business. It ensures you have the liquidity needed to meet obligations and seize opportunities as they arise. Regular tracking of cash flow, through detailed cash flow statements, gives you a clear picture of money coming in and going out. These statements help you spot potential shortfalls before they become problematic, allowing you to take action early. By reviewing these regularly, you can maintain enough liquidity to cover expenses and avoid unpleasant financial surprises.

Taking it a step further, cash flow forecasting provides even greater insight. By using historical data and projecting future changes in revenue and expenses, you can anticipate cash needs and make informed decisions regarding investments, financing, and cost management. Accurate forecasting allows you to plan for seasonal shifts, manage significant expenditures, and ensure you have sufficient funds to sustain operations. For instance, if your business typically experiences a surge in sales during the holiday season, a cash flow forecast helps you prepare for increased inventory and staffing needs to capitalize on that demand.

Another important aspect of cash flow management is efficiently handling receivables and payables. Streamlining your invoicing process ensures that billing and payment collections are timely, which is vital for keeping cash flowing steadily into your business. Utilizing automated invoicing systems, such as QuickBooks or FreshBooks, can reduce delays and errors, resulting in quicker payments and stronger cash flow. These tools automate invoice delivery and follow-up reminders, which helps ensure you get paid promptly.

Negotiating favorable payment terms with suppliers is another smart strategy for improving cash flow. Extending your payables without incurring penalties allows you to keep more cash on hand for longer periods, giving you flexibility to cover operating expenses or invest in growth. For example, securing net sixty payment terms instead of net thirty gives you an additional thirty days to pay your suppliers, which can significantly enhance your cash management and provide more breathing room for other financial commitments.

Carefully tracking cash flow, anticipating future needs, and handling both receivables and payables with strategic insight enables you to maintain a solid financial foundation. This approach ensures that your business remains financially stable, supporting not only daily operations but also paving the way for sustainable long-term growth.

Optimize Cost Management

Optimizing cost management is essential for boosting profitability and ensuring the long-term success of your business. One key approach is to consistently review and analyze your operating expenses. A thorough expense analysis allows you to pinpoint areas where you can cut costs or optimize spending. For example, you may discover opportunities to renegotiate contracts with suppliers to secure better pricing or terms. Additionally, implementing energy-saving measures, such as upgrading to energy-efficient lighting or optimizing heating and cooling systems, can result in significant cost reductions. Reducing waste in your operations—whether through improved inventory management or refining processes—can further help lower your overall operating costs.

Benchmarking your expenses against industry standards offers another powerful tool for cost optimization. By comparing your costs to those of similar businesses, you can identify areas where your spending may be higher than necessary or where there is potential for improvement. Industry benchmarks provide a clear reference point, helping to ensure that your expenses are aligned with best practices. For instance, if you find that your utility expenses are above the industry average, this may indicate a need to adopt more energy-efficient practices or upgrade equipment.

Leveraging technology is also a highly effective way to improve cost management. Automation tools can streamline repetitive tasks, reducing labor costs and allowing employees to focus on more strategic, high-value activities. Technology investments also tend to enhance productivity and efficiency across the board. Implementing project management software, for instance, helps ensure that projects stay on track and within budget by providing better oversight and coordination.

Data analytics plays a pivotal role in driving smarter cost management decisions. By utilizing data, you can gain deeper insights into your cost drivers and identify specific areas for savings. Data-driven decision-making allows you to allocate resources more effectively, leading to improved financial performance. For example, analyzing sales data can reveal which products or services yield the highest profit margins, helping you direct your efforts toward the most profitable areas. Similarly, examining operational data can uncover inefficiencies or bottlenecks, which, once addressed, can result in substantial savings and improved cost efficiency.

Effective cost management strategies such as these will help you reduce expenses, increase profitability, and ensure that your business remains financially sustainable in the long term.

Secure Funding

Securing the right funding is a crucial step for any business aiming to grow or maintain stability. The first step is to carefully evaluate your funding options. Debt financing, such as loans, lines of credit, or issuing bonds, offers immediate capital for business initiatives. While this approach requires regular repayments with interest, it is essential to ensure that your business can manage the debt without risking financial health. For instance, a small business loan can be useful for acquiring new equipment or expanding operations, but accurately forecasting cash flow is vital to ensure that debt repayments remain manageable.

Another viable option is equity financing, which involves issuing new shares or seeking venture capital. This method provides significant funding without the obligation of repayment, making it particularly attractive for high-growth startups. However, equity financing often comes with the trade-off of diluted ownership and control. For example, bringing in venture capital can offer not only substantial funds but also valuable strategic guidance, though it may also result in ceding some decision-making power and ownership stakes.

Internal funding through retained earnings or profits can be another effective route. This approach allows you to fund growth or stabilize the business without taking on external debt or interest costs. Although internal funding might limit the amount of capital available, it allows the business to maintain full control and ownership. Reinvesting profits, for instance, can finance marketing initiatives, research and development, or other strategic projects without incurring additional financial obligations.

Maintaining strong credit is vital for accessing favorable funding options. Proper credit management, such as paying bills on time and keeping debt levels manageable, helps preserve your business's credit rating. A strong credit score can improve your ability to secure financing on better terms, such as lower interest rates or more flexible repayment schedules. These favorable terms can significantly enhance both your financial stability and growth potential.

Building and nurturing financial relationships is another critical aspect of securing funding. Developing strong connections with banks, investors, and financial institutions can lead to better funding opportunities, tailored advice, and even strategic insights. For instance, maintaining open and transparent communication with your bank can result in more customized financial solutions, while forging relationships with investors may open doors to not only capital but also valuable networking opportunities and business expertise.

By carefully considering your funding options, managing your credit, and building strong financial relationships, you can ensure that your business secures the capital needed to thrive while safeguarding its financial health and long-term success.

Build Financial Resilience

Building financial resilience is essential for safeguarding your business against unexpected challenges and ensuring long-term stability. One of the most critical steps in this process is establishing a robust financial reserve. An emergency fund acts as a safety net, enabling your business to cover unforeseen expenses or navigate economic downturns without disrupting operations. This reserve provides the cushion needed to sustain stability during tough times, such as sudden shifts in the market or unexpected repairs. Financial experts typically recommend setting aside three to six months' worth of operating expenses, ensuring your business is well-prepared for any emergencies that may arise.

Securing appropriate insurance coverage is another pivotal component of financial resilience. Insurance shields your business from various risks, including property damage, liability claims, and interruptions to your operations. For example, property insurance can cover the costs of damages from natural disasters, while liability insurance protects against lawsuits that could otherwise cripple your business. Business interruption insurance, on the other hand, guarantees that your business continues to generate income even when operations are temporarily halted due to unforeseen events. Having the right insurance coverage not only reduces the financial impact of these events but also provides peace of mind, allowing you to focus on running your business effectively.

Diversifying your revenue streams is also vital for maintaining financial resilience. Expanding your offerings by introducing new products or services can reduce your dependence on a single source of income, thereby spreading financial risk across multiple channels. For instance, if demand for your primary product decreases, additional offerings can help sustain your revenue. Additionally, exploring new markets or targeting different customer segments can open up fresh opportunities for growth. By entering new markets or expanding your customer base, you reduce your exposure to downturns in specific sectors or demographics. For example, if your business has traditionally focused on one demographic, branching out to new regions or segments can provide a more stable financial foundation.

Preparing for the unexpected through these strategies ensures your business can adapt and sustain growth even in challenging times.

Monitor Financial Performance

Consistently monitoring financial performance ensures that your business stays on track and meets its financial goals. Regular financial reviews are at the heart of this process. By routinely examining key financial documents, such as income statements, balance sheets, and cash flow statements, you gain a holistic view of your business's financial position. These reviews give you insight into your revenue streams, expenses, assets, liabilities, and cash flow. For example, an income statement outlines your profitability over a specific period, while a balance sheet offers a snapshot of your assets and liabilities. Through regular analysis of these reports, you can identify areas for improvement and ensure that your business is progressing as planned.

In addition to reviewing these statements, it is vital to monitor key performance indicators (KPIs) like profitability, liquidity, and return on investment (ROI). KPIs provide clear metrics that reflect how effectively your business is meeting its financial objectives. For instance, tracking profitability helps you assess how well you are managing expenses in relation to earnings, while liquidity ratios measure your ability to cover short-term obligations. Monitoring ROI allows you to gauge the success of your investments. Keeping a close watch on these indicators enables you to spot trends, measure your progress, and make informed, data-driven decisions that improve your business's financial performance.

Adaptability is critical when financial data reveals underperformance or when market conditions shift. The business environment is constantly evolving, and your financial strategies need to be flexible enough to keep pace. If your financial reviews or KPIs indicate that certain areas are not meeting expectations, it may be necessary to adjust budgets, reallocate resources, or revise your investment strategy. Being flexible enables you to respond proactively to both challenges and opportunities, helping your business remain resilient and competitive.

Creating a culture of continuous improvement is another important aspect of maintaining strong financial performance. Regularly reviewing and refining your financial processes can lead to increased efficiency and better resource management. Encourage your team to propose enhancements in financial management, whether that involves refining expense tracking, optimizing invoicing procedures, or improving cash flow management. This ongoing focus on improvement ensures that your financial practices grow alongside your business, positioning you to stay ahead of potential issues and thrive in a dynamic market.

Human Capital Management: Hiring, Training, and Retention

Effectively managing human capital is key to building a skilled, motivated, and productive workforce that drives your business toward its goals. By focusing on strategic hiring, comprehensive training, and strong retention programs, you ensure the right talent is in place to support long-term success. These approaches work together to create a strong foundation for growth, with each element contributing to a workforce that is engaged, adaptable, and committed to your organization's future.

Strategic Hiring

Building a strong and effective workforce starts with a strategic approach to hiring. It begins by clearly defining job roles and requirements. Crafting detailed job descriptions that outline specific responsibilities, qualifications, and expectations is key to attracting the right candidates. This clarity helps potential hires understand their role within the company and sets the stage for success from the very beginning. Complementing these descriptions with competency profiles adds another layer of precision, highlighting the skills, knowledge, and attributes essential for each position. These profiles serve as a roadmap throughout the hiring process, ensuring that new hires are well-aligned with the company's overall objectives.

The next step is implementing targeted recruitment strategies. Casting a wide net by diversifying your talent-sourcing channels broadens your candidate pool. Leveraging job boards, social media, professional networks, and recruitment agencies increases your chances of finding top talent. At the same time, developing a strong employer brand is crucial. Showcasing your company's values, culture, and benefits makes your business stand out in a competitive market, attracting candidates who are not just qualified but also a great cultural fit.

Encouraging employee referrals is another effective tactic. Offering incentives for successful referrals taps into your existing workforce to identify high-quality candidates who are more likely to integrate well within the company. This approach can streamline the hiring process while enhancing the overall quality of your recruitment efforts.

Conducting a rigorous selection process is vital to making informed hiring decisions. Structured interviews with standardized questions ensure a consistent and fair evaluation of candidates, allowing you to assess both technical skills and cultural fit. Utilizing assessment tools such as aptitude tests, personality assessments, and job simulations provides valuable insights into a candidate's potential and abilities, offering objective data to support your decisions.

Lastly, thorough background checks are an indispensable part of the hiring process. Verifying references, qualifications, and past employment ensures that your new hires meet the company's standards of integrity and reliability, reducing risks and fostering a trustworthy workforce.

Comprehensive Training and Development

Cultivating a skilled and motivated workforce requires implementing comprehensive training and development programs. A strong onboarding process is crucial to this foundation. Begin with a thorough orientation that immerses new hires in your company's culture, values, and expectations, helping them feel a sense of belonging from day one. Beyond orientation, role-specific training ensures that new employees gain the knowledge and skills they need to succeed in their roles. Tailored training programs enhance their abilities and boost confidence, allowing them to contribute meaningfully right from the start.

Continuous learning is also essential in maintaining a competitive and innovative workforce. By offering ongoing training programs, you keep your employees updated on industry trends, evolving technologies, and best practices. This commitment to regular learning fosters an environment of constant improvement and keeps skills sharp and relevant. Investing in professional development through advanced education, certifications, or workshops further demonstrates your dedication to employee growth. Not only does this benefit individual career paths, but it also strengthens the overall capability and adaptability of your team.

Leadership development plays a key role in preparing your business for future growth. Succession planning is critical to ensure that high-potential employees are ready to step into leadership roles when needed. By grooming future leaders from within, you secure continuity and stability for your business. Mentorship programs can enhance this process by pairing experienced leaders with emerging talent. These partnerships provide valuable guidance, support, and insights, helping mentees grow into strong, capable leaders.

Another vital aspect of training and development is performance management. Regular performance reviews give you the opportunity to assess employees' progress, provide constructive feedback, and set clear goals for the future. These reviews help to identify areas for growth while also recognizing accomplishments, fostering a culture of continuous development. Individual development plans can further align employee aspirations with company objectives, creating a clear path for personal growth that contributes to the organization's success.

Robust Retention Programs

Keeping your top talent engaged, satisfied, and loyal depends on establishing strong retention programs. The key to this lies in offering competitive compensation and benefits. Providing fair compensation that aligns with industry standards not only attracts top performers but also keeps them committed. Employees who feel they are compensated fairly are more likely to stay long-term and put forth their best efforts. Beyond salary, comprehensive benefits, such as health insurance, retirement plans, and wellness programs, play a pivotal role in job satisfaction. Offering these benefits shows employees that you are invested in their well-being and future, making them feel valued and secure in their roles.

Cultivating a positive work environment is equally important for retention. A company culture that fosters collaboration, respect, and inclusivity boosts morale and deepens employee engagement. When employees feel respected and included, they are more likely to be committed to their work. Promoting work-life balance through flexible arrangements, such as remote work options, flexible hours, and generous paid time off, helps prevent burnout and supports overall well-being. Prioritizing work-life balance sends a clear message that you respect employees' personal lives and health, which in turn nurtures loyalty and long-term commitment.

Recognition and rewards are powerful motivators that reinforce positive behaviors and drive performance. Creating employee recognition programs that celebrate achievements not only elevates morale but also encourages employees to maintain high performance. Whether through formal awards or simple, heartfelt acknowledgments, recognition lets employees know their efforts are appreciated. Incentive programs that reward employees for meeting performance targets, completing significant projects, or driving innovation further enhance engagement by offering tangible rewards for their hard work.

Offering career growth opportunities is another essential element of a strong retention strategy. Promoting from within and supporting internal mobility allows employees to envision long-term career paths within the company. Opportunities for advancement and lateral moves help retain ambitious and skilled employees who might otherwise seek growth elsewhere. Encouraging skill development through cross-training, job rotations, and special projects ensures employees continue to grow and evolve within the organization. This not only enhances job satisfaction but also keeps employees energized about their future with your company.

Finally, fostering employee feedback and engagement strengthens retention. Regularly seeking employee input through surveys, focus groups, and one-on-one meetings demonstrates that you value their perspectives. Actively listening to employees and acting on their feedback builds trust and strengthens their sense of belonging. When employees see their input leading to tangible improvements, they feel more valued and loyal to the organization, knowing that their voices are heard and their contributions matter.

CHAPTER 8

MARKETING AND SALES STRATEGIES

Tailoring Marketing Strategies for Growth

Crafting marketing strategies that drive growth requires a deep understanding of your target audience, the smart use of data and analytics, and a willingness to adopt innovative tactics that capture attention. The goal is to develop campaigns that not only resonate with your audience but also increase brand visibility, attract new customers, and build lasting loyalty. Start by thoroughly researching your market to discover what your audience truly needs and desires. Leveraging data and analytics helps you track customer behavior and evaluate the effectiveness of your campaigns, offering valuable insights to fine-tune your approach for greater impact. Incorporating creative tactics like personalized marketing, engaging social media content, and strategic content marketing further extends your reach and enhances your effectiveness. By focusing on these key elements, you can tailor your marketing efforts to not only attract new customers but also strengthen relationships with your existing ones. Here are the essential steps to develop customized marketing strategies that fuel business growth.

Understand Your Target Audience

Truly understanding your target audience is fundamental to creating marketing strategies that resonate and foster business growth. Start by conducting in-depth market research with a focus on customer segmentation. Segmenting your audience by demographics, psychographics, behaviors, and specific needs allows you to craft personalized and relevant marketing messages. Demographic factors such as age, gender, and income level provide a basic framework, while psychographics dig deeper, offering insights into lifestyle choices, values, and personal interests. Additionally, analyzing customer behaviors—like purchase history and engagement patterns—enables you to align your marketing more precisely with how your audience interacts and what they prefer.

Developing detailed buyer personas for each audience segment further refines your approach. These personas represent data-driven, fictional characters that embody the key characteristics of your ideal customers, including their pain points, motivations, and preferences. For example, if one of your buyer personas is a tech-savvy young professional, your messaging might focus on convenience, innovation, and cutting-edge technology to better appeal to this group's needs and desires.

Another critical component in understanding your audience is customer journey mapping. By charting the journey from the first interaction with your brand to the final purchase and beyond, you can identify the key touchpoints that shape the customer experience. Whether they encounter your brand on social media, through your website, or via customer service, understanding these touchpoints allows you to create a consistent, engaging experience across every channel.

Through customer journey mapping, you can also uncover pain points that may be hindering conversion. Identifying and addressing obstacles, such as complicated checkout processes or lack of payment options, can lead to significant improvements in customer satisfaction and higher conversion rates. Proactively refining these elements ensures a smoother journey, resulting in stronger engagement and more successful outcomes.

Leverage Data and Analytics

Harnessing the power of data and analytics is essential for developing impactful marketing strategies. By utilizing advanced analytics tools such as Google Analytics, Adobe Analytics, and customer relationship management (CRM) systems, you can collect valuable insights into customer behavior, preferences, and interactions. These insights allow you to make informed decisions that optimize your marketing efforts. For instance, Google Analytics provides detailed reports on website traffic, user behavior, and conversion paths, helping you identify which channels are driving the most engagement and sales.

Tracking key performance metrics is another critical component of data-driven marketing. Metrics such as customer acquisition cost (CAC), customer lifetime value (CLV), conversion rates, and return on marketing investment (ROMI) are vital in measuring the success of your marketing strategies. Regularly monitoring these metrics enables you to evaluate what is working and where adjustments are needed. For example, if your CAC is higher than expected, it may signal the need to refine your targeting approach or explore more cost-effective marketing channels. Conversely, a low CLV may indicate the need to focus on customer retention and relationship-building efforts.

Personalized marketing is where data truly makes a difference. Leveraging customer data to create targeted campaigns allows you to tailor your messaging to specific segments, making it more relevant and impactful. Personalization increases engagement and conversion rates by speaking directly to individual needs and preferences. For instance, segmenting your email lists based on past purchase behavior and offering personalized product recommendations can lead to higher open rates and click-through rates, ultimately driving more sales.

Automation and artificial intelligence (AI) tools further enhance personalization and efficiency. Platforms like HubSpot, Marketo, and Pardot automate various marketing tasks, such as email campaigns and social media posting, allowing you to deliver personalized content at scale. AI tools analyze vast amounts of data to identify patterns and predict customer behavior, making your marketing more targeted and effective. For example, AI can help optimize email send times for maximum engagement or suggest product recommendations based on a customer's browsing and purchase history.

Incorporating data and analytics into your marketing strategies ensures that your efforts are data-driven, personalized, and efficient. These insights not only help optimize your current campaigns but also guide your long-term marketing strategy, driving consistent growth and delivering strong returns on investment.

Multi-Channel Marketing Approach

Taking a multi-channel marketing strategy allows you to reach a wider audience and build stronger connections across various platforms. By engaging potential customers across various digital platforms, you can build a strong, cohesive brand presence that resonates with different demographics. This approach ensures that you meet your customers where they are, delivering consistent and engaging experiences.

Social media marketing is an excellent way to engage with your audience on platforms like Facebook, Instagram, LinkedIn, and Twitter. Each platform caters to different segments of your target audience, so creating tailored content for each one is key. Develop a content calendar that blends promotional posts, educational insights, and user-generated content to maintain a steady connection with your followers. For instance, Instagram stories and reels are ideal for offering behind-the-scenes glimpses or sharing quick tips, while LinkedIn is perfect for publishing in-depth articles that establish your brand as an authority in your field. This combination builds a community around your brand while positioning you as a trusted voice in your industry.

Search engine optimization (SEO) is equally important in your multi-channel approach. Optimizing your website and content for search engines helps attract more organic traffic to your site. Identify the keywords your target audience frequently searches for, and incorporate them naturally into high-quality, valuable content. Pay attention to technical aspects like site speed, mobile optimization, and secure connections (HTTPS), as these factors influence your search rankings and visibility. Keep your content fresh and relevant to sustain strong SEO performance over time.

Content marketing, including blogs and articles, serves as a valuable tool for drawing in and retaining a dedicated audience. Creating content that speaks to your audience's needs and interests establishes your brand as an industry expert, helping to build trust and credibility. Regularly publishing useful, relevant content boosts organic traffic and strengthens your relationship with your audience. Video marketing should also be part of your strategy—whether through product demonstrations, customer testimonials, educational clips, or behind-the-scenes content. Video offers a dynamic way to engage your audience, delivering messages more effectively than text alone.

Email marketing continues to be a powerful tool for direct communication. Segmenting your email lists based on customer behavior and preferences enables you to send personalized, relevant content that drives engagement. Personalized email campaigns result in higher open and click-through rates, enhancing your ability to nurture leads and turn them into loyal customers. Automated email sequences, such as welcome emails, cart abandonment reminders, and re-engagement campaigns, ensure timely and meaningful communication with your subscribers, further boosting conversions and customer retention.

Incorporating these channels into a cohesive, multi-channel marketing approach enhances your brand's reach, strengthens customer engagement, and drives measurable growth.

Leverage Influencer and Affiliate Marketing

Collaborating with influencers and affiliates offers a powerful way to expand your brand's reach and enhance credibility by tapping into their established audiences and trust.

For influencer partnerships, the key is to identify individuals who not only have a strong following but also align closely with your brand values. The authenticity of the connection between the influencer and your brand is far more important than the size of their audience. When you choose influencers whose followers genuinely care about your product or service, the content they create will resonate deeply with potential customers. For example, if you are a beauty brand, partnering with a respected beauty vlogger can result in credible product reviews that generate both interest and sales. Ensuring that your influencer campaigns align with your broader marketing strategy also helps maintain consistency across all channels. This approach enhances the overall impact of the campaign while ensuring that it works in harmony with your other marketing efforts. It is also essential to measure the success of these collaborations—track metrics like engagement, reach, and return on investment (ROI) to fine-tune future campaigns based on performance data.

Affiliate marketing offers another highly effective avenue for driving sales and boosting brand visibility. Building a successful affiliate program means offering appealing incentives that motivate partners to promote your products or services. Providing affiliates with marketing materials, personalized tracking links, and competitive commissions encourages them to actively spread the word about your brand. An effective affiliate program transforms customers, bloggers, and industry professionals into passionate advocates who help extend your reach. Monitoring affiliate performance regularly enables you to identify top contributors and make strategic adjustments to maximize results. By analyzing data on conversions, sales, and affiliate impact, you can identify which affiliates are adding the most value and optimize your program accordingly.

Focus on Customer Engagement and Retention

Engaging and retaining customers is fundamental for cultivating a loyal customer base and securing long-term success. A great way to keep customers coming back is by introducing loyalty programs that reward them for their repeat business, referrals, and continued engagement. These programs encourage customers to return and increase their overall value to your business. Offering points, discounts, or exclusive rewards creates strong incentives for customers to remain loyal. For example, a points-based system where customers accumulate rewards with each purchase can significantly boost repeat business and brand loyalty.

Providing exclusive perks, such as special discounts or early access to new products, further strengthens customer relationships. These VIP-style benefits make customers feel valued and appreciated, deepening their emotional connection to your brand. Such privileges often lead to stronger customer loyalty and retention. Offering early access to sales or new product releases, for instance, can make loyal customers feel like insiders, reinforcing their preference for your brand.

Another way to enhance customer engagement is by fostering a sense of community around your brand. Creating online spaces where customers can connect, share their experiences, and engage directly with your brand helps build loyalty. Whether through Facebook Groups, Reddit threads, or dedicated forums, these communities provide a platform for customers to interact with one another and your brand, generating a vibrant and supportive environment. This sense of belonging can significantly boost satisfaction and loyalty, as customers feel more personally connected to your brand.

Additionally, actively engaging with customer feedback on social media, review sites, and through surveys shows that you truly value their opinions. Listening and responding to feedback, both positive and negative, reflects your commitment to continuous improvement. Being responsive builds trust and fosters stronger relationships. For instance, when a customer expresses dissatisfaction on social media and you resolve their issue promptly and publicly, you can transform a negative experience into loyal advocacy for your brand.

Monitor and Adjust Strategies

To achieve sustained success, continually monitoring and adjusting your marketing strategies is crucial. Regular performance reviews allow you to measure the effectiveness of your campaigns and make informed, data-driven decisions. Start by analyzing key metrics such as engagement, conversion rates, and return on investment (ROI). This evaluation helps you determine what is working well and identify areas that need refinement. For example, if a social media campaign garners high engagement but low conversions, you might need to revise your call-to-action or improve your landing page to better convert leads into customers.

Incorporating A/B testing into your strategy is another powerful way to fine-tune your marketing efforts. By testing different variations of your marketing messages, landing pages, and email content, you can discover which elements resonate best with your audience. This method provides valuable insights into customer preferences and enables you to optimize your approach for maximum impact. For instance, testing two different subject lines in an email campaign can reveal which one generates higher open rates, helping you craft more compelling content moving forward.

Adaptability is key in today's dynamic market landscape. Remaining agile allows you to adjust your marketing strategies as market conditions, customer preferences, and competitive forces evolve. Keeping a close eye on industry trends and shifts in consumer behavior ensures that your marketing stays relevant and effective. For instance, if consumer interest shifts toward sustainability, quickly highlighting the eco-friendly aspects of your products can help keep your messaging aligned with your audience's values.

Embracing innovation is essential for keeping your marketing fresh and engaging. Continuously exploring new technologies, trends, and platforms helps you stand out in a crowded marketplace. Experimenting with emerging strategies—such as using augmented reality for product demonstrations or incorporating interactive features on social media—creates unique customer experiences that differentiate your brand from the competition.

By regularly reviewing your performance, implementing A/B testing, staying adaptable, and fostering innovation, you can ensure that your marketing strategies remain effective and impactful. This proactive approach enables you to make timely adjustments, optimize your efforts, and ultimately drive stronger results for your business.

Effective Marketing for Small Businesses

Marketing is essential for small businesses seeking to attract new customers, build brand recognition, and succeed in a competitive landscape. Even with limited resources, small businesses can make a substantial impact by concentrating on strategies that maximize both reach and engagement. Focusing on the right tactics and tools allows small businesses to craft compelling campaigns that connect with their audience and drive meaningful growth. In the following sections, we will look into key marketing strategies that can help small businesses enhance their efforts, ensuring they make the most of their resources while reaching their business objectives.

Define Your Unique Value Proposition

To make a lasting impact in a crowded market, defining your unique value proposition (UVP) is indispensable. Start by pinpointing what distinguishes your business from the competition. Whether it is superior product quality, exceptional customer service, distinctive features, or competitive pricing, these strengths should serve as the core of your UVP. For example, if your business offers handcrafted products made from sustainably sourced materials, this sets you apart and can be a key selling point. Emphasizing these advantages not only demonstrates your uniqueness but also builds trust and credibility with potential customers.

Think about the specific benefits your products or services provide. Consider how your offerings solve problems or meet needs more effectively than others in the market. For instance, if your software streamlines complex tasks and saves businesses time and money, that benefit should take center stage. By clearly highlighting these value points, you help customers see why choosing your business is the best decision.

Crafting a clear and engaging message is equally important. Develop a succinct elevator pitch that quickly conveys your UVP in a compelling way. This pitch should be straightforward and resonate with your target audience. Imagine you have only 30 seconds to explain your business to someone—what would you say to spark their interest? The power of a well-crafted message lies in its ability to capture attention and leave a lasting impression.

Consistency is key when communicating your UVP. Make sure it is prominently featured across all your marketing channels, from your website to social media and advertising. Every customer interaction should reinforce the same message. If your UVP focuses on delivering fast and friendly customer service, for example, ensure that this is reflected not just in your marketing materials but also in your social media engagement, website copy, and customer communications. Maintaining a unified message across all touchpoints strengthens your brand and solidifies your position in the minds of your customers.

Leverage Digital Marketing

Digital marketing offers small businesses a powerful way to expand reach and engage with a wider audience. Start by creating a well-optimized website that leaves a lasting impression on potential customers. As the first point of contact for many, your website should be professional, easy to navigate, and provide visitors with quick access to the information they seek. Ensuring it is mobile-responsive is crucial, given the increasing reliance on smartphones for browsing. A fast-loading website is also key, as slow performance can lead to potential customers abandoning your site before exploring further.

Search engine optimization (SEO) plays an important role in driving organic traffic to your website. By carefully selecting relevant keywords that align with your target audience's search behavior, you can improve your site's visibility. Integrate these keywords naturally into your content, ensuring it remains high-quality and valuable to your visitors. In addition to content optimization, focus on the technical aspects of SEO, such as incorporating meta tags, descriptive alt text for images, and maintaining a well-structured layout. For instance, adding accurate alt text to images not only improves search rankings but also enhances the user experience for those with disabilities.

Social media is another valuable tool for boosting your digital presence. Selecting the right platforms is key—focus on those that align with your target audience. For visually driven content and broad appeal, platforms like Facebook and Instagram are excellent choices, while LinkedIn is better suited for B2B marketing. Keep your audience engaged by posting a variety of content, from product updates and industry news to customer testimonials and behind-the-scenes looks at your business. Mixing different formats—such as images, videos, and text—helps keep your content fresh and engaging. Additionally, consider using social media advertising to reach specific demographics. Platforms like Facebook and Instagram offer detailed targeting options that allow you to reach users based on their interests, behaviors, and location, ensuring your ad spend is used effectively.

Email marketing continues to be one of the most effective methods for directly engaging with your audience. By building an email list through incentives like sign-up bonuses, lead magnets, or special promotions, you create a valuable channel for communication. Once your list is established, personalizing your campaigns to match different audience segments can boost engagement and drive conversions. Email platforms such as Mailchimp, Constant Contact, and SendinBlue allow you to streamline this process through automation, segmentation, and performance tracking. Make sure your emails deliver value by offering exclusive deals, sharing insightful content, or providing timely product updates. When crafted with care and purpose, email campaigns can significantly strengthen customer relationships and foster long-term loyalty, ending your marketing efforts on a powerful note.

Focus on Local Marketing

Focusing on local marketing is an effective strategy to connect with your community and attract nearby customers. Start by optimizing your business for local SEO, which can greatly improve your visibility in local searches. One of the useful steps is claiming and optimizing your Google My Business listing. This ensures that potential customers can easily find you when they search for services in your area. Be sure to include accurate business details such as your address, phone number, and hours of operation. Enhance your listing by adding high-quality images of your products, services, and location. Encouraging satisfied customers to leave positive reviews will also boost your credibility and draw in new customers.

Incorporating local keywords into your website content, meta tags, and online profiles can further improve your search rankings. For instance, if you operate a bakery in Austin, using phrases like "best bakery in Austin" or "fresh homemade bread in Austin" can help local searchers find your business more easily. This targeted approach increases the chances that potential customers in your area will discover your offerings when they are searching for products or services similar to yours.

Getting involved in your community also strengthens your local presence. Participating in or sponsoring local events, fairs, and activities raises your visibility while showing your commitment to the community. This involvement helps build goodwill and loyalty among local customers.

Additionally, networking with other local businesses, organizations, and influencers can lead to valuable partnerships, referrals, and joint marketing opportunities. For example, collaborating with a nearby coffee shop for a cross-promotion could introduce both businesses to new customers.

Local advertising is another impactful tool. Advertising in local print and online directories that your target audience frequents can drive traffic to your business while boosting your local SEO. Many customers still use these directories to find businesses in their area, so maintaining a presence there can enhance both your credibility and accessibility. Geotargeted ads on platforms like Google Ads and Facebook Ads can also help you reach potential customers within your specific geographic area. By focusing your marketing efforts on the local community, you increase the likelihood of attracting customers who are ready and able to visit your business.

Utilize Content Marketing

Creating valuable content effectively attracts and engages your audience while positioning your brand as an industry leader. A good place to start is blogging. Consistently publishing educational content related to your industry draws organic traffic to your website, builds credibility, and provides genuine value to your readers. For example, if you run a fitness business, blog posts covering workout tips, nutritional guidance, and wellness trends can appeal to those searching for this type of information. Each blog should be optimized for search engines by incorporating relevant keywords, internal and external links, and compelling headlines, which in turn improves your rankings and drives traffic over time.

Video marketing plays a vital role in content strategies as well. Creating engaging videos such as product demos, how-to tutorials, customer testimonials, or brand stories greatly boosts engagement on both social media and your website. Video content tends to be highly shareable, increasing its potential reach. Establishing a YouTube channel to host and share your videos can further expand your audience. To maximize effectiveness, optimize videos with relevant keywords in titles and descriptions, detailed summaries, and eye-catching thumbnails. For instance, a cooking brand could attract food lovers by producing recipe videos and kitchen tips, deepening engagement.

Visual content like infographics offers another opportunity to captivate and educate your audience quickly. Infographics are especially useful for distilling complex information into a visually appealing, easy-to-understand format. This makes them highly shareable on social media platforms and an excellent way to drive traffic to your website. For example, a health-focused brand could create an infographic explaining the benefits of various vitamins, appealing to an audience seeking quick, digestible insights. Similarly, incorporating high-quality images and visually-driven posts can capture your audience's attention and increase shares, further boosting your reach.

Encourage Customer Reviews and Testimonials

Encouraging customer reviews and testimonials can be an excellent way to build trust and attract new customers. Positive reviews serve as social proof, demonstrating to potential customers that others have had great experiences with your products or services. Begin by actively requesting reviews on well-known platforms such as Google, Yelp, Facebook, and industry-specific sites. A strong presence across these platforms ensures that prospective customers can find positive feedback no matter where they search. After a customer completes a purchase, follow up with an email expressing your gratitude and inviting them to share their feedback. Simplify the process by providing direct links to your review profiles in the email, making it easy for customers to leave their comments.

Displaying testimonials prominently on your website can significantly influence potential buyers' decisions. When visitors see that others have had positive experiences, it builds credibility and trust in your brand. Consider placing a dedicated testimonials section on your homepage or product pages for maximum impact. Social media is another excellent venue for showcasing positive reviews and testimonials. Sharing customer feedback on your profiles not only highlights your satisfied customers but also encourages others to share their experiences. Regularly posting testimonials on platforms like Instagram, Facebook, and LinkedIn can boost your brand's credibility and expand your reach.

Additionally, using follow-up emails and direct requests can effectively increase the number of testimonials you receive. Research indicates that customers are more likely to leave reviews when asked, especially if the process is made quick and straightforward.

Furthermore, positive reviews and testimonials contribute to improved search engine rankings. Search engines view reviews as fresh, user-generated content, which can enhance your visibility. Businesses with a steady flow of positive reviews are more likely to appear in local search results, further increasing the chances of attracting nearby customers.

Measure and Analyze Performance

Measuring and analyzing performance is vital to understanding the impact of your marketing efforts. Tools like Google Analytics, social media insights, and email marketing reports provide a comprehensive view of key performance metrics such as website traffic, conversion rates, engagement levels, and return on investment (ROI). These analytics platforms offer real-time data that shows how your campaigns are performing. For example, Google Analytics can pinpoint which sources are driving the most visitors to your site and how they are interacting with your content, while social media insights reveal which posts generate the highest engagement.

Consistent review of your performance data helps you uncover trends, strengths, and areas that need improvement. By analyzing this information regularly, you can identify patterns that may not be immediately obvious. You might discover, for instance, that certain types of content perform best on specific days or that certain demographics are more responsive to your campaigns. Armed with these insights, you can make informed adjustments to your strategies. If a campaign is underperforming, you can refine your messaging, shift your targeting, or reallocate your budget to more effective channels.

A/B testing further sharpens your marketing approach by comparing different variations of key elements such as email subject lines, ad creatives, landing pages, and call-to-action buttons. Testing allows you to determine which versions resonate most with your audience, helping you optimize campaigns for better performance. This data-driven experimentation identifies what works best and leads to more effective strategies.

Iterative improvement is the cornerstone of long-term marketing success. The insights gathered from A/B testing and performance analysis should be continuously applied to refine and enhance your marketing efforts. This ongoing process of testing, learning, and optimizing results in small but meaningful improvements that can dramatically boost your ROI. For example, discovering that a particular call-to-action color consistently drives higher conversion rates enables you to implement this across all campaigns, maximizing your outcomes.

By integrating these strategies, small businesses can amplify their marketing impact, driving growth and establishing a strong presence in their markets.

Sales Techniques Suitable for Both Growing and Small Businesses

Generating revenue and fueling growth hinges on effective sales techniques, whether your business is scaling quickly or operating on a smaller, more focused level. Employing strategies that emphasize understanding customer needs, nurturing strong relationships, and embracing technology can greatly enhance sales outcomes and help you reach your goals. These approaches are not only effective in attracting new customers but also in retaining loyal ones, which is critical for ensuring long-term stability and success. Below, we will explore some of the most impactful sales techniques that work across both growing and small businesses, empowering them to achieve steady growth and maintain a competitive edge in their respective markets.

Consultative Selling

Consultative selling shifts the focus from simply selling a product to building meaningful conversations aimed at helping the customer. This approach is all about understanding your customer's unique needs and delivering tailored, value-driven solutions that resonate with them.

Start by practicing active listening during sales interactions. Truly engage with the customer, listening closely to their pain points, objectives, and challenges. Ask open-ended questions to encourage more in-depth discussions. For instance, rather than asking, "Do you need this product?" try asking, "What specific challenges are you experiencing in your daily operations?" This uncovers underlying problems that your product or service can effectively solve.

After gathering this valuable insight, perform a thorough needs assessment. Analyze what you have learned to identify how your products or services can directly solve the customer's problems. By demonstrating a keen understanding of their needs, you build trust and position yourself as a credible and knowledgeable partner.

Once you have identified their needs, present personalized solutions that address those specific challenges. Highlight the features and advantages of your offerings that will bring the most value to the customer. For instance, if the customer wants to boost team productivity, emphasize how your software can automate repetitive tasks, giving their team more time to focus on higher-priority projects.

Clearly articulate your value proposition by focusing on the results that matter most to the customer, such as reducing costs, improving efficiency, or driving better outcomes. When customers see the value that your solution offers, they are far more likely to commit to the purchase.

Relationship Building

Building strong relationships with prospects and customers not only boosts sales but also cultivates loyalty and long-term partnerships.

Start by establishing trust and rapport. Building genuine connections goes beyond remembering names; it involves understanding individual preferences, taking a sincere interest in their needs, and maintaining a positive and respectful tone in every interaction. For example, if a customer shares a personal interest or milestone, make it a point to ask about it during future conversations. This simple yet meaningful gesture shows that you care about them as people, not just as business contacts.

Consistency is equally critical. Following through on promises and delivering on your commitments strengthens trust over time. If you tell a client you will send information or check in by a certain date, be sure to do so. This dependability not only solidifies trust but also creates a foundation of reliability, which is essential for fostering long-term relationships.

Regular follow-ups show that you value the relationship and are invested in the customer's success. Whether it is checking in to address any concerns, sharing additional insights, or simply keeping the conversation going, regular touchpoints keep you connected and engaged. This ongoing communication reinforces your dedication and helps maintain a positive relationship.

Keeping your customers informed about new products, features, or promotions is another effective way to maintain engagement and encourage repeat business. Sharing updates that directly benefit your customers keeps your offerings relevant and strengthens their interest in your brand. For instance, if your company introduces a feature that resolves a common customer pain point, letting them know could enhance their satisfaction and generate further sales.

Leverage Technology

Incorporating technology into your sales processes can dramatically improve both efficiency and effectiveness. Customer relationship management (CRM) systems like Salesforce, HubSpot, or Zoho CRM enable you to accurately organize customer data. These tools allow you to track customer interactions, manage sales pipelines, and gain valuable insights into customer behavior. For instance, you can easily monitor which customers are engaging with your content, track deal progress, and assess the effectiveness of your communication strategies. This level of organization ensures that you never miss an opportunity and allows you to tailor your approach based on detailed customer profiles.

Automation is another major benefit of CRM tools. By automating tasks such as follow-up emails, appointment scheduling, and data entry, your sales team can free up time to focus on higher-value activities that require a personal touch. Automation can enhance efficiency while simultaneously reducing the likelihood of human error. For example, setting up automated reminders for follow-ups ensures that no potential lead is overlooked, and using standardized templates for communications helps maintain consistency and professionalism across the board.

Sales analytics tools further enhance your ability to make informed, data-driven decisions. By analyzing sales performance data, you can gain insights into customer preferences, understand market trends, and identify areas for improvement. For instance, data analysis might show that a particular demographic is particularly responsive to certain product features, allowing you to fine-tune your marketing and sales strategies to better target that group. These insights enable you to refine your sales approach and reach the right audience with the most compelling message.

Tracking key performance indicators (KPIs) like conversion rates, average deal size, and sales cycle length is crucial for evaluating the success of your sales efforts. Regularly reviewing these metrics gives you valuable insights into what is driving success and where adjustments can be made. For example, if you find that your sales cycle is taking longer than expected, you can pinpoint any bottlenecks and refine your approach by offering more tailored information earlier in the process. With these ongoing adjustments, your sales strategy becomes more agile and effective, helping you consistently move toward your goals.

Solution Selling

Solution selling revolves around deeply understanding your customer's challenges and positioning your products or services as the ideal solutions to address their needs. By identifying specific pain points, you can tailor your approach to show exactly how your offerings will meet their needs, demonstrating empathy and alignment with their goals. This approach not only illustrates your awareness of their struggles but also highlights how your solutions can have a real, positive impact. During your sales conversations, ask insightful questions like "What difficulties are you currently experiencing" or "How is this challenge affecting your business outcomes?" These questions help uncover underlying issues that your products or services can effectively resolve.

Incorporating case studies and testimonials into your pitch is another way to build trust and credibility. Sharing examples of how you have successfully solved similar problems for other customers provides reassurance to potential clients. Real-life success stories show that your solutions work and can be trusted. For instance, a detailed case study explaining how your product improved efficiency for another company in the same industry can be highly persuasive. Similarly, testimonials from satisfied customers reinforce the positive outcomes your solutions can deliver.

Product demonstrations offer a powerful way to connect the features of your product with the customer's needs. By showcasing your offerings in action, you give customers a clear and hands-on understanding of how the product can address their pain points. For example, if you are promoting a software tool, walking customers through a live demo that illustrates how it simplifies project management tasks, such as organizing workflows or meeting deadlines, can be incredibly convincing.

Offering free trials or limited-time access to your product also can encourage potential customers to commit. Trials provide a risk-free way for them to experience the product in their own environment without the pressure of making an immediate purchase. This hands-on opportunity lets them evaluate the benefits firsthand, helping to overcome any hesitations and build confidence in your solution. For instance, offering a 30-day free trial of your software allows potential customers to explore its capabilities, ultimately helping them make a more informed and confident decision about moving forward with your product.

Social Selling

Social selling harnesses the power of social media to engage with prospects, nurture customer relationships, and cultivate meaningful professional connections. When used effectively, social media can become a powerful tool for transforming your sales strategy and driving measurable results.

Start by being an active participant on platforms like LinkedIn, Twitter, and Facebook. These channels give you direct access to potential customers and industry leaders. Regularly share valuable content that highlights industry insights, solutions to common challenges, or innovative trends. By positioning yourself as a resource, you keep your audience engaged while also building credibility as a thought leader. For instance, if you work in the tech industry, sharing updates on software innovations or cybersecurity developments can help establish your expertise and attract a dedicated following.

Building relationships on social media is just as important. Connecting with key decision-makers, influencers, and peers within your industry expands your network and opens up new opportunities. These connections can lead to referrals, partnerships, or even collaborations that have a meaningful impact on your business. Engaging in online discussions, forums, or industry groups allows you to showcase your expertise and increase your visibility. Demonstrating your knowledge in these spaces helps create a reputation for being approachable and insightful, both of which are valuable traits in building trust.

In addition, sharing content that directly addresses your audience's needs can greatly enhance your credibility. Post articles, videos, infographics, or reports that offer solutions to industry problems or provide fresh perspectives. By consistently offering useful and relevant content, you show your commitment to delivering value, which strengthens trust and fosters loyalty over time.

Contributing to meaningful conversations is another critical aspect of social selling. By actively participating in industry-specific forums and groups, you can offer valuable insights and provide input on trending topics. This type of engagement keeps you informed about the latest developments while simultaneously broadening your audience and solidifying your expertise. For example, by joining relevant LinkedIn groups and contributing regularly, you can increase your visibility, build credibility, and ultimately strengthen your professional reputation in the field. Through consistent and thoughtful interaction, you establish yourself as a go-to resource for others in the industry.

Customer-Centric Selling

Customer-centric selling places the customer's needs and experiences at the heart of every interaction, fostering greater satisfaction, loyalty, and word-of-mouth referrals. By focusing on delivering personalized service, you can cultivate deeper connections and more meaningful relationships with your customers.

Delivering outstanding customer service is fundamental to this approach. This means being attentive, responsive, and proactive in addressing each customer's unique needs and concerns. Whether answering inquiries quickly, offering in-depth product details, or resolving any issues promptly, every interaction should leave the customer feeling appreciated and well cared for.

Personalization is a critical aspect of customer-centric selling. By tailoring your communications and engagement based on each customer's preferences and past behavior, you create a more relevant and enjoyable experience. This could include recommending products that complement previous purchases, sending customized emails, or remembering and acting on details specific to the customer's preferences.

Post-sale support also plays a vital role in this strategy. Providing ongoing assistance ensures that customers can fully utilize your products or services, which ultimately boosts their satisfaction and encourages continued loyalty. This support might take the form of detailed user guides, training sessions, or a dedicated customer service team ready to help with any questions or challenges that arise.

Additionally, consistently seeking and acting on customer feedback demonstrates a genuine commitment to their experience. Regularly requesting feedback and using it to improve your offerings shows customers that their opinions matter. This input not only helps enhance your products and services but also strengthens the bond between you and your customers by demonstrating a commitment to their satisfaction.

Effective Negotiation

Effective negotiation plays a crucial role in shaping positive business outcomes, helping you secure successful deals while building strong, long-term relationships. Thorough preparation is the foundation of any successful negotiation. Before entering discussions, invest time in understanding the customer's needs, budget, and constraints. This involves researching the client's business, industry trends, and specific challenges they are facing. Equipped with this knowledge, you can present persuasive solutions that are directly aligned with their goals, making your proposal far more compelling. It is also essential to clarify your own objectives and limits during this preparation phase, ensuring that you know what you are willing to negotiate and what your bottom line is.

Defining clear objectives is another key element of effective negotiation. Determine your desired outcomes, acceptable concessions, and non-negotiable points ahead of time. Having these objectives firmly in mind keeps you focused during the negotiation process and helps prevent impulsive decisions that could compromise your position. For example, knowing your absolute minimum terms ensures you do not agree to anything that undermines your business interests.

A collaborative mindset is vital for achieving win-win outcomes. Rather than viewing the negotiation as a competitive battle where one side wins and the other loses, approach it as an opportunity to find mutual benefits. This collaborative attitude not only improves the overall negotiation experience but also lays the groundwork for future partnerships. By seeking common ground, you can craft solutions that satisfy both parties, fostering a stronger, more positive relationship.

Flexibility is equally important in successful negotiations. Being open to compromise and willing to adjust your position as the conversation unfolds shows that you are committed to finding a solution that works for everyone involved. Flexibility does not mean giving in on critical points; rather, it is about being adaptable and creative in addressing both parties' needs. For example, if budget constraints arise, you could propose alternative payment terms or a phased approach to the project to ease the burden.

By integrating these negotiation strategies into your approach, you can enhance your sales outcomes, build lasting customer relationships, and achieve sustainable growth, whether you are a small business or a larger enterprise.

CHAPTER 9

PERSONAL DEVELOPMENT AND LEADERSHIP

Developing the Right Mindset for Your Business Path

Successfully navigating the challenges and opportunities of the business world requires cultivating the right mindset. Whether you aim to expand your enterprise into a large corporation or maintain a small, sustainable operation, the mindset you adopt will shape your decisions, resilience, and long-term success. Embracing a growth mindset, staying adaptable, and building resilience are critical to thriving through the highs and lows of your journey. Here are strategies to help you foster the mindset that aligns with your business goals, keeping you focused, motivated, and prepared to overcome any challenges that arise.

Embrace a Growth Mindset

Think of your business as a garden that flourishes with consistent care, attention, and a readiness to adapt to changing conditions. Embracing a growth mindset is like being a diligent gardener, always looking for ways to nurture improvement and foster development. This mindset encourages you to see challenges not as obstacles, but as opportunities for learning and innovation.

A strong commitment to learning is at the heart of this approach. Imagine yourself as a lifelong learner, constantly seeking out new knowledge and insights. You can nurture this by regularly reading industry-related materials, attending workshops, engaging in networking events, and pursuing courses that expand your skill set. Staying curious and informed helps you remain adaptable and innovative, positioning you to tackle new challenges and seize emerging opportunities with confidence.

When setbacks happen, resist the urge to see them as failures. Instead, view them as important lessons on your path to success. Every misstep provides a chance to improve and refine your approach. Take inspiration from Thomas Edison's words: "I have not failed. I have just found 10,000 ways that would not work." By adopting this outlook, you enhance your problem-solving skills and drive innovation within your business.

Another vital aspect of a growth mindset is seeking feedback. Constructive input from employees, customers, mentors, and peers offers invaluable insights that highlight areas for improvement. It helps you spot blind spots and make better decisions, ultimately strengthening your leadership and business strategies. Additionally, engaging in regular self-reflection allows you to assess your actions, recognize your strengths and weaknesses, and fine-tune your approach. Leaders who prioritize feedback and self-reflection often inspire their teams and lead with greater effectiveness.

Foster an Entrepreneurial Spirit

Cultivating an entrepreneurial spirit within your business fuels innovation and drives growth. Picture a workplace where creativity thrives, risks are embraced, and adaptability and resilience become second nature to everyone. This environment promotes innovation, empowers employees to take ownership, and keeps your business agile and competitive, leading to sustained growth and a motivated, engaged workforce.

Start by creating a culture that celebrates innovation. Inspire your team to think creatively and question conventional approaches. Hold regular brainstorming sessions, offer innovation workshops, and provide a space for employees to share their ideas, whether through suggestion boxes or digital platforms. Celebrating both successes and learning from attempts that did not go as planned reinforces the message that continuous improvement is central to your business's evolution.

Taking calculated risks is another critical component of an entrepreneurial spirit. Encourage yourself and your team to evaluate opportunities thoroughly, weighing potential rewards against possible downsides. This is not about taking reckless chances but about making informed decisions that can lead to major breakthroughs and growth. Calculated risks are often the gateway to seizing new opportunities that can push your business to the next level.

In a constantly evolving business landscape, adaptability is a must. Being able to pivot your strategies and adjust to market changes, shifting customer needs, or technological advancements keeps your business relevant and competitive. Embracing flexibility might mean adopting new tools, exploring new markets, or reshaping your business model. The quicker you adapt to external changes, the more likely you are to maintain momentum and drive long-term success.

Resilience is equally vital, helping you and your team navigate challenges without losing sight of your goals. By developing strategies to manage stress and maintain a positive outlook, you build the strength needed to face adversity head-on. This could involve practicing mindfulness, seeking guidance from mentors, or fostering a strong support network within your business. Resilience is more than just bouncing back—it is about learning, growing, and emerging stronger with each experience, preparing you for whatever comes next.

Focus on Vision and Goals

A clear vision and well-defined goals serve as the compass that guides your business through the complexities of the market. Think of your vision as the North Star, offering direction and purpose for every strategic decision you make.

Start by crafting a compelling vision for your business. This vision should reflect your long-term aspirations and core values, painting a vivid picture of what you strive to achieve. It is not just about setting targets; it is about creating a powerful narrative that drives your strategy and actions. Your vision should inspire your team and stakeholders, motivating them to work toward a shared goal. Consider how Elon Musk's vision for SpaceX—making space travel accessible and eventually enabling life on Mars—not only shaped the company's strategy but also energized and united employees and stakeholders.

Consistently communicating your vision is just as important. Make sure your vision is clear and regularly shared with your team, stakeholders, and even customers. This constant communication ensures that everyone is working toward the same objectives, fostering a unified sense of purpose. You can keep the vision top of mind through regular meetings, newsletters, or visual reminders around the workplace. When employees feel connected to the company's mission, they tend to be more engaged and productive.

Setting SMART goals—specific, measurable, achievable, relevant, and time-bound—provides the clarity and focus you need to track progress and measure success. For example, instead of a vague objective like "increase sales," a SMART goal would be "increase sales by 20% over the next quarter through targeted marketing campaigns." This level of detail helps you plan, execute, and evaluate more effectively.

Breaking down long-term goals into smaller, manageable milestones can make the journey to success more tangible and less overwhelming. Each milestone represents a step toward the larger goal and offers opportunities to celebrate progress, keeping both you and your team motivated. For instance, if your long-term goal is to launch a new product line, milestones could include completing market research, finalizing product design, securing suppliers, and rolling out a marketing campaign. These smaller achievements help maintain momentum and focus as you work toward the bigger picture.

Cultivate a Customer-Centric Approach

Placing your customers at the center of your business strategy is crucial for building lasting relationships and ensuring long-term success. Every interaction with your business should leave customers feeling valued, appreciated, and understood, fostering a deeper connection and loyalty to your brand.

The first step in prioritizing customer needs is developing a thorough understanding of their preferences, pain points, and desires. Conducting comprehensive market research and crafting detailed customer personas helps you gain insight into their profiles. This allows you to tailor your products, services, and interactions to align with their specific needs. Such a personalized approach not only enhances satisfaction but also fosters loyalty, as customers feel a deeper connection to your brand.

Personalization takes this customer-centric focus even further. Offering personalized experiences, such as product recommendations based on previous purchases or targeted marketing messages, shows customers you truly understand them. CRM systems and data analytics tools can play a vital role in gathering and analyzing customer data, enabling you to deliver tailored experiences that resonate with individual preferences.

Listening closely to customer feedback is another key element of a customer-centric approach. Actively seek feedback through surveys, online reviews, social media interactions, and direct conversations. These insights offer a window into what your customers appreciate and where improvements are needed.

Showing responsiveness to customer feedback is equally important. By making timely adjustments to your products or services based on customer suggestions, you demonstrate that their voices are heard. Whether you are refining a feature or enhancing your customer service processes, responding to feedback reinforces your commitment to improving their experience. This kind of responsiveness strengthens trust and deepens the bond between your business and your customers.

Leadership and Team Building

Leadership and team building are foundational to any thriving business. Strong leadership guides your team toward collective goals, while effective team building creates a cohesive, productive workforce.

Leading by example establishes the benchmark for your team. When you demonstrate the qualities you expect, such as integrity, dedication, and transparency, you foster an environment of accountability and mutual respect. Your behavior influences how your team approaches their work, encouraging them to adopt the same high standards of professionalism and commitment, which in turn drives higher engagement and productivity.

Motivating your team is equally vital. Sharing your vision helps your team connect with the company's broader purpose. Recognizing their achievements, no matter the size, reinforces their value and encourages them to stay motivated. Offering support—whether through guidance, resources, or simply being available to listen—shows that you are invested in their success, which strengthens team morale and commitment.

Empowering your team by delegating authority and fostering autonomy enables them to take ownership of their work. Trusting them with decision-making responsibilities enhances their investment in the company's success. This empowerment often leads to greater innovation and creativity as employees feel more confident in exploring new ideas and solutions.

Developing your team through continuous learning is also crucial. Investing in their professional growth through training, skill-building opportunities, and mentorship programs not only improves their abilities but also demonstrates your commitment to their long-term success. By encouraging ongoing learning, you prepare them for future challenges while fostering a culture of continuous improvement that strengthens the entire organization.

Balance Work and Life

Balancing work and life is essential for maintaining overall well-being and achieving long-term success in both personal and professional areas. Prioritizing your well-being is a key aspect of this balance. Taking care of your physical and mental health through regular exercise, adequate sleep, and healthy eating habits helps you stay energized and focused. These self-care practices not only support your physical health but also enhance your mood and cognitive function, ensuring that you can perform at your best.

Managing stress is another important factor. Mindfulness and meditation can help you stay present and manage stress more effectively, offering moments of calm during a busy day. Pursuing hobbies and activities that bring joy and relaxation also serves as a great way to recharge, providing a mental break from work and helping you maintain a healthy perspective.

Achieving work-life integration requires setting clear boundaries between your professional and personal responsibilities. Establishing specific times for work and personal activities helps create structure and prevents burnout. By maintaining this separation, you ensure that you devote time to relaxation and leisure without letting work dominate your day.

Effective time management also plays a significant role. Prioritizing tasks based on their importance allows you to focus on what truly matters, while delegating responsibilities when possible can help lighten your workload. This strategic approach enables you to make room for personal pursuits without sacrificing productivity.

Incorporating these strategies into your daily routine allows you to strike a balance that fosters both professional success and personal happiness, creating a fulfilling and resilient life.

Leadership Styles for Growing Businesses vs. Small Businesses

Selecting the right leadership style is crucial for guiding your business toward success and long-term sustainability. The challenges and opportunities faced by growing businesses and small businesses often call for different leadership approaches. In growing businesses, leaders need to focus on scaling operations, managing increased complexity, and fostering innovation to fuel expansion. The ability to delegate, strategize for the long term, and encourage a culture of innovation becomes critical as the organization grows.

On the other hand, small businesses benefit from a more hands-on and personal leadership approach. In these environments, leaders are closer to their teams, directly influencing company culture and building strong relationships with employees and customers alike. This personal touch allows small business leaders to stay agile and responsive to changes while ensuring that their vision remains central to all operations. Adapting your leadership style to align with the stage and scale of your business is essential to successfully navigating the demands of growth or preserving the advantages of being small and nimble.

The following sections explore key leadership styles and strategies that can be tailored to fit the unique needs of both growing and small businesses.

Leadership Styles for Growing Businesses

1. Visionary Leadership

Leading a growing business requires more than just managing day-to-day operations; it demands visionary leadership that drives the organization toward greater heights. Visionary leaders are skilled at crafting and communicating a compelling vision of the future, one that unites and motivates the entire team. This clarity of purpose becomes a powerful tool for guiding the organization as it scales and enters new markets. By articulating an ambitious and shared goal, visionary leaders ignite enthusiasm, inspire commitment, and foster a culture where everyone works together toward a common purpose.

Visionary leaders do not just inspire—they are actively involved in shaping the long-term strategic direction of the business. They prioritize innovation, encourage creativity, and take calculated risks, all of which are essential for achieving transformative growth. Companies like Tesla and Amazon have thrived under such leadership by continually pushing the boundaries of what is possible, driven by a clear and forward-thinking strategy. Visionary leaders create a roadmap that not only envisions the future but also positions their companies to actively shape it.

Adaptability is another important characteristic of visionary leaders. They are keenly aware that the marketplace is constantly evolving and understand the need to pivot when necessary. Whether it involves seizing new opportunities or adjusting strategies to overcome unforeseen challenges, visionary leaders ensure their growing businesses remain competitive and resilient. By balancing bold long-term goals with the agility to respond to change, they steer their organizations toward sustained growth and success.

Visionary leadership is more than just dreaming big—it is about turning those dreams into a strategic plan and rallying a team that is fully engaged in making that vision a reality.

2. Transformational Leadership

A transformational leader is one who drives change and fosters a culture of continuous improvement within the organization. In growing businesses, this style of leadership plays a pivotal role in nurturing creativity and innovation. Transformational leaders create an environment where employees are encouraged to bring forward fresh ideas and solutions, feeling empowered to contribute to the company's evolution. This approach is particularly effective in fast-moving business environments, where adaptability and resilience are key to thriving. By constantly questioning the status quo and seeking new ways to improve, transformational leaders push their organizations to become more efficient and effective.

These leaders inspire and motivate their teams to embrace change with optimism and enthusiasm. They communicate a clear and compelling vision of the future, helping their employees see challenges as opportunities for personal and professional growth. This inspiration cultivates a deep sense of responsibility and dedication within the team. When employees feel valued and understand the impact of their contributions, they are more likely to invest their energy and creativity into achieving the company's goals.

Transformational leaders also prioritize employee development, recognizing that the growth of the business is directly tied to the growth of its people. They provide mentorship, training, and opportunities for career advancement, ensuring that their teams are continuously learning and evolving. This focus on nurturing talent helps to build a skilled and capable workforce ready to meet the demands of a rapidly growing organization.

Collaboration and inclusivity are also core to transformational leadership. By encouraging open communication and valuing diverse perspectives, these leaders enhance decision-making and problem-solving within the team. Creating a culture of trust and mutual respect allows employees to work together more effectively, fostering an environment where innovation can flourish. When employees feel safe to share their ideas and take risks, the entire organization benefits from a more dynamic and forward-thinking approach.

Transformational leadership goes beyond simply managing change; it is about embedding a mindset of continuous improvement, innovation, and employee development into the fabric of the company. By driving progress and investing in their people, transformational leaders set the stage for sustained growth and long-term success in a constantly evolving market.

3. Delegative Leadership

As businesses expand and operations become more complex, adopting a delegative leadership style can be highly effective in managing the growing demands. Delegative leadership, often referred to as laissez-faire leadership, centers on empowering teams by giving them the authority to make decisions and take ownership of their roles. This approach fosters a culture of accountability and autonomy, driving higher levels of motivation and performance among team members. When employees are trusted to take the lead in their areas of expertise, they feel more valued and committed to delivering their best work.

One key advantage of delegative leadership is that it allows leaders to shift their focus toward strategic priorities and high-level decision-making. By entrusting operational tasks to skilled team members, leaders free up time and resources to concentrate on steering the company toward its long-term objectives. For example, a CEO might delegate the day-to-day management of various departments to trusted leaders, giving them the capacity to focus on innovation, market expansion, and other key growth initiatives.

This leadership approach also promotes a culture of trust and teamwork. Delegative leaders equip their teams with the necessary resources and support, while also granting them the freedom to experiment and make decisions independently. This autonomy boosts employee confidence, encourages innovation, and cultivates creative problem-solving. Studies show that organizations that grant employees more autonomy tend to experience higher levels of job satisfaction and lower turnover rates, which are critical for sustaining growth over the long term.

However, for delegative leadership to succeed, it is essential to carefully select the right team members and clearly communicate expectations. Leaders must ensure that employees have the skills, knowledge, and support needed to manage their responsibilities effectively. Regular check-ins and feedback sessions help monitor progress, address challenges, and provide guidance when needed. Maintaining open communication allows leaders to strike a balance between supporting their teams and avoiding micromanagement, promoting both independence and accountability.

Delegative leadership enables teams to take the initiative, drive the business forward, and make critical decisions while allowing leaders to focus on overarching strategic goals. This leadership style is particularly effective in growing businesses where the ability to scale and adapt quickly is crucial for continued success.

4. Data-Driven Leadership

Navigating a growing business successfully requires precision, and data-driven leadership offers that precision by guiding decisions through insights and analytics. Leveraging data allows leaders to identify emerging trends, measure performance, and optimize operations. This approach is especially valuable in dynamic business environments where staying ahead of market shifts and customer needs is critical. For example, data can uncover customer behavior patterns, highlight operational inefficiencies, and pinpoint areas of opportunity, helping leaders make strategic adjustments that fuel growth and enhance efficiency.

At the core of data-driven leadership is informed decision-making. Leaders who rely on data are better equipped to evaluate the success of their strategies and adapt based on clear evidence rather than relying solely on instinct. For instance, by using data analytics tools, a leader can monitor sales performance across different regions, identifying which areas excel and which require additional focus. This detailed insight allows for more targeted actions, ensuring that resources are directed to areas that drive the most impact.

A key aspect of this leadership style is establishing clear performance metrics. Data-driven leaders set measurable goals and consistently track progress using key performance indicators (KPIs) such as revenue growth, customer acquisition costs, and employee productivity. Regularly reviewing these KPIs allows leaders to see whether their strategies are working and where they may need to adjust. For example, if a decline in customer satisfaction scores is detected, a leader can immediately investigate and implement improvements to address any issues before they escalate.

Data-driven leaders also foster transparency and accountability within their organizations. By sharing relevant data with teams, they ensure that everyone is aligned with the company's goals and understands how their efforts contribute to overall success. This transparency creates a collaborative environment where employees feel empowered to act on data and make informed decisions. For instance, sharing sales performance data with the marketing team can help them craft more effective campaigns by focusing on high-performing regions or customer segments.

Furthermore, data-driven leadership extends to using predictive analytics to forecast future trends. By analyzing historical data, leaders can anticipate market demands and make proactive decisions that prepare the business for future growth. For example, predictive analytics might help a retail business forecast seasonal inventory needs, reducing the likelihood of stockouts or overstocking.

Embracing data-driven leadership equips your business with the ability to make informed decisions, stay agile in a competitive landscape, and set the foundation for sustained growth.

5. Collaborative Leadership

Collaborative leadership is a dynamic approach that emphasizes teamwork and open communication, both of which are crucial for growing businesses. As your company expands, fostering cross-functional collaboration becomes increasingly important. This style of leadership encourages departments and teams to work together seamlessly toward shared goals, reducing redundancies and capitalizing on the collective expertise of your organization. When efforts are unified, the business benefits from increased efficiency, better decision-making, and stronger overall performance.

Central to collaborative leadership is creating an environment where open communication flourishes. Leaders who embrace this style promote transparency and actively encourage team members to share ideas, thoughts, and feedback. When employees feel heard and valued, it fosters trust and engagement, leading to greater motivation and productivity. This sense of empowerment makes employees more committed to their work and to the company's success. Open communication also ensures that vital information flows freely across the organization, helping everyone stay aligned and informed.

Another pillar of collaborative leadership is inclusive decision-making. Leaders who prioritize collaboration seek input from all levels and departments, recognizing the importance of diverse perspectives. By involving a wide range of voices, you can unearth ideas and insights that might otherwise be overlooked. This inclusive approach not only results in more innovative solutions but also promotes a sense of ownership among employees. For example, when facing a complex issue, bringing together team members from various departments to brainstorm ideas can lead to more creative and well-rounded strategies.

Collaboration also strengthens problem-solving within your business. When employees from different backgrounds work together, they bring unique viewpoints that can lead to more innovative solutions. This diversity of thought is essential in an ever-changing business landscape where agility and creativity are necessary for staying competitive. For instance, by encouraging your marketing and product development teams to collaborate closely, you can create marketing campaigns that effectively showcase the product's strengths and resonate more deeply with customers.

Building a collaborative culture also nurtures strong relationships between employees, which enhances team dynamics and creates a positive work environment. When employees enjoy working together, they are more likely to share knowledge, support one another, and collaborate effectively on projects. This camaraderie boosts morale and job satisfaction, fostering a sense of unity across the organization. Activities like team-building exercises and regular cross-departmental meetings can further strengthen these relationships and reinforce a collaborative spirit.

By adopting collaborative leadership, you position your business for long-term success. Teams become more aligned, motivated, and equipped to tackle challenges while seizing opportunities together. This approach not only drives innovation and problem-solving but also fosters a cohesive, resilient organization ready to thrive in a competitive market.

Leadership Styles for Small Businesses

1. Hands-On Leadership

In small businesses, hands-on leadership is often one of the most impactful approaches. Rather than simply overseeing operations, hands-on leaders dive into the daily workings of the business, actively participating in a wide range of functions. Whether they are on the production floor, managing customer service inquiries, or assisting with sales, these leaders are directly involved in ensuring every aspect of the business runs efficiently. This level of engagement allows them to gain a deep understanding of the business, making it easier to spot potential issues early and implement effective solutions. A leader who is side by side with their team exemplifies commitment and work ethic, which sets a powerful example for everyone else in the organization.

Another key element of hands-on leadership is maintaining open and direct lines of communication. Leaders who embrace this style often build close-knit relationships with their employees, fostering a strong sense of community within the business. This communication style allows for the free flow of information, which minimizes misunderstandings and enhances collaboration. Regular team meetings where progress is discussed, concerns are addressed, and solutions are brainstormed together, can create an environment of transparency and teamwork. Such practices help keep everyone aligned and promote a culture where employees feel valued and involved in the decision-making process.

Approachability is another hallmark of hands-on leadership. Employees tend to view these leaders as more relatable and accessible, which helps build trust and loyalty within the team. When employees see their leader working alongside them—especially during high-pressure situations—they are more motivated to go above and beyond in their efforts. For example, when a leader steps in to help meet a tight deadline or resolve an urgent issue, it inspires the team to match that level of dedication, fostering a culture of mutual support and shared success.

The personal connections forged through hands-on leadership can also lead to improved employee retention. When team members feel a strong connection to their leader and know that their efforts are both recognized and appreciated, they are more likely to stay with the company. This is particularly beneficial for small businesses, where high turnover can be both costly and disruptive. For instance, a hands-on leader who regularly acknowledges individual and team achievements, offers personalized feedback, and provides opportunities for growth can create a loyal and motivated workforce.

Hands-on leadership, with its focus on active participation and direct communication, strengthens relationships within the business and builds a motivated team that is ready to take on any challenge.

2. Servant Leadership

Servant leadership places a strong focus on prioritizing the well-being, growth, and success of employees, customers, and the community. This approach is particularly effective in small businesses, where fostering a people-first culture can have a profound impact on overall success. Servant leaders cultivate a supportive and inclusive work environment where every team member feels valued, heard, and empowered. By prioritizing the needs of their team, these leaders build a culture of trust, collaboration, and mutual respect. For example, a servant leader may take time to understand each employee's strengths and goals, offering tailored support to help them develop and thrive within the company.

Empowering employees is a key component of servant leadership. Leaders who follow this approach ensure their teams have the resources, training, and autonomy to excel in their roles. This sense of empowerment leads to higher job satisfaction and deeper engagement—both of which are crucial for retaining top talent in a small business setting. For instance, a servant leader might delegate meaningful responsibilities to employees, trust them with important decisions, and provide guidance when challenges arise. This will enhance morale while also instilling a sense of ownership and accountability among the team.

In addition to focusing on employees, servant leaders place great importance on community and customer relationships. They often engage in community service and encourage their teams to do the same, strengthening the connection between the business and the local community. Servant leaders also prioritize exceptional customer service, understanding that happy customers are essential to business success. For example, a servant leader might introduce feedback loops to continuously improve products and services, ensuring that the business consistently meets or exceeds customer expectations.

The impact of servant leadership extends beyond individual employee satisfaction. By fostering a culture centered on respect, collaboration, and continuous growth, servant leaders set the stage for sustainable success. This leadership style not only improves employee retention and productivity but also strengthens customer loyalty and enhances the business's reputation within the community. Embracing servant leadership can be a powerful strategy for small businesses looking to create lasting, positive change and build strong, resilient teams.

3. Adaptive Leadership

Adaptive leadership thrives in small businesses because it is rooted in flexibility and a proactive approach to solving problems. This leadership style allows leaders to adjust strategies swiftly in response to changing circumstances, giving them the agility to handle market fluctuations and seize new opportunities. For example, when a new competitor emerges or customer preferences shift, an adaptive leader can pivot quickly, adjusting marketing tactics, altering product lines, or exploring new market segments to ensure the business stays competitive and continues to thrive.

Problem-solving is at the core of adaptive leadership, which is critical in the fast-moving world of small businesses. Adaptive leaders not only address challenges head-on but also encourage their teams to think creatively and develop innovative solutions. By fostering a culture of collaborative problem-solving, these leaders ensure that the business can tackle issues efficiently and maintain smooth operations. For instance, when a challenge arises, an adaptive leader might gather the team for a brainstorming session, seeking diverse perspectives to identify the root cause and develop effective solutions, which promotes continuous improvement and innovation.

Another key aspect of adaptive leadership is the openness to feedback and learning. Adaptive leaders understand that the business environment is constantly evolving, so they actively seek new information, industry trends, and best practices. This learning-oriented mindset helps them make informed decisions and implement changes that benefit the business. Whether through attending industry conferences, joining professional networks, or encouraging team members to pursue professional development, adaptive leaders ensure their organization stays ahead of industry changes and is prepared to adapt when new challenges and opportunities arise.

Ultimately, adaptive leadership combines flexibility, effective problem-solving, and a commitment to continuous learning—qualities that are particularly valuable for small businesses. This leadership style creates a culture of agility and innovation, empowering employees to contribute their ideas and solutions. It helps businesses remain resilient and capable of navigating the complexities of a dynamic market while driving sustainable growth.

4. Relationship-Oriented Leadership

In the close-knit world of small businesses, relationship-oriented leadership shines by focusing on personal connections that directly impact success. Leaders who prioritize relationships build strong bonds with employees, customers, and stakeholders, fostering an environment that thrives on support and collaboration. This approach does more than just improve team morale and cohesion; it nurtures loyalty and trust, both within the business and with its customers and partners.

In small businesses, building relationships goes beyond the professional. Relationship-oriented leaders take the time to understand their employees on a personal level, learning about their strengths, goals, and challenges. By offering personalized feedback and tailored support, these leaders help employees feel appreciated and respected. When employees sense they are truly valued, their job satisfaction rises, they contribute their best work, and they remain dedicated to the business's success.

Customer satisfaction is also at the heart of relationship-oriented leadership. These leaders go the extra mile to ensure that every customer interaction leaves a positive impact. Actively seeking feedback and addressing customer needs promptly and effectively strengthens the relationship between the business and its customers. Delivering outstanding customer service consistently leads to stronger loyalty, repeat business, and powerful word-of-mouth recommendations—essential elements for small business growth and sustainability.

Open communication is another strength of relationship-oriented leaders. By encouraging employees to share ideas, raise concerns, and engage in decision-making, these leaders create a culture of inclusion and collaboration. When team members feel their voices are heard and their input matters, they become more invested in the business's success. This collective wisdom fuels innovation and helps the business adapt to challenges with greater agility.

Relationship-oriented leadership in small businesses focuses on creating deep, meaningful connections. By building trust and fostering a culture of open communication and collaboration, these leaders strengthen both their team and their customer base, positioning their business for long-term success.

5. Entrepreneurial Leadership

Entrepreneurial leadership is crucial for small businesses looking to carve out a unique place in competitive markets. These leaders are defined by their commitment to innovation and a willingness to embrace risk. Continuously seeking new opportunities, they encourage fresh ideas and are unafraid of change. This proactive mindset cultivates a culture of creativity and dynamism, which not only fuels growth but also helps the business stand apart from competitors.

In small businesses, innovation can take many forms, whether through launching new products, enhancing services, or finding more efficient ways to operate. Entrepreneurial leaders push their teams to challenge the status quo and develop creative solutions to problems. This approach not only drives meaningful improvements in the business but also keeps employees engaged, as they see their ideas come to life and feel that their contributions are making a real difference.

Risk-taking is another defining trait of entrepreneurial leaders. They understand that progress often requires stepping into unknown territory. By taking calculated risks, these leaders pursue new growth opportunities that others might shy away from. What sets them apart is their ability to carefully weigh potential rewards against the risks, ensuring that their decisions are informed and strategic, with the potential for significant impact.

Equally important are vision and passion. Entrepreneurial leaders possess a deep passion for their business and its mission, which inspires and motivates their teams. Their enthusiasm drives a shared commitment to achieving common goals. By articulating a clear vision and demonstrating unwavering dedication, these leaders instill a strong sense of purpose in their teams, propelling the business forward with energy and direction.

Moreover, these leaders know how to maintain motivation and morale, even in challenging times. They celebrate successes, learn from setbacks, and always strive for improvement. This positive, high-energy leadership style fosters a resilient business culture that is adaptable and ready to seize opportunities as they arise.

In essence, entrepreneurial leadership in small businesses focuses on nurturing innovation, embracing calculated risks, and fostering a clear, passionate vision. By driving a culture of creativity and purpose, these leaders empower their teams to push boundaries, explore new possibilities, and build a business capable of thriving in competitive markets.

Adapting Leadership Styles

Step #1: Assess Business Needs

Tailoring your leadership style to the specific needs of your business is vital for ensuring success and overcoming the challenges that arise along the way. The first step is to assess the context in which your business operates. Factors such as the size of your business, its growth stage, the industry you are in, and the nuances of your organizational culture all influence which leadership style will yield the best results.

For instance, a tech startup may flourish under visionary or transformational leadership, where innovation and long-term objectives inspire creativity and drive employees to push boundaries. Conversely, a small retail business might benefit more from a hands-on or relationship-oriented leadership style, where close attention to daily operations and strong personal connections with employees and customers foster a positive work environment and customer loyalty.

Flexibility is key when adapting your leadership style to meet the evolving needs of your business. What works in the initial stages of a small business may become less effective as the company grows and scales. Being open to adjusting your leadership approach ensures that you stay in tune with the demands of your business as it matures. For example, a leader who begins with a hands-on style might need to shift toward a more delegative approach as the business expands, empowering the team to take on more responsibility while the leader focuses on strategic direction and decision-making.

Recognizing that different circumstances require different leadership styles is also essential. In times of crisis or when swift, decisive action is necessary, an authoritative leadership style might be more effective. Conversely, during periods of stability and growth, fostering a collaborative environment where team input and innovation are encouraged can lead to better outcomes.

By evaluating your business needs and staying adaptable, you ensure that your leadership style grows in sync with your business, helping you navigate new challenges and seize opportunities as they arise.

Step #2: Develop Leadership Skills

To become an effective leader, you must commit to continuous improvement while leveraging your strengths and addressing any areas for growth. Developing strong leadership skills is an ongoing journey that requires feedback, education, and staying informed about the latest best practices. As your business evolves, so too must your ability to lead through different stages of growth and adapt to new challenges.

One critical aspect of leadership development is actively seeking feedback from your team, peers, and mentors. Constructive feedback provides valuable insights into how you can improve and helps you understand the impact of your leadership style on others. Being open to this feedback not only demonstrates humility but also fosters a culture of growth within your organization.

Continuing education is another essential component of sharpening your leadership abilities. Enrolling in leadership courses, attending workshops, and participating in seminars will broaden your knowledge and refine your approach. Reading books and articles on leadership trends and industry advancements further equips you with fresh insights. Additionally, working with a mentor or coach can provide personalized guidance, helping you tackle challenges and further develop your leadership skills.

Staying informed about leadership trends is also crucial for your development. Follow industry experts, engage in professional networks, and participate in conferences to learn from others' experiences. This exposure to proven strategies and innovative techniques allows you to refine your own leadership approach, ensuring that you stay adaptable and effective in your role.

Recognizing and leveraging your strengths is vital in leadership. Understand what you excel at and capitalize on those skills. At the same time, be mindful of any weaknesses and take proactive steps to address them. This might mean delegating tasks to team members whose strengths complement yours or seeking additional training to build up areas where you need improvement.

Building a diverse team that complements your leadership style is equally important. A well-rounded team with varied perspectives and expertise enhances problem-solving and decision-making, helping your business thrive. By fostering a culture of collaboration, where every team member feels valued and empowered, you can leverage their strengths to drive the business forward.

Leadership development is a continuous process of learning, self-awareness, and adaptation. By focusing on growth, harnessing your strengths, and addressing your challenges, you will build the skills needed to effectively lead your business through each phase of its growth.

Step #3: Foster a Positive Culture

Fostering a positive culture is key to ensuring the long-term success and sustainability of your business. When your leadership aligns with the values of your organization, you create an environment where employees feel valued, engaged, and motivated. This alignment strengthens employee satisfaction and performance, laying the foundation for a thriving workplace.

To build a strong culture, make sure your actions and decisions consistently reflect the core values of your business. For example, if innovation is one of your values, actively encourage creative thinking and reward those who bring forward new ideas. If teamwork is a priority, create opportunities for collaboration and celebrate group achievements. By staying true to your company's values, you reinforce the culture you want to cultivate and ensure that it permeates every level of your organization.

Leading by example is also critical. Exhibit the behaviors and attitudes you want your team to emulate. If punctuality and professionalism are important to you, show up on time and carry yourself with professionalism in all interactions. When your team sees you modeling the behavior you want to see, they are more likely to adopt those same standards, creating a cohesive and driven workplace.

A culture built on open and transparent communication fosters trust and strengthens team relationships. Encourage employees to voice their ideas, concerns, and feedback openly, without fear of judgment. Communicate your vision, goals, and expectations clearly, while remaining receptive to input from your team. This transparency builds trust and ensures everyone feels heard, which fosters a stronger sense of belonging.

Recognizing and celebrating achievements is another powerful way to maintain a positive culture. Celebrate both individual and team successes, regardless of their size. Recognition not only boosts morale but also reinforces the behaviors and outcomes you want to see replicated, motivating your team to continue striving for excellence.

Additionally, offering opportunities for professional growth enhances your culture by showing employees that you are invested in their development. Provide avenues for learning, mentorship, and career advancement. When employees see that the company supports their personal and professional growth, they are more likely to stay committed and contribute to the business's long-term success.

By fostering a positive culture, you create a workplace where employees feel supported, valued, and motivated to succeed, ultimately driving performance and securing the future success of your business.

Balancing Work-Life Dynamics and Personal Fulfillment

Finding harmony between your professional responsibilities and personal life is essential for sustaining both success and well-being. As a business leader, achieving this balance can lead to increased productivity, better health, and a greater sense of happiness. When you strike the right balance, it positively impacts not only your mental and physical health but also contributes to a more positive work environment and deeper personal satisfaction. Next, we will explore strategies to help you achieve this balance effectively.

Set Clear Boundaries

Establishing distinct boundaries is fundamental for maintaining a balance between work and personal life, leading to greater fulfillment in both areas. One effective way to create this balance is by setting clear work hours within a structured schedule. Define specific start and end times for your workday and stick to them consistently. This not only ensures that you dedicate time to both professional and personal activities but also helps prevent overworking, allowing you to be fully present in each part of your day without feeling pulled in different directions.

Creating a dedicated workspace is another key strategy, especially if you work from home. Set up a designated area specifically for work that is separate from your living spaces. This physical separation helps you mentally transition between work and personal time, boosting focus and productivity during work hours. Additionally, organizing your workspace to minimize distractions is vital for maintaining concentration. Let family members or housemates know about your work hours so they can respect your need for a focused environment.

By setting clear boundaries through a structured schedule and a dedicated workspace, you create the foundation for a healthier work-life balance, enhancing your overall well-being and productivity.

Prioritize and Delegate

Prioritizing tasks and effectively delegating responsibilities are necessary for balancing work-life dynamics and enhancing personal fulfillment. To begin, it is important to identify and focus on the most critical tasks that drive progress in both your professional and personal life. Use a clear prioritization method, such as ranking tasks by urgency and importance, to ensure you are dedicating time and energy to what truly matters. By honing in on these high-priority tasks, you can prevent burnout and make better use of your time, leaving space for personal activities and relaxation.

Delegation is another powerful strategy that contributes to a more balanced life. Learn to trust your team by assigning tasks that do not require your direct involvement. Delegating responsibilities allows you to focus on high-impact areas while empowering others to contribute and develop their skills. For example, if you are running a business, delegating routine administrative tasks to a capable team member can free up your time to focus on strategic decisions and personal priorities.

By carefully prioritizing your responsibilities and delegating effectively, you create more time for both work and personal fulfillment, fostering a healthier and more balanced lifestyle.

Embrace Flexibility

Adopting a flexible work routine can significantly improve your ability to balance professional responsibilities with personal commitments, leading to increased productivity and fulfillment. Embracing flexible work arrangements, such as remote work or adjustable schedules, provides you with the freedom to manage your time more effectively. This flexibility allows you to choose where and when you work, helping you optimize your day around both work tasks and personal needs. For instance, eliminating long commutes gives you more time to dedicate to work and personal activities, enhancing your overall efficiency. Being able to adjust your schedule also enables you to handle unexpected events or pursue personal enrichment, such as attending a midday yoga class or managing family responsibilities, without compromising your professional obligations.

Prioritizing self-care is an essential aspect of flexibility. Taking regular breaks throughout your workday—whether it is a short walk, a few stretches, or a quick snack—helps recharge your energy and maintain focus. These small moments of rest prevent burnout and keep you motivated, ultimately boosting your productivity when you return to work.

Incorporating mindfulness into your daily routine further supports mental clarity and stress management. Simple practices such as meditation, deep breathing, or moments of quiet reflection can help you stay centered and focused. These mindful pauses allow you to be more present in your work, leading to better decision-making and a more balanced approach to your day.

Flexibility in your work routine not only enhances professional productivity but also supports personal well-being. By creating a work-life structure that accommodates both career ambitions and personal happiness, you can cultivate a more sustainable and fulfilling way of working.

Foster a Supportive Work Environment

Fostering a supportive work environment is important for enhancing employee well-being, satisfaction, and overall productivity. Building a positive workplace culture begins with promoting work-life balance. Encourage your team to take breaks, use their vacation time, and establish clear boundaries between their work and personal lives. When employees feel empowered to balance their responsibilities, they are not only happier but also more productive. As a leader, you are instrumental in establishing this tone. By prioritizing your own well-being and maintaining a healthy work-life balance, you lead by example, inspiring your team to follow suit. This approach fosters a culture where everyone feels comfortable valuing their personal time just as much as their professional commitments.

Providing resources and support is equally important in creating a nurturing environment. Implementing employee assistance programs offers access to services like mental health support, counseling, and financial advice, which can be incredibly beneficial for employee well-being. Wellness initiatives, including fitness programs, health screenings, and mindfulness workshops, further contribute to a healthier and more engaged workforce. Additionally, policies that offer flexibility—such as adjustable work hours, remote work options, and generous parental leave —signal your commitment to addressing the diverse needs of your team, significantly improving morale and retention.

By prioritizing employee well-being and fostering work-life balance, you create a work environment that not only enhances job satisfaction but also builds loyalty and reduces turnover. When employees feel valued and supported, they are more likely to stay engaged, motivated, and productive, contributing to the overall success of your business. While building such a culture requires ongoing effort and genuine care, the positive impact on both employees and the organization makes it an investment that pays off in the long run.

In short, a supportive work environment nurtures well-being and productivity, fostering loyalty and contributing to long-term business success.

Pursue Personal Fulfillment

Achieving a balanced and fulfilling life as an entrepreneur or business leader means making time for personal fulfillment. Start by setting personal goals that align with your passions and interests beyond work. Reflect on what excites you—whether it is a hobby, creative project, or personal aspiration—and pursue activities that enrich your life. Investing in personal development through courses, workshops, or even new hobbies can give you fresh perspectives that invigorate both your personal and professional life. This commitment to growth keeps you energized and continuously evolving, fueling your endeavors with new ideas and motivation.

Spending quality time with loved ones is also key to personal fulfillment. Nurturing relationships with family and friends strengthens your emotional well-being, creating a support system that helps you navigate life's challenges. Sharing experiences, engaging in meaningful conversations, and simply being present with those who matter most provide you with a sense of connection and belonging. Pursuing activities you love—whether that means traveling, volunteering, or diving into a creative pursuit—adds joy and purpose to your life. These moments allow you to step away from work pressures, recharge, and reconnect with what truly matters.

Sustaining personal fulfillment requires regular reflection and adjustment. Periodically assess your work-life balance and the satisfaction you gain from your personal pursuits. Be mindful of what is working well and where there might be room for improvement. Flexibility is essential; remain open to adjusting your routines, habits, or priorities as your life and needs evolve. This self-awareness helps you stay aligned with your values and ensures that you are living a life that is both balanced and deeply fulfilling.

By focusing on personal goals, nurturing relationships, and engaging in activities that bring you joy, you cultivate a life that supports both your well-being and your professional success.

CHAPTER 10

BUILDING NETWORKS AND COMMUNITY

The Importance of Networking for Business Success

Networking goes far beyond just exchanging business cards—it is about building meaningful relationships that can have a profound impact on your business. Imagine attending a conference where every conversation has the potential to unlock new opportunities, forge valuable partnerships, or offer fresh insights. This is the true essence of networking. It is a vital practice that plays a key role in driving business growth, and we will explore why it serves as a cornerstone of long-term success.

Access to Opportunities

Think of networking as holding the key to a vast treasure trove of opportunities. At an industry event, you strike up a conversation with someone whose business needs align perfectly with what you offer. These chance encounters often blossom into lucrative deals, simply because you were there, engaging with the right people.

But it is not just about immediate gains. Networking paves the way for strategic alliances and collaborations. The relationships you build can lead to joint ventures, opening doors to new markets and driving innovation. Imagine meeting an investor at a seminar who provides both funding and mentorship, turning your ambitious plans into reality and fueling your company's growth.

The power of networking does not stop there. It keeps you informed about market trends and emerging technologies, helping you stay competitive. The connections you cultivate become a rich source of knowledge and support, enabling you to seize new opportunities and guide your business toward sustained success.

Knowledge and Expertise

The knowledge gained through networking is invaluable. Connecting with a mentor who has extensive industry experience can help navigate complex challenges with greater confidence. Their guidance provides direction, helping to avoid common pitfalls while offering clarity during critical decision-making moments.

Engaging with fellow business owners also opens the door to a rich exchange of lessons learned. You share your struggles and successes, and in return, you gain practical solutions and fresh insights. These conversations expand your problem-solving toolkit, equipping you with new strategies to tackle obstacles head-on.

Networking also drives continuous learning and professional growth. Attending conferences and workshops exposes you to diverse perspectives and the latest industry standards. Each interaction, whether at a seminar or in a casual discussion, can ignite innovative ideas and introduce cutting-edge practices that elevate your business to the next level.

Building Relationships and Trust

Building strong relationships and trust is fundamental to long-term business success. Regular interactions with peers, clients, and partners help reinforce your credibility and reliability, laying the foundation for enduring collaborations and customer loyalty. Trust is a powerful driver of these connections, ensuring that partnerships thrive and customers remain loyal over time.

Being actively engaged in your industry enhances your reputation as a knowledgeable and dependable professional. Surrounding yourself with a network of like-minded individuals who understand the challenges of running a business provides not only emotional support but also practical advice and valuable insights.

Networking fosters a collaborative atmosphere where resources, information, and contacts are freely exchanged. This culture of mutual support strengthens your ability to tackle business challenges, leading to innovative solutions. The relationships you build not only open doors to new opportunities but also provide the foundation for navigating the highs and lows of business with greater resilience.

Enhancing Visibility and Brand Awareness

Enhancing visibility and brand awareness is essential for business growth, and networking is a powerful tool in this process. Word-of-mouth referrals and recommendations from satisfied clients and business partners can significantly expand your reach. When trusted individuals endorse your brand, new customers are more likely to be drawn to your business with confidence.

The strong relationships you cultivate through networking often transform clients and peers into natural brand ambassadors. Their personal experiences with your products or services become authentic promotions within their own circles, boosting your credibility and drawing in more potential customers.

Building connections with journalists and influencers also opens doors to valuable media coverage. Positive exposure increases your brand's visibility, helping to establish trust and attract attention. A well-placed article or feature can introduce your business to a broader audience, generating excitement and interest in what you offer.

Attending industry events and conferences further elevates your brand. Participating as a speaker or expert at these events not only amplifies your brand recognition but also positions you as a thought leader in your field, helping you connect with a wider audience while showcasing your expertise.

Innovation and Collaboration

Innovation and collaboration are key factors in fostering business growth and sustaining success. When you connect with a diverse range of professionals, countless opportunities for collaboration emerge. These connections can lead to joint ventures and strategic alliances that enable you to pool resources and venture into new markets, expanding your business's reach and capabilities.

Through networking, you gain access to valuable resources, including top talent. Building relationships within your industry helps you identify and attract skilled candidates through trusted referrals. This approach creates a more cohesive and efficient team, which is vital for achieving your business goals.

Strong relationships with suppliers can also lead to advantages such as better pricing and a more reliable supply chain. A solid partnership with suppliers might even grant you early access to new products, giving your business a competitive advantage in the marketplace. Ultimately, networking fosters innovation and collaboration by establishing relationships that propel your business toward growth and success.

Personal Growth and Confidence

Networking goes beyond driving business success; it also plays a pivotal role in personal growth and building confidence. As you regularly engage in networking activities, your ability to confidently present yourself and your business improves. With each interaction, the anxiety surrounding public speaking and social interactions diminishes, allowing you to feel more at ease in professional settings.

Opportunities to participate in speaking engagements, community events, and leadership roles within your network further enhance your personal development. These experiences sharpen your communication skills, strengthen your strategic thinking, and foster empathy. Each leadership opportunity helps you grow both personally and professionally, expanding your influence and confidence.

Additionally, networking opens the door to diverse perspectives and ideas. Engaging with people from various backgrounds broadens your understanding of the business landscape and fuels creativity. This exposure to different viewpoints enhances your decision-making and allows you to approach challenges with fresh, innovative solutions.

Strategies for Building a Strong Business Community

Building a strong business community creates a foundation where collaboration, support, and shared success enable businesses to thrive. In a well-connected network, businesses can access valuable resources, share knowledge, and explore new growth opportunities. By fostering a sense of community, you tap into collective wisdom and cooperative efforts that drive innovation and progress. Next, we will explore key strategies to effectively build and nurture a vibrant business community.

Foster Open Communication

Fostering open communication is key to building a strong and engaged business community, and it all starts with creating the right channels for everyone to connect. Think about setting up online spaces like LinkedIn groups, Slack channels, or even Facebook groups where everyone can share insights, ask questions, and collaborate. These platforms will keep the conversation going and help strengthen the bonds within your community.

It is also important to keep everyone in the loop. Regular updates through newsletters, emails, or social media posts can ensure everyone knows what is happening—whether it is about upcoming events, community news, or even success stories. These consistent touchpoints make sure nobody feels left out, and everyone remains engaged.

Encouraging participation is another big part of building this community. Get everyone involved by sparking discussions and inviting them to share their perspectives. The more voices you bring to the table, the richer your community becomes.

And do not forget about feedback—it is crucial. Asking for input on what is working, what could be better, and what people would like to see more of shows that you are listening and that their opinions matter. By acting on that feedback, you can create a space that evolves with the needs of your community and keeps everyone connected and valued.

Organize Networking Events

Networking events give you the perfect chance to connect, exchange ideas, and build lasting relationships with others in your community. Whether you are attending in-person meetups like business breakfasts, happy hours, or industry mixers, these gatherings offer relaxed environments where deeper professional connections can flourish, often sparking new opportunities for collaboration.

If your community is spread out geographically, virtual events can be just as effective in keeping everyone connected. Webinars, online workshops, and virtual coffee chats provide the convenience of participating from anywhere, so no one has to miss out, regardless of location.

You might also find that themed events are a great way to deepen those connections. When you focus on specific industries or topics of interest, you bring together people who share the same challenges and interests. This targeted approach encourages richer conversations, more meaningful exchanges of knowledge, and stronger bonds. And if you are looking to take things further, organizing collaborative projects or hackathons can promote teamwork and creative problem-solving, leading to fresh ideas and potential business growth.

Provide Valuable Resources

Providing valuable resources is a powerful way to help your community members grow personally and professionally. Offering educational content and expert insights builds a foundation for collaboration and mutual support. Hosting workshops and seminars on topics like business development, marketing strategies, technological advancements, and leadership skills keeps everyone up to date and sharpens their expertise. Regular sessions can keep the community engaged and ensure everyone stays informed about industry trends.

Creating a resource library filled with articles, eBooks, templates, and toolkits is another way to support your community. Having a go-to place for guidance and inspiration makes it easier for members to access the information they need to grow. You can also invite industry experts and thought leaders to share their knowledge through guest lectures, Q&A sessions, and interviews, adding even more value to your network.

Mentorship programs offer a more personal touch by pairing seasoned professionals with those who are just starting out or looking to improve. These relationships provide ongoing guidance, encouragement, and real-world advice, helping mentees navigate challenges and reach their goals. The exchange of knowledge and experience strengthens the community and fosters lasting bonds.

Facilitate Collaboration and Partnerships

Facilitating collaboration and partnerships within your community fosters mutual growth and innovation. When members come together for joint ventures or collaborative projects, they unlock new opportunities and create synergies that benefit everyone involved. By encouraging peer support groups, you help build camaraderie and trust, giving members a space to openly discuss challenges, share advice, and offer emotional support. These interactions strengthen the community, leading to deeper connections and a more unified group.

Connecting members with potential collaborators, suppliers, and clients creates valuable business partnerships that drive growth. Imagine a member finding a reliable supplier within the community—this connection could lead to cost savings and better product quality. Co-branding efforts can also be powerful; when members collaborate on marketing campaigns, events, or product launches, they leverage each other's strengths and audiences. This not only amplifies their reach but also enhances the credibility of everyone involved, creating a win-win situation that reinforces the community's success.

Recognize and Celebrate Achievements

Recognizing and celebrating achievements creates a positive and motivating atmosphere within your community. By establishing awards and recognition programs, you highlight the efforts of individuals and teams who set a standard of excellence. Categories like "Innovator of the Year," "Top Collaborator," or "Community Champion" allow you to honor different kinds of contributions, encouraging others to strive for success.

Spotlighting member achievements through newsletters, social media, or during community events not only showcases individual success but also inspires the broader community. Sharing these stories emphasizes the value of being part of a supportive network. Celebrating milestones, such as hosting anniversary events to mark major accomplishments, strengthens community pride and unity. These moments demonstrate how members have benefited from the connections, resources, and encouragement within the community, reinforcing the spirit of collaboration and collective growth.

Promote Inclusivity and Diversity

Promoting inclusivity and diversity within your community brings together a variety of perspectives and ideas, sparking innovation and growth. Actively inviting members from different backgrounds, industries, and experiences creates a richer, more dynamic environment. It is essential to foster a welcoming atmosphere where everyone feels respected, valued, and able to contribute. This means implementing inclusive practices, addressing potential barriers, and ensuring that events and activities are accessible to all.

Creating equal opportunities for participation and contribution is vital to fostering a sense of belonging and reinforcing the community's commitment to equity. When everyone feels they have a voice and a role to play, it strengthens the bonds within the group and builds trust. By encouraging collaboration, empathy, and mutual respect, you not only deepen relationships but also boost overall satisfaction, as members feel more connected and supported. Offering mentorship opportunities and peer support networks further solidifies this sense of unity, while celebrating teamwork showcases the community's collective strength and reinforces a culture of shared success.

Measure and Evaluate Community Impact

To ensure your community remains vibrant and effective, regularly measuring and evaluating its impact is crucial. Tracking key performance metrics such as event attendance, participation rates, and online engagement helps you understand what resonates with members and what may need adjusting. Gathering direct feedback through surveys offers invaluable insights into their experiences, needs, and levels of satisfaction. This information allows you to align your community's initiatives with the evolving needs of its members.

Focusing on continuous improvement is key. By evaluating how your efforts contribute to members' personal and professional development, you can ensure that the community remains a valuable resource. Adapting strategies based on feedback and performance data enables you to refine existing programs, introduce fresh initiatives, or phase out those that are less impactful. Ultimately, this ongoing process of measuring, listening, and evolving guarantees your community stays dynamic, relevant, and responsive to the needs of its members.

Leveraging Networks for Growth and Support

Leveraging networks effectively can be a powerful driver of business growth and resilience. A well-built network does more than offer surface-level connections; it opens the door to valuable resources, insights, and opportunities that can accelerate your business's success. By focusing on cultivating meaningful relationships, you create a network that benefits both parties, offering mutual support and shared opportunities. These relationships can provide critical assistance during tough times, insightful guidance from experienced mentors, and connections to potential clients, partners, and investors. As we explore key strategies, you will discover how to harness your network's potential to fuel your growth and build the support system you need to overcome challenges along the way.

Expanding Business Opportunities

Expanding business opportunities through networking requires a strategic approach to identifying potential partners and accessing new markets. Start by seeking out partnerships with businesses that offer complementary products or services. These strategic alliances can create synergy by allowing you to tap into new customer bases, enhance your product offerings, and utilize each other's strengths. For instance, collaborating on product development, sharing distribution channels, or launching joint marketing campaigns can help you maximize resources and capabilities while reducing costs.

Joint ventures are another effective way to expand your reach, especially for larger projects or entering new markets. By pooling resources, sharing risks, and drawing on the expertise of both parties, you can tackle complex projects more effectively. Joint ventures not only combine the strengths of both partners but also help mitigate individual risks, making them particularly beneficial for exploring unfamiliar markets.

To make informed decisions when entering new markets, tap into your network to gain insights into customer preferences, industry trends, and regulatory landscapes. Engaging with industry experts and peers will provide valuable information to guide your strategies. For international growth, global networks are essential. Connecting with local businesses can help you navigate cultural differences, regulatory requirements, and logistical challenges, ensuring a smoother transition into new markets.

By focusing on strategic alliances and joint ventures, and leveraging your network for market insights and international connections, you will drive growth and strengthen your competitive position.

Gaining Insights and Knowledge

Gaining insights and knowledge is essential for staying competitive and driving your business forward. One effective way to achieve this is by seeking out mentors within your network who have successfully navigated similar business challenges. Their guidance, experience, and strategic advice can help you avoid common mistakes and make more informed decisions.

Engaging with thought leaders through conferences, webinars, and social media can also be invaluable. These industry experts share cutting-edge insights and ideas that can inspire innovation and enhance your business strategies. Peer learning is equally powerful. By participating in learning groups, roundtables, and mastermind sessions, you can exchange best practices, gain fresh perspectives, and learn from the successes and failures of others.

Studying case studies of successful network members provides practical, real-world examples that you can apply to your own business. Additionally, networking keeps you informed about industry trends, emerging technologies, and regulatory changes, helping you stay agile and competitive. By engaging with diverse professionals across various sectors, you gain access to a wealth of perspectives and expertise that can fuel your innovation and adaptability.

Leveraging your network for mentorship, thought leadership, and peer learning gives you the insights and knowledge needed to stay ahead of the curve and continuously refine your business strategies.

Enhancing Visibility and Credibility

Enhancing your visibility and credibility within your industry is crucial for business growth. One effective way to achieve this is by actively attending networking events such as conferences and trade shows. These gatherings offer opportunities to showcase your business, connect with potential clients, and engage with key industry influencers. Not only do these events increase your exposure, but they also keep you informed about the latest trends and innovations shaping your industry.

Volunteering to speak at events like webinars, industry panels, or conferences is another powerful strategy. Sharing your knowledge in front of an audience establishes you as a thought leader and demonstrates your expertise. This visibility builds credibility and fosters trust, which can lead to valuable networking opportunities and new business connections.

Media relationships are equally important for boosting your credibility. Establishing connections with journalists, bloggers, and influencers can lead to positive coverage for your brand. Collaborating with them on articles, podcasts, or videos expands your reach and attracts a broader audience. These media relationships also position you as a trusted expert in your field, further solidifying your reputation.

By embracing these strategies—attending key events, speaking publicly, building media relationships, and collaborating on content—you will enhance your visibility, establish credibility, and open doors to exciting growth opportunities for your business.

Accessing Resources and Support

Accessing resources and support through your network can be a game-changer for your business. One of the biggest benefits is financial backing. Networking often connects you with potential investors and lenders through trusted referrals and personal introductions. These warm introductions can build trust right from the start, making it easier to have meaningful conversations and explore new opportunities for funding.

Your network can also keep you informed about grants, subsidies, and funding programs that could give your business a financial boost. By sharing tips about eligibility and the application process, your contacts can help streamline your efforts and increase your chances of success.

Recruiting talent through network referrals is another advantage. Traditional recruitment methods do not always reach the best candidates, but recommendations from people who understand your business needs can lead to high-quality hires. Referrals often come with an added layer of trust, ensuring that the people you hire are a great fit.

Collaboration within your network can enhance your team's skills as well. By teaming up with other businesses to offer joint training programs and workshops, you create opportunities for skill-building that benefit everyone. These shared initiatives do more than develop your workforce—they strengthen community ties and promote mutual growth.

Building a Support System

Building a strong support system is essential for staying motivated and achieving success in your entrepreneurial journey. Engaging with peers through community groups provides a valuable space to discuss challenges, share advice, and offer mutual support. Whether you join an existing group or create your own, these connections foster a sense of camaraderie and collective problem-solving, making the often-isolating journey of entrepreneurship feel more collaborative.

Establishing accountability partners within your network can be a game-changer. Regular check-ins with someone who understands your goals and challenges help keep you focused and motivated. These partners offer fresh perspectives and constructive feedback, which can be instrumental in navigating obstacles and staying on track.

Emotional support is equally important. In times of stress or uncertainty, having a network of fellow entrepreneurs who have faced similar challenges provides a safe space to share experiences and receive encouragement. Their empathy and understanding help alleviate stress and build resilience, contributing to your overall mental well-being.

Mentoring relationships within your network offer not only professional guidance but also emotional support. Mentors bring valuable insights from their own experiences, helping you make informed decisions and avoid common pitfalls. They also boost your confidence, providing clarity and reassurance as you face difficult choices.

By actively cultivating your support system, you create a network that nurtures both your professional growth and personal well-being. This holistic support makes the entrepreneurial journey more manageable, helping you thrive in both your business and your personal life.

Facilitating Innovation and Collaboration

Facilitating innovation and collaboration within your network can significantly boost your business's creative potential. When you collaborate on projects, you tap into diverse expertise and resources that push your business toward breakthrough solutions. Innovation hubs, incubators, and accelerators provide the perfect environment for this, offering not just access to cutting-edge technology but also mentorship and funding opportunities that fuel creativity.

Cross-industry partnerships are particularly powerful, bringing together unique skills, knowledge, and perspectives. These collaborations often lead to the development of new products, services, and business models that you might not have imagined on your own. For instance, when a tech company partners with a healthcare provider, they might create innovative health tech solutions that open up new market opportunities for both.

Knowledge exchange plays a crucial role in driving innovation. Participating in workshops and seminars focused on best practices and emerging trends keeps you and your team thinking creatively and continuously learning. These events provide opportunities to share experiences, learn from leaders in your field, and gain fresh insights that can shape your strategies.

Organizing brainstorming sessions with members of your network can also stimulate the free flow of ideas. By tapping into the collective intelligence of participants from diverse backgrounds, you unlock highly creative solutions to problems and generate concepts that could transform your business.

By fostering collaboration and facilitating the exchange of knowledge through innovation hubs, cross-industry partnerships, workshops, and brainstorming sessions, you enhance your ability to innovate. This not only strengthens your product and service offerings but also positions your business as a leader in innovation within your industry.

Maintaining and Growing Your Network

For long-term business success, it is crucial to focus on maintaining and expanding your network. The key to keeping your network vibrant is consistent and meaningful communication. Regularly engage with your contacts through emails, phone calls, or social media, not just when you need something. Show genuine interest in their progress, share updates, and keep the relationship strong. This ongoing interaction signals that you value your connections and strengthens your professional relationships.

Equally important is the idea of value exchange. Focus on what you can contribute to your network, whether by sharing helpful information, offering support on projects, or introducing people who could benefit from knowing each other. When you consistently offer value, you build trust and goodwill, positioning yourself as a valuable member of the network. Even something as simple as sharing a relevant article with a personal note can enhance your connections.

Expanding your network should always be a priority. Actively seek out new contacts across different industries and areas of expertise to broaden your perspectives and open up more opportunities for growth. Attend industry events, webinars, and conferences to meet new people, and do not hesitate to introduce yourself to speakers and other attendees. These interactions often lead to valuable new relationships.

Finally, take an active role in your network. Volunteer for leadership roles, join committees, and contribute to discussions in professional groups. Your involvement not only increases your visibility but also helps establish you as a leader within your network. This can lead to deeper connections and more opportunities to collaborate on meaningful projects.

By staying engaged, contributing value, expanding your reach, and actively participating, you can maintain and grow a strong network that not only supports your current goals but also opens doors to future success.

CHAPTER 11

REAL-LIFE CASE STUDIES: BUSINESSES THAT GREW BIG

Case Study 1: Netflix's Journey from Startup to Streaming Giant

Background:

In 1997, Reed Hastings and Marc Randolph founded Netflix as a DVD rental-by-mail service. The idea was sparked by Hastings' frustration with late fees from renting a video. At the time, Netflix's initial model allowed consumers to rent and buy physical DVDs online, which was quite novel. In 1999, they introduced a subscription service that enabled customers to rent unlimited DVDs for a fixed monthly fee, setting the stage for their future business model.

Growth Decision:

The turning point for Netflix arrived in 2007 when the company decided to pivot from DVD rentals to streaming content online. Recognizing the Internet's potential to deliver media more conveniently and the increasing availability of high-speed internet, Netflix's executives foresaw a shift in consumer preferences towards on-demand entertainment. They also wanted to stay ahead of competitors and adapt to the rapidly changing technological landscape.

Execution:

To execute this transformation, Netflix invested heavily in developing its streaming technology and acquiring streaming rights for a diverse array of content. This required substantial capital and technical innovation. The company shifted its business model to a subscription-based streaming service, allowing users to access a vast library of films and TV shows for a monthly fee. As they phased out the DVD rental business, they focused entirely on streaming, marking a significant transition in their operational focus.

The execution phase also involved expanding into original content production, starting with the release of "House of Cards" in 2013. This move differentiated Netflix from other streaming services and established it as a content creator. By producing high-quality original series and films, Netflix attracted and retained subscribers with exclusive content.

Outcomes:

This strategic shift revolutionized the entertainment industry. By 2022, streaming services, including Netflix, had more viewers than traditional cable or broadcast TV. Netflix's ability to predict and adapt to market trends allowed it to dominate the streaming industry. Today, valued at over $210 billion, Netflix continues to innovate with original content and international expansions, boasting a subscriber base of over 200 million worldwide. The journey of Netflix, from a startup to a major corporation, is a testament to the importance of innovation, adaptability, and strategic foresight in business. By recognizing and responding to emerging trends, Netflix not only survived but thrived in a competitive industry, setting a standard for other businesses aiming to grow and scale successfully.

Case Study 2: Starbucks - Expanding from a Local to a Global Brand

Background:

Starbucks began in 1971 as a single coffee bean store in Seattle's Pike Place Market, founded by Jerry Baldwin, Zev Siegl, and Gordon Bowker. At first, the company focused on selling premium coffee beans and equipment. In the early 1980s, Howard Schultz joined as Director of Retail Operations and Marketing. During a trip to Italy, Schultz was inspired by the Italian coffeehouse culture and saw an opportunity to bring a similar experience to the United States.

Growth Decision:

In 1987, Schultz acquired Starbucks with the support of local investors and started its transformation into a coffeehouse chain. His vision was to create a "third place" between home and work where people could relax and enjoy a high-quality coffee experience. This decision marked a significant shift from selling coffee beans and equipment to serving brewed coffee and espresso beverages. Recognizing the potential for rapid expansion, Schultz focused on creating a scalable business model that could be replicated in multiple locations, building a strong brand identity and providing a consistent customer experience across all stores.

Execution:

To execute this vision, Starbucks adopted an aggressive expansion strategy, initially focusing on major urban centers in the United States. The company also invested in training programs to ensure that employees, known as "partners," could deliver the high level of service and quality the brand promised. In the 1990s, Starbucks began its international expansion, entering markets in Asia, Europe, and the Middle East. The company adapted its store formats and product offerings to cater to local tastes and preferences while maintaining its core brand identity. For instance, in Japan, Starbucks introduced green tea-flavored beverages, while in the Middle East, it adjusted its menu for regional preferences and cultural norms.

Starbucks also embraced technology to enhance the customer experience and streamline operations. The introduction of the Starbucks Card in 2001 and the mobile app in 2009 provided convenient payment options and helped build customer loyalty. Additionally, the company's investment in digital platforms allowed it to engage with customers through personalized marketing and loyalty programs.

Outcomes:

Starbucks' expansion from a local coffee shop to a global brand has been phenomenally successful. As of 2022, Starbucks operates over 34,000 stores in more than 80 countries, making it the largest coffeehouse chain in the world. The company's consistent focus on quality, customer experience, and innovation has helped build a strong global brand with a loyal customer base. The financial success of Starbucks is evident in its revenue growth, which reached $29 billion in 2021. The company has also diversified its revenue streams by introducing products like ready-to-drink beverages, coffee machines, and merchandise, further strengthening its market position. Starbucks' journey from a local coffee shop to a global brand illustrates the importance of a clear vision, strategic planning, and the ability to adapt and innovate. The company's success story provides valuable insights for businesses looking to expand their operations and build a strong global presence.

Lessons Learned from Businesses That Scaled Up

Scaling a business presents a mix of opportunities and challenges. Companies like Netflix and Starbucks have expertly managed this journey, providing valuable insights for entrepreneurs looking to grow their operations. These lessons shed light on strategic moves and decisions that have driven their success, offering guidance for those on a similar path. Here are some key takeaways drawn from their experiences.

Lesson #1: Embrace Innovation and Adaptability

Innovation and adaptability are vital for growth, keeping businesses competitive and ready to seize new opportunities. Netflix and Starbucks are prime examples of how these principles can fuel success.

For Netflix, innovation was the driving force that transformed it from a DVD rental service into a global streaming leader. By embracing the potential of internet technology early on, Netflix opened up new revenue streams and redefined how people consume entertainment.

Starbucks took a different route, focusing on customer experience and continually enhancing its offerings. By creating a "third place" between home and work, Starbucks not only sold coffee but built a lifestyle brand. Through thoughtful store designs, a diverse menu, and digital innovations, Starbucks continuously evolved to meet customer needs.

Adaptability is just as critical for long-term success. Netflix showcased this when it shifted to producing original content like "House of Cards." This move set it apart from competitors and built a loyal subscriber base. Similarly, Starbucks adapted to changing consumer preferences by introducing healthier menu options and plant-based foods, keeping its brand relevant to a diverse audience.

For entrepreneurs, the takeaway is clear: proactively embrace innovation and be ready to adapt. Whether that means investing in new technology, exploring new markets, or adjusting your product line, staying flexible and open to change will help your business thrive in an ever-evolving market.

Lesson #2: Focus on Customer Experience

Delivering an exceptional customer experience is a powerful way to differentiate your business and foster loyalty. Starbucks and Netflix excel in this area, offering valuable insights into how businesses can enhance customer satisfaction and build lasting relationships.

Starbucks' concept of the "third place" between home and work has been central to its global success. By creating a welcoming atmosphere with comfortable spaces, personalized service, and a sense of community, Starbucks turned coffee shops into more than just places to grab a drink. The company has continuously innovated to meet changing preferences, introducing popular cold beverages, plant-based options, and healthier choices to cater to evolving tastes.

Adaptation to the digital age has also been a key element of Starbucks' strategy. With mobile ordering, drive-thru services, and partnerships with delivery platforms, Starbucks has increased its convenience and reach. The Starbucks app, which allows mobile orders and rewards loyalty, further strengthens customer engagement and encourages repeat visits.

Netflix has similarly transformed the customer experience. By shifting from DVD rentals to streaming, Netflix tapped into the growing demand for on-demand entertainment. Personalized recommendations based on viewing history ensure users feel catered to, while original content like "House of Cards" keeps subscribers invested in the platform, reinforcing long-term loyalty.

Both companies prove that placing the customer at the center of your strategy pays dividends in terms of repeat business and long-term success. For entrepreneurs, the takeaway is this: deeply understand and respond to customer needs, whether that means refining your service delivery, creating personalized experiences, or building an inviting and accessible environment.

When you focus on delivering exceptional customer experiences, you not only enhance satisfaction but also build a loyal following that drives growth and strengthens your business reputation.

Lesson #3: Invest in Technology and Infrastructure

Strategic investments in technology and infrastructure are vital for scaling efficiently and achieving long-term success. Both Netflix and Starbucks illustrate the power of this approach. Netflix's rise to a global streaming leader was driven by its continuous investment in technology, enabling seamless content delivery and personalized user experiences. This commitment kept Netflix ahead of industry trends and in tune with evolving consumer demands.

Similarly, Starbucks' focus on technology and standardized processes ensures consistent quality and service across the globe. Innovations like the Starbucks app enhance customer convenience, while new technologies like the Siren Craft System streamline beverage customization and boost operational efficiency.

Scalable infrastructure is another critical component for expansion. Netflix's global content distribution network and Starbucks' standardized processes enable smooth international growth while maintaining quality and brand consistency.

For entrepreneurs, prioritizing investments in technology and infrastructure is a forward-thinking strategy that ensures sustainable growth and secures a competitive edge in the marketplace.

Lesson #4: Build a Strong Brand Identity

A strong brand identity is essential for building customer trust and loyalty, and it plays a pivotal role in driving market expansion. Netflix and

Starbucks provide excellent examples of how a well-defined brand fuels business growth.

Netflix has built its global brand on simplicity, innovation, and a customer-first approach. By investing in original content like "House of Cards" and "Stranger Things," Netflix reinforces its identity as a leader in entertainment. Their personalized recommendations further enhance the user experience, deepening customer loyalty.

Similarly, Starbucks has crafted a brand identity centered on customer experience and quality. The idea of the "third place" between home and work creates a welcoming atmosphere that draws customers in. Coupled with digital innovations like the Starbucks app and a robust loyalty program, Starbucks continually strengthens its relationship with customers by offering convenience and personalized experiences.

These examples illustrate the power of a strong brand identity to attract and retain customers, fueling sustained growth. Entrepreneurs should focus on building a brand that clearly communicates their values, resonates with their audience, and sets them apart from competitors, ensuring a lasting connection with customers.

Lesson #5: Leverage Strategic Partnerships and Acquisitions

Strategic collaborations and acquisitions are key drivers of rapid growth and market expansion. By strategically aligning with partners and acquiring complementary businesses, companies like Netflix and Starbucks have successfully tapped into new markets, embraced emerging technologies, and gained access to critical resources that fuel their growth.

Netflix forms partnerships with content creators, production companies, and tech firms to continuously expand its content library. Collaborating with filmmakers and studios helps Netflix deliver high-quality original content that keeps subscribers engaged. Strategic acquisitions, such as Millarworld, allow Netflix to tap into valuable intellectual property, enriching its content lineup and diversifying its offerings.

Similarly, Starbucks has used acquisitions like that of the Seattle Coffee Company to facilitate international growth. Its partnership with Nestlé has expanded Starbucks' product reach beyond its stores, bringing its products to millions of homes worldwide. By forging digital partnerships with tech companies, Starbucks enhances its operational efficiency and improves customer experiences, ensuring it stays ahead in the ever-evolving coffee industry.

Entrepreneurs can learn from these examples by strategically leveraging partnerships and acquisitions to accelerate growth. These collaborations provide access to new markets, enhance product offerings, and position businesses to scale faster and more effectively.

Lesson #6: Establish Effective Financial Management and Strategic Investment

Sound financial management paired with strategic investment decisions forms the backbone of successful business growth. Netflix and Starbucks showcase how balancing cash flow, securing necessary funding, and directing investments toward key initiatives can set the stage for sustained expansion. Their stories highlight the importance of financial foresight in maintaining both stability and momentum on the path to long-term success.

Netflix's journey is marked by bold investments in technology and original content, backed by raising significant capital. Despite large expenditures, Netflix focused on generating positive cash flow to reinvest in its business. By producing exclusive, high-quality content, Netflix attracted more subscribers, ensuring its growth and competitive standing in the entertainment industry.

Starbucks, on the other hand, exemplifies a balanced approach to financial stability and growth. While maintaining short-term financial health, the company invests in standardized store formats that guarantee quality and consistency across its global operations. Its digital innovations, such as the Starbucks app, not only streamline service but also deepen customer engagement. Additionally, investments in sustainability initiatives align with customer values, further strengthening the brand.

For entrepreneurs, mastering financial management means securing the right funding, carefully managing cash flow, and making investments that position the business for long-term success. Strategic financial decisions help maintain agility while preparing the business to seize future opportunities and overcome challenges.

Lesson #7: Talent Acquisition and Development

Building a skilled and motivated team is critical when scaling a business. Netflix and Starbucks provide standout examples of how to approach talent acquisition and development effectively.

Netflix places a strong emphasis on attracting top talent by cultivating a culture of freedom and responsibility. By empowering employees and investing in their professional growth, Netflix fosters an innovative and adaptive workforce that directly contributes to the company's continued success.

At Starbucks, employee training is at the heart of its customer service excellence. The company offers structured programs that ensure every team member delivers a high level of service. Starbucks also prioritizes continuous learning, offering career development opportunities that enhance employee skills while demonstrating a genuine commitment to their growth. Comprehensive benefits packages reinforce employee satisfaction and retention, further strengthening the team.

Entrepreneurs aiming to scale their businesses should prioritize talent acquisition and invest in development programs that align with their company culture and values. A well-trained, motivated team not only elevates customer experience but also fuels the company's growth and long-term success.

Lesson #8: Cultivate a Long-Term Vision and Strong Leadership

Having a clear long-term vision and strong leadership is fundamental to driving business growth. Howard Schultz's vision for Starbucks and Reed Hastings' leadership at Netflix exemplify how guiding principles and focused leadership can transform companies. Schultz's concept of Starbucks as a "third place" between home and work shaped the brand's expansion and operations, while his dedication to ethical sourcing and community engagement strengthened the brand's values and connection with customers. Hastings' foresight into the potential of streaming technology led Netflix from a DVD rental service to a global streaming leader, focusing on innovation and customer experience to navigate this transformation successfully.

For entrepreneurs, defining core values and long-term goals is essential for aligning teams around shared objectives. Strong leadership provides the inspiration and empowerment needed to foster innovation, maintain focus, and drive continuous improvement. This approach helps build a resilient, sustainable business capable of thriving amid the challenges of growth.

CHAPTER 12

REAL-LIFE CASE STUDIES: BUSINESSES THAT STAYED SMALL

Case Study 1: Thriving as a Boutique Business - The Painted Pretzel

Background:

The Painted Pretzel, founded by Raven Thomas in 2008, began as a small home-based business creating gourmet chocolate-covered pretzels. Raven, a stay-at-home mom, started making these unique treats in her kitchen, focusing on high-quality ingredients and creative designs. Her commitment to excellence and innovation quickly attracted a local customer base, and she began selling her products at local events and through a small website.

Decision to Stay Small:

Despite receiving offers for large-scale distribution and mass production, Raven made a conscious decision to keep The Painted Pretzel relatively small. She believed that maintaining a boutique approach would allow her to focus on product quality and customer satisfaction. This decision was driven by a desire to ensure each product was handcrafted and met her high standards. By staying small, Raven could also maintain a work-life balance that suited her family's needs.

Execution:

To execute her vision, Raven implemented several strategies to grow her business sustainably without sacrificing quality or personal touch. She continued to produce each pretzel by hand, ensuring that every product met her meticulous standards. This commitment to handcrafted quality set The Painted Pretzel apart from mass-produced competitors and built a loyal customer base that appreciated the artisanal approach. Customers knew that when they purchased from The Painted Pretzel, they were getting a product made with care and attention to detail, which was a key differentiator in a crowded market.

Raven expanded her online presence while maintaining local sales through events and small retailers. She created an engaging website and leveraged social media to reach a broader audience without the need for large-scale distribution. This dual approach allowed her to scale her business at a manageable pace, balancing the expansion of her market reach with the ability to maintain her high standards of quality and personal touch. The online platform also enabled her to connect with customers across the country, turning a small local business into a brand with national recognition.

Additionally, Raven partnered with local businesses and event organizers to promote her products. These collaborations increased brand visibility and provided opportunities for growth without the risks associated with rapid expansion. For instance, her products were featured in local gift shops and at corporate events, further establishing The Painted Pretzel's reputation as a premium handcrafted treat. These partnerships allowed her to tap into new customer bases and build a stronger presence in the community.

Customer engagement was another critical component of Raven's strategy. She prioritized responding personally to feedback and incorporating customer suggestions into her product line. This responsiveness not only improved customer satisfaction but also fostered a strong community around her brand. By valuing and acting on customer input, Raven built a loyal following that felt connected to the business and its success. This close relationship with her customers created a sense of community and trust, which is invaluable for any small business looking to thrive in the long term.

Raven's approach to executing her vision for The Painted Pretzel combined meticulous craftsmanship with strategic growth and deep customer engagement. Her commitment to quality, balance between local and online sales, strategic partnerships, and strong customer relationships all contributed to the sustainable growth of her business. This case study illustrates how a small business can thrive by staying true to its core values and focusing on building strong, meaningful connections with its customers.

Outcomes:

The Painted Pretzel's approach led to significant success while staying true to its values. The company gained national attention when it appeared on the television show "Shark Tank" in 2012, where Raven secured an investment from billionaire Mark Cuban. This investment provided the resources needed to grow the business sustainably.

Financially, The Painted Pretzel achieved impressive growth, with annual revenues reaching hundreds of thousands of dollars. By focusing on quality and maintaining a boutique approach, Raven built a brand known for its exceptional products and personalized customer service. The company's success demonstrates that it is possible to thrive by staying small and focusing on what matters most to the entrepreneur. This case study illustrates that small businesses can achieve significant success by maintaining a focus on quality, customer satisfaction, and sustainable growth. The Painted Pretzel's journey offers valuable lessons for other entrepreneurs looking to build a successful boutique business.

Case Study 2: The Success of a Niche Market Approach - Entrepreneur on Fire (EOFire), a One-Man Business

Background:

In 2009, John Lee Dumas, an aspiring entrepreneur, realized there was a gap in the podcasting world for content that featured interviews with successful entrepreneurs. At the time, most business podcasts were released infrequently and did not cater to the demand for daily, consistent content. Dumas decided to fill this niche by creating "Entrepreneur on Fire" (EOFire), a daily podcast that would provide value to listeners looking for entrepreneurial inspiration and practical advice.

Decision to Focus on a Niche Market:

John Lee Dumas identified a specific need in the podcasting market: a daily show featuring in-depth interviews with successful entrepreneurs. His target audience was aspiring entrepreneurs and business owners seeking motivation, strategies, and insights from those who had already achieved success. By focusing on this niche, Dumas aimed to build a loyal audience that craved regular, high-quality content.

Execution:

John Lee Dumas executed his niche market approach for EOFire through several key strategies that set his podcast apart and ensured its success.

One of the standout strategies was the daily podcast format. Unlike many other podcasts that were released weekly or sporadically, EOFire was designed to be a daily podcast. This unique format distinguished EOFire from other business podcasts and quickly attracted a dedicated following of listeners who appreciated the consistency and frequency of new content.

Another crucial element was the high-quality content. Each episode featured an in-depth interview with a successful entrepreneur. Dumas focused on extracting valuable insights and actionable advice from his guests, ensuring that each episode provided significant value to his audience. His interviewing style and thorough preparation contributed significantly to the high quality of the content, making EOFire a go-to resource for aspiring entrepreneurs.

As a one-man business, Dumas leveraged technology to streamline his production process. He used podcasting software, automated scheduling tools, and efficient editing techniques to manage the daily production schedule. This technological approach allowed him to maintain high standards while operating independently, ensuring the podcast's sustainability and growth.

Monetization strategies were also a key aspect of EOFire's execution. Dumas explored various revenue streams, including sponsorships, affiliate marketing, and selling his own products and services. He created online courses, wrote books, and offered coaching programs, all of which contributed to his income while providing additional value to his listeners. These diverse revenue streams not only supported the podcast financially but also expanded its reach and impact.

Finally, building a community was a cornerstone of EOFire's success. Dumas actively engaged with his audience through social media, email newsletters, and online communities. He built a strong connection with his listeners by responding to their questions, gathering feedback, and fostering a sense of community among aspiring entrepreneurs. This engagement not only strengthened listener loyalty but also helped Dumas continuously improve and adapt his content to meet the needs of his audience.

Through these strategies, John Lee Dumas successfully executed a niche market approach that turned EOFire into a leading podcast for entrepreneurs. His dedication to consistency, quality, technological efficiency, diverse monetization, and community engagement has set a benchmark for others in the podcasting industry.

Outcomes:

The niche market approach of EOFire led to significant success for John Lee Dumas. His podcast quickly gained popularity, reaching millions of downloads and earning numerous awards in the podcasting industry. EOFire became a go-to resource for aspiring entrepreneurs, and Dumas himself became a recognized authority in the entrepreneurial podcasting space.

Financially, EOFire generated substantial revenue through sponsorships, affiliate marketing, and sales of Dumas's own products and services. His ability to monetize his niche content allowed him to build a profitable business while maintaining the flexibility and independence of a one-man operation.

John Lee Dumas's journey with EOFire illustrates how a one-man business can thrive by focusing on a niche market, providing consistent and high-quality content, leveraging technology, and engaging with a dedicated community. His success provides valuable insights for solo entrepreneurs looking to carve out a niche and build a profitable business.

Lessons Learned from Businesses That Chose to Stay Small

Success does not always come from expanding rapidly; many businesses have thrived by choosing to stay small, prioritizing quality, sustainability, and meaningful customer relationships. These companies have shown that profitability and influence can be achieved without chasing aggressive growth. By deliberately focusing on staying small, they have found a way to remain nimble and true to their core values while still making a significant impact. Below are some key takeaways from businesses like The Painted Pretzel and EOFire, which have embraced the power of staying small and thriving through strategic focus and dedication to their core values.

Lesson #1: Commitment to Quality

Both The Painted Pretzel and EOFire highlight the power of prioritizing quality as a foundation for success. Raven Thomas, founder of The Painted Pretzel, focused on ensuring every pretzel was handcrafted with exceptional care. By using top-quality ingredients and a meticulous production process, she created gourmet chocolate-covered pretzels that set her apart from mass-produced alternatives. This attention to detail helped build a loyal customer base that valued the artisanal touch and the unique flavor experience, driving her business forward in a crowded market.

Similarly, John Lee Dumas of EOFire built his brand on a commitment to high-quality podcast content. Each episode of EOFire is designed to offer substantial value, featuring in-depth interviews with successful entrepreneurs and packed with actionable insights. Dumas's dedication to delivering consistently engaging and well-prepared content helped EOFire amass millions of downloads, earning trust and loyalty from listeners around the world.

These examples illustrate a powerful lesson for entrepreneurs: placing quality at the forefront of your business can differentiate you from larger competitors and attract a dedicated following. Whether it is through handcrafted products or carefully curated content, a commitment to excellence fosters trust, loyalty, and long-term success.

Lesson #2: Focus on Niche Markets

Concentrating on a niche market can be a game-changer for small businesses, as demonstrated by Raven Thomas of The Painted Pretzel and John Lee Dumas of EOFire. Both entrepreneurs embraced this strategy, using it to build distinct, thriving brands.

Raven Thomas discovered her niche within the gourmet food industry by specializing in artisanal chocolate-covered pretzels. Rather than competing with mass-market snack companies, she honed in on a specific product and perfected it. Her focus on handcrafted quality and unique flavors allowed her pretzels to stand out in the crowded snack aisle, attracting a customer base that valued gourmet, high-quality treats. This commitment to her niche enabled her to maintain exceptional standards and develop a brand that became synonymous with artisanal excellence.

In a similar fashion, John Lee Dumas spotted an opportunity in the podcasting space by identifying an unmet demand. Instead of following the trend of weekly or irregular podcast releases, he launched EOFire as a daily podcast that featured interviews with successful entrepreneurs. This daily format catered to listeners who craved frequent inspiration and actionable business insights, quickly building a loyal and engaged audience. By focusing on this specific need, Dumas carved out a niche for EOFire in the entrepreneurial podcast world, leading to millions of downloads and a strong following.

The key takeaway here is that focusing on a niche market allows small businesses to leverage their strengths and address specific needs that larger companies may overlook. By zeroing in on a unique product or service, entrepreneurs can create strong brand identities, cultivate loyal customers, and achieve lasting success, even in competitive industries.

Lesson #3: Personalized Customer Experience

Staying small offers the unique advantage of creating truly personalized customer experiences, a strategy both The Painted Pretzel and EOFire have mastered.

Raven Thomas, the founder of The Painted Pretzel, prioritized personal connections with her customers. She actively listened to their feedback, incorporated their ideas into her products, and made sure that each interaction was genuine and meaningful. This hands-on approach fostered a sense of community and trust around her brand. Customers felt valued because they knew their voices were heard and their input mattered. This not only increased customer satisfaction but also cultivated loyalty and repeat business. By nurturing these personal connections, Raven built a dedicated customer base that supported the growth and longevity of her brand.

Similarly, John Lee Dumas of EOFire created a deep connection with his audience through personalized engagement. Whether interacting on social media or in online communities, Dumas made sure to address listener questions and feedback. His dedication to delivering valuable content tailored to his audience's needs created a strong sense of community among listeners. This bond transformed casual listeners into loyal followers who felt personally invested in EOFire's success, helping the podcast flourish.

For entrepreneurs, taking the time to personalize customer interactions can dramatically boost satisfaction and loyalty. Engaging with customers, listening to their feedback, and acting on their suggestions strengthens relationships and builds a devoted community around your brand. This personal touch, often more feasible for small businesses, differentiates you from larger competitors and drives lasting success.

Lesson #4: Flexibility and Agility

Small businesses have a distinct advantage when it comes to flexibility and agility. This ability to adapt swiftly to market shifts and customer preferences has been a key factor in the success of both The Painted Pretzel and EOFire.

Raven Thomas demonstrated agility with The Painted Pretzel by consistently adapting and expanding her product offerings. As she identified the growing demand for high-quality gourmet treats, she was quick to innovate, experimenting with new flavors and designs. This responsiveness kept her product line fresh and appealing, allowing her to remain competitive in a constantly changing market. By staying nimble, Raven ensured that The Painted Pretzel could quickly align with customer tastes, keeping her business both relevant and thriving.

John Lee Dumas exhibited agility by continually producing high-quality content for his daily podcast, EOFire. Dumas streamlined his production processes with the help of technology, which allowed him to meet the demands of a daily show without sacrificing quality. He also demonstrated adaptability by listening to audience feedback and tailoring his content accordingly. This responsiveness helped EOFire stay valuable and engaging for listeners, contributing to its sustained growth.

For small businesses, flexibility and agility offer a significant edge in today's dynamic marketplace. Whether it is adjusting product offerings like The Painted Pretzel or refining content to meet audience needs like EOFire, the ability to pivot quickly ensures relevance and long-term success. Without the bureaucratic barriers that can slow down larger companies, small businesses can seize opportunities and adapt swiftly to challenges, making flexibility a cornerstone of sustainable growth.

Lesson #5: Sustainable Growth and Financial Stability

Both The Painted Pretzel and EOFire illustrate the power of sustainable growth and financial stability through strategic decision-making and deliberate pacing. Rather than chasing rapid expansion, these businesses focused on quality, consistency, and financial health, which ultimately led to long-term success.

Raven Thomas started her journey in her home kitchen, crafting each gourmet chocolate-covered pretzel by hand. Her emphasis on quality over quantity allowed her to build a loyal customer base and create consistent demand. When a $2 million order from Sam's Club presented itself, Raven recognized the need for strategic growth. Instead of over-leveraging her business by expanding too quickly, she sought investment from partners who aligned with her values. This careful approach helped The Painted Pretzel grow steadily without sacrificing quality, ultimately resulting in a 1500% increase in sales after her appearance on "Shark Tank."

Similarly, John Lee Dumas of EOFire achieved financial stability by diversifying his revenue streams. Through sponsorships, affiliate marketing, and his own product offerings, Dumas built multiple income sources that provided consistent cash flow. By keeping his business manageable, he was able to maintain a high standard of content while connecting deeply with his audience. This focus on sustainable income generation allowed him to grow his business steadily while protecting the integrity of his brand.

The key takeaway is that sustainable growth requires balancing expansion with the capacity to maintain quality and manage resources effectively. Whether it is through careful scaling, strategic investment, or diversified revenue streams, businesses that prioritize stability over speed create a foundation for long-term success. Small businesses, in particular, can benefit by focusing on manageable growth, minimizing financial risks, and ensuring that every decision aligns with their values and long-term goals.

Lesson #6: Strong Community and Network

Fostering a strong community and network is a key ingredient for small business success. Both The Painted Pretzel and Entrepreneur on Fire (EOFire) exemplify how local collaborations, partnerships, and meaningful community engagement can lead to significant growth and deep customer loyalty.

Raven Thomas began her journey by embedding herself within her local community. Selling her gourmet pretzels at local events and small retailers allowed her to build a strong reputation for quality and creativity. This grassroots approach helped her grow her brand organically, earning a loyal following that appreciated her attention to detail. After appearing on "Shark Tank" and receiving an investment from Mark Cuban, she continued to harness the power of her local connections. Her brand expanded to high-end retailers like Neiman Marcus, solidifying her pretzels as a premium product with a dedicated customer base.

John Lee Dumas of EOFire leveraged his network to create a thriving community around his podcast. By engaging consistently with his audience on social media and within online forums, he cultivated a loyal and interactive listener base. This consistent interaction helped create a close-knit community that extended beyond just the podcast itself. Dumas's focus on delivering valuable content and responding to his audience's needs helped build a network of dedicated listeners who not only supported the podcast but also referred it to others, driving EOFire's organic growth.

For small businesses, investing time in building strong relationships within their community and networks can provide invaluable support. Whether through local collaborations, online engagement, or community events, fostering these connections helps cultivate loyalty and opens up new opportunities. By prioritizing these relationships, small businesses can establish a solid foundation for sustained success, standing out in a crowded market while maintaining their connection with customers.

CONCLUSION

Launching your entrepreneurial journey is like navigating uncharted waters, with each decision steering you toward your destination. The strategies and insights shared throughout this book can serve as both your map and compass, guiding you toward success.

The moment to act is now. With your vision in focus, your knowledge honed, and your tools ready, step forward with conviction. Every choice you make is a step toward building the future of your business. You have laid a solid foundation—now it is time to trust in your preparation and take the bold actions necessary to achieve your goals.

As you progress, keep in mind that each step draws you closer to realizing your aspirations. The path may present obstacles, but it is also full of opportunities. Believe in your abilities, lean into your preparation, and move forward with determination.

Your entrepreneurial journey is shaped by thoughtful decisions. Let each one reflect your vision and your commitment. As you continue forward, may your business flourish and your ambitions be fulfilled, step by step, with purpose and confidence.

THANK YOU

Thank you for taking the time to read this book. Your support means the world to me, and I truly hope the insights shared have been valuable to your journey.

If you found this book helpful or inspiring, I would greatly appreciate it if you could leave a review to help others discover it as well. Your feedback is an important source of encouragement as I continue to write.

Thank you again!

APPENDIX 1

BUSINESS PLAN TEMPLATE

Executive Summary

- Business Name:
- Business Address:
- Contact Information:
- Date:
- Business Overview: *(Briefly describe your business and its products or services.)*
- Market Opportunity: *(Summarize the market needs your business addresses.)*
- Objectives: *(Outline your business goals and key milestones.)*
- Funding Requirements: *(State the amount of funding needed and how it will be used.)*

Company Description

- Business Structure: *(Describe the legal structure of your business, e.g., Sole Proprietorship, LLC, Corporation.)*
- Ownership: *(List the owners and their stakes in the business.)*
- Location: *(Describe your business location and any facilities.)*
- History: *(Provide a brief history of the business, if applicable.)*

Market Analysis

- Industry Overview: *(Outline the current state of your industry.)*
- Target Market: *(Define your target market and customer segments.)*
- Market Needs: *(Describe the needs or problems your business addresses.)*

- Competition: *(Analyze your competitors and your competitive advantage.)*

Organization and Management

- Organizational Structure: *(Provide an organizational chart of your business.)*
- Management Team: *(List key members of your team, their roles, and their backgrounds.)*
- Advisors: *(Mention any advisors or board members.)*

Products or Services

- Product/Service Description: *(Detail your products or services.)*
- Features and Benefits: *(Highlight key features and benefits.)*
- Research and Development: *(Describe any ongoing R&D activities.)*

Marketing and Sales Strategy

- Marketing Plan: *(Outline your marketing strategies, including online and offline tactics.)*
- Sales Strategy: *(Describe your sales process and sales tactics.)*
- Pricing Strategy: *(Explain your pricing model.)*

Operations Plan

- Production: *(Describe your production process or how you deliver services.)*
- Facilities: *(Detail your facilities and equipment.)*
- Supply Chain: *(Explain your supply chain and inventory management.)*

Financial Plan

- Revenue Model: *(Explain how your business makes money.)*
- Funding Requirements: *(Detail the funding you need and its purpose.)*
- Financial Projections: *(Provide income statements, cash flow statements, and balance sheets for the next three to five years.)*
- Break-Even Analysis: *(Calculate your break-even point.)*

Appendix

- Resumes: *(Include resumes of key team members.)*
- Additional Information: (Provide any additional information or documents that support your business plan.)

APPENDIX 2

GROWTH STRATEGY OUTLINES

Growth Strategy Outline for Startups

1. Market Research and Analysis

- **Identify Target Market:** Define your primary and secondary target markets, including demographics, psychographics, and behavioral characteristics.

- **Competitive Analysis:** Analyze your competitors' strengths, weaknesses, opportunities, and threats (SWOT). Identify gaps in the market and areas where your startup can differentiate itself.

- **Market Trends:** Research industry trends, customer preferences, and technological advancements that could impact your market.

2. Value Proposition and Positioning

- **Unique Selling Proposition (USP):** Clearly define what makes your product or service unique and valuable to customers.

- **Brand Positioning:** Develop a positioning statement that captures your brand's place in the market and how it differs from competitors.

3. Product Development and Innovation

- **Product Roadmap:** Create a product development roadmap that outlines key features, enhancements, and future offerings.

- **Minimum Viable Product (MVP):** Develop and test an MVP to gather customer feedback and iterate quickly based on insights.

4. Marketing and Customer Acquisition

- **Digital Marketing Strategy:** Utilize digital marketing channels such as social media, search engine optimization (SEO), content marketing, and email marketing to reach your target audience.

- **Paid Advertising:** Implement paid advertising campaigns on platforms like Google Ads, Facebook Ads, and LinkedIn Ads to drive traffic and conversions.

- **Referral Programs:** Develop referral programs to incentivize existing customers to refer new ones.

5. Sales Strategy

1. **Sales Funnel:** Define your sales funnel stages, from lead generation to closing the sale. Develop strategies for each stage to optimize conversion rates.

- **Sales Team:** Build and train a sales team focused on customer acquisition and retention. Provide them with the tools and resources needed to succeed.

6. Funding and Financial Planning

- **Funding Sources:** Identify potential funding sources, such as venture capital, angel investors, crowdfunding, or loans. Prepare a compelling pitch deck to attract investors.

- **Financial Projections:** Develop detailed financial projections, including revenue, expenses, and cash flow for the next 3-5 years. Use these projections to guide strategic decisions.

7. Scalability and Operations

- **Scalable Infrastructure:** Invest in scalable technology and systems to support growth, such as cloud computing, customer relationship management (CRM) software, and automation tools.

- **Operational Efficiency:** Streamline operations to improve efficiency and reduce costs. Implement processes that can scale as the business grows.

8. Metrics and Performance Monitoring

- **Key Performance Indicators (KPIs):** Establish KPIs to measure the success of your growth strategy. Regularly review and analyze these metrics to make data-driven decisions.

- **Continuous Improvement:** Foster a culture of continuous improvement by regularly assessing performance and making necessary adjustments.

Growth Strategy Outline for Small Businesses

1. Market Analysis and Customer Insights

- **Customer Segmentation:** Segment your customer base to better understand their needs and preferences. Tailor your offerings to meet these specific segments.

- **Local Market Research:** Conduct research to understand local market conditions, competition, and customer behavior.

2. Strengthening Your Value Proposition

- **Customer Feedback:** Gather and analyze customer feedback to refine your value proposition and ensure it meets customer needs.
- **Brand Differentiation:** Clearly communicate what sets your business apart from competitors.

3. Enhancing Products and Services

- **Product Line Expansion:** Explore opportunities to expand your product or service line based on customer needs and market demand.
- **Quality Improvement:** Focus on continuous improvement of your products or services to enhance customer satisfaction and loyalty.

4. Marketing and Community Engagement

- **Local Marketing:** Implement local marketing strategies such as community events, sponsorships, and partnerships with local businesses.
- **Content Marketing:** Create valuable content that addresses the interests and pain points of your target audience. Use blogs, videos, and social media to engage with customers.
- **Email Campaigns:** Develop targeted email campaigns to nurture leads and keep existing customers informed about promotions and updates.

5. Sales and Customer Relationship Management

- **CRM Systems:** Implement a CRM system to manage customer relationships and streamline sales processes.
- **Customer Retention:** Develop customer loyalty programs and personalized experiences to increase retention rates.

6. Financial Management

- **Budgeting:** Create a detailed budget that outlines expected revenue and expenses. Monitor financial performance against this budget.
- **Cost Control:** Identify areas where you can reduce costs without compromising quality. Implement cost-saving measures where possible.

7. Operational Improvements

- **Process Optimization:** Review and optimize business processes to improve efficiency and reduce waste.
- **Technology Upgrades:** Invest in technology that can streamline operations, such as inventory management systems or accounting software.

8. Performance Measurement

- **KPIs:** Establish KPIs to track the effectiveness of your growth strategy. Regularly review these metrics and adjust your approach as needed.

- **Customer Satisfaction:** Measure customer satisfaction through surveys and feedback to ensure you are meeting their needs.

General Business Growth Strategy Outline

1. Strategic Planning

- **Vision and Mission:** Revisit your business vision and mission to ensure they align with your growth objectives.

- **SWOT Analysis:** Conduct a SWOT analysis to identify strengths, weaknesses, opportunities, and threats.

2. Market Expansion

- **Market Research:** Conduct thorough market research to identify potential new markets and customer segments.

- **Expansion Plan:** Develop a plan for entering new markets, including market entry strategies, marketing plans, and resource allocation.

3. Product and Service Diversification

- **Innovation:** Encourage innovation to develop new products or services that meet emerging customer needs.

- **Diversification:** Explore opportunities to diversify your product or service offerings to reduce dependence on a single revenue stream.

4. Marketing and Brand Building

- **Integrated Marketing Campaigns:** Develop integrated marketing campaigns that use a mix of online and offline channels to reach your target audience.

- **Brand Positioning:** Strengthen your brand positioning to clearly communicate your unique value proposition.

5. Sales Optimization

- **Sales Strategy:** Develop a comprehensive sales strategy that includes lead generation, customer acquisition, and retention tactics.

- **Sales Training:** Invest in training programs to enhance the skills and performance of your sales team.

6. Financial Strategy

- **Capital Management:** Develop a capital management strategy to ensure you have the necessary funds to support growth initiatives.

- **Financial Projections:** Create detailed financial projections to guide decision-making and attract potential investors.

7. Operational Excellence

- **Process Improvement:** Continuously review and improve business processes to enhance efficiency and effectiveness.

- **Technology Integration:** Integrate technology solutions that support business operations and scalability.

8. Performance Tracking and Adjustment

- **KPIs:** Define and track KPIs that are aligned with your growth objectives. Use these metrics to measure progress and inform strategic adjustments.

- **Feedback Loop:** Establish a feedback loop to continuously gather insights from customers, employees, and other stakeholders. Use this feedback to refine your strategies.

APPENDIX 3

FINANCIAL PLANNING WORKSHEETS

Financial Planning Worksheet 1: Budgeting Worksheet

Monthly Budget Worksheet

Category	Planned ($)	Actual ($)	Difference ($)
Income			
Sales Revenue			
Service Revenue			
Other Income			
Total Income			
Expenses			
Salaries and Wages			
Rent			
Utilities			
Marketing and Advertising			
Travel and Entertainment			
Insurance			
Professional Services			
Loan Payments			
Taxes			
Miscellaneous			
Total Expenses			
Net Income (Total Income - Total Expenses			

Financial Planning Worksheet 2: Cash Flow Management Worksheet

Cash Flow Management Worksheet

Period	Starting Cash ($)	Cash Inflows ($)	Cash Outflows ($)	Ending Cash ($)
January				
February				
March				
April				
May				
June				
July				
August				
September				
October				
November				
December				
Total Yearly Cash Flow				

Financial Planning Worksheet 3: Financial Projections Worksheet

3-Year Financial Projections

Year	Year 1 ($)	Year 2 ($)	Year 3 ($)
Income			
Sales Revenue			
Service Revenue			
Other Income			
Total Income			
Expenses			
Salaries and Wages			
Rent			
Utilities			
Marketing and Advertising			
Travel and Entertainment			
Insurance			
Professional Services			
Loan Payments			
Taxes			
Miscellaneous			
Total Expenses			
Net Income (Total Income - Total Expenses			

Break-Even Analysis

Category	Amount ($)
Fixed Costs	
Variable Costs per Unit	
Selling Price per Unit	
Break-Even Point (Units)	
Break-Even Point (Revenue)	

Instructions for Using the Worksheets

Monthly Budget Worksheet:

- **Planned Column:** Enter your projected income and expenses for each category at the beginning of the month.

- **Actual Column:** Track your actual income and expenses throughout the month.

- **Difference Column:** Calculate the difference between the planned and actual amounts to identify variances and adjust your budget accordingly.

Cash Flow Management Worksheet:

- **Starting Cash:** Begin with the amount of cash you have at the start of the period.

- **Cash Inflows:** Record all incoming cash, including sales revenue, loans, and other sources.

- **Cash Outflows:** Track all outgoing cash, such as expenses, loan payments, and purchases.

- **Ending Cash:** Calculate the ending cash balance by adding cash inflows and subtracting cash outflows from the starting cash.

3-Year Financial Projections Worksheet:

- **Income and Expenses:** Project your income and expenses for the next three years, using historical data and market trends to inform your estimates.

- **Net Income:** Calculate your net income for each year by subtracting total expenses from total income.

- **Break-Even Analysis:** Determine your break-even point by calculating fixed costs, variable costs per unit, and the selling price per unit. Use these figures to find the number of units you need to sell to cover all costs and start generating profit.

APPENDIX 4

FURTHER READING MATERIALS

Business Growth and Scaling

"Scaling Up: How a Few Companies Make It...and Why the Rest Don't" by Verne Harnish

This book provides practical tools and techniques for scaling a business, focusing on four key areas: people, strategy, execution, and cash.

"The Lean Startup: How Today's Entrepreneurs Use Continuous Innovation to Create Radically Successful Businesses" by Eric Ries

A guide to implementing lean startup principles, including validated learning, rapid experimentation, and pivoting based on customer feedback.

"Blitzscaling: The Lightning-Fast Path to Building Massively Valuable Companies" by Reid Hoffman and Chris Yeh

This book explores the concept of blitzscaling, or rapidly scaling up a business, and the strategies and tactics used by companies like LinkedIn and PayPal.

Small Business Management

"The E-Myth Revisited: Why Most Small Businesses Don't Work and What to Do About It" by Michael E. Gerber

"Small Business Management: Launching & Growing Entrepreneurial Ventures" by Justin G. Longenecker, J. William Petty, Leslie E. Palich, and Frank Hoy

"Profit First: Transform Your Business from a Cash-Eating Monster to a Money-Making Machine" by Mike Michalowicz

Marketing and Sales

"Building a StoryBrand: Clarify Your Message So Customers Will Listen" by Donald Miller

"Contagious: How to Build Word of Mouth in the Digital Age" by Jonah Berger

"Influence: The Psychology of Persuasion" by Robert B. Cialdini

Financial Management

"Financial Intelligence for Entrepreneurs: What You Really Need to Know About the Numbers" by Karen Berman and Joe Knight

"Accounting Made Simple: Accounting Explained in 100 Pages or Less" by Mike Piper

"The Barefoot Investor: The Only Money Guide You'll Ever Need" by Scott Pape

Leadership and Personal Development

"Leaders Eat Last: Why Some Teams Pull Together and Others Don't" by Simon Sinek

"Drive: The Surprising Truth About What Motivates Us" by Daniel H. Pink

"Atomic Habits: An Easy & Proven Way to Build Good Habits & Break Bad Ones" by James Clear

Networking and Community Building

"Never Eat Alone: And Other Secrets to Success, One Relationship at a Time" by Keith Ferrazzi

"The Art of Community: Seven Principles for Belonging" by Charles Vogl

"Superconnector: Stop Networking and Start Building Business Relationships that Matter" by Scott Gerber and Ryan Paugh

www.ingramcontent.com/pod-product-compliance
Lightning Source LLC
Chambersburg PA
CBHW071449220526
45472CB00003B/738